Sweet Freedom

For all our sisters,
especially Judy, Belinda and Tina

Sweet Freedom

The Struggle for Women's Liberation

Anna Coote and Beatrix Campbell

Basil Blackwell

Copyright © Anna Coote and Beatrix Campbell 1982, 1987

Copyright in the illustrations © Christine Roche 1982 for all illustrations except that on p. 253; for that on p. 253, 1987

First published 1982
Second edition 1987

Basil Blackwell Ltd
108 Cowley Road, Oxford, OX4 1JF, UK

Basil Blackwell Inc.
432 Park Avenue South, Suite 1503
New York, NY 10016, USA

British Library Cataloguing in Publication Data
Coote, Anna
  Sweet freedom : the struggle for women's
  liberation — 2nd ed.
  1. Women — Great Britain — Social
  conditions   2. Feminism — Great Britain
  I. Title   II. Campbell, Beatrix
  305.4'2'0941   HQ1597

  ISBN 0-631-14957-0
  ISBN 0-631-14958-9 Pbk   20022633

Library of Congress Cataloging in Publication Data
Coote, Anna.
  Sweet freedom.

  Includes bibliographical references and index.
  1. Feminism—Great Britain.   2. Feminism.
  3. Women's rights.   I. Campbell, Beatrix.
  II. Title.
  HQ1597.C74   1987   305.4'2   86—30959
  ISBN 0-631-14957-0
  ISBN 0-631-14958-9 (pbk.)

Typeset in 10 on 11½ pt. Baskerline
by Pioneer Associates, Perthshire
Printed in Great Britain by
Billing & Son Ltd, Worcester

Contents

Preface to the second edition

We wrote this account originally in 1981, and updated it in late 1986. In those intervening years, the women's movement changed, the political climate changed and, inevitably, we changed too.

Five years ago, what we wrote seemed like contemporary journalism: women's liberation was still 'here and now'; we felt a part of it and able to contribute to its politics. By 1986 we were writing about something that was no longer with us in the same form: women's liberation as a self-contained and singular movement had become part of our recent history. That is not to say that 'feminism' was over — on the contrary, feminist politics were stronger, more dynamic and more widespread than ever. Nor had the women's movement gone into abeyance: it had been with us throughout the century and remained, though its character had changed. What was over was a particular phase of the women's movement that was a product of the 1960s, had peaked in the 1970s and faded in the 1980s — which called itself the women's liberation movement.

We cannot predict how feminism or the women's movement will change in the future. The second edition of *Sweet Freedom*, unlike the first, is mainly in the past tense, to indicate that we are writing about a particular period, and that we cannot account for how women's politics and perceptions will change in the late 1980s and beyond. At certain points in the text we have abandoned prescription for description — another sign of our changed relation to the time in which we write.

We have added new material on the Black women's movement, on Greenham Common and the peace movement, on Women Against Pit Closures, on the women's committees of the GLC and other local authorities, on health and reproductive rights, on changes in the law and in benefits and services, on developments in the Labour Party and the trade unions, on the formation of the SDP, on changes in education and in sexual politics . . . and more. More generally, the atmosphere around the women's movement seems to have changed, and we have tried to convey this too. It has to do with the passing of an era, with feminism diversifying, spreading outwards and making links with other kinds of politics, with a new confidence among women, but perhaps with a certain loss of anger and urgency, because we carry with us the history of our struggle.

Yet while so much has changed, there is even more that hasn't — and this should be apparent in the chapters that follow. We may have a better understanding of how men are privileged and women subordinate, but we have not yet transformed the economic and social patterns that make them so.

We hope this book will be read alongside other books about the women's liberation movement, some already published, others still to be written. This is our account of what happened: it is just one side of the story.

Anna Coote
Beatrix Campbell

Acknowledgements

Love and thanks to Melissa Benn for her excellent, painstaking research and likewise to Candida Lacey and Mary Newton, who worked on the revised edition; to Carol Fisher who scrutinized every chapter and gave such sterling advice; to Dale Spender for her invaluable help and support; to Angela Lloyd and Jessica Sacret for their care and attention; to Neil Myers for Kung Fu; to Margaret Bluman for everything; to Rosalind Coward for her rigorous criticism and timely intervention; to *Red Rag* and the NCCL women's group, with whom some of the ideas in this book originated; and to Christine Jackson, Fran Bennett, Patricia Hewitt and Tess Gill for giving us their time, and such useful comments on the manuscript.

1 New beginnings

If all Men are born free, how is it that all Women are born slaves? As they must be if the being subjected to the inconstant, uncertain, unknown, arbitrary will of Men, be the perfect Condition of Slavery?

Mary Astell, 1700

Consider . . . whether, when men contend for their freedom . . . it be not inconsistent and unjust to subjugate women, even though you firmly believe that you are acting in the manner best calculated to promote their happiness? Who made man the exclusive judge, if woman partake with him the gift of reason?

Mary Wollstonecraft, 1792

The great social injustices are the subjection of labour and the subjection of women. They are co-equal manifestations of the spirit of tyranny . . . It is the characteristic of sex rule as much as of class rule that those in power dictate the activities as well as withhold the rights of the rest.

Christabel Pankhurst, 1902

At regular intervals throughout history, women rediscover themselves — their strengths, their capabilities, their political will. In short, there is a women's uprising. But they have never yet secured the means of communicating their endeavours truthfully beyond the boundaries of their own movements. And since men have not found it in their interests to convey an accurate picture, the ideas and activities of these rebellious women have largely been omitted from the records. Their writings have been left to gather dust in corners. Children are not taught about them in schools — except as curiosities which seem to have no root or reason.

Men are often heard to lament their children's innocence of war. No less lamentable are the generations of girls who have grown up in ignorance of their grandmothers' politics. Only when they reinvent rebellion for themselves do they begin to disinter the buried remains of that knowledge. Each time, they find that although the setting is new, the battle they are fighting is essentially the same.

This book is about our time. Our women's liberation movement. We are not writing from nostalgia, bidding a fond farewell to the struggle that began in the 1960s. We are aware that there is a danger, in the bitter climate of the late 1980s, of being forced into retreat. It has happened before. Shall we late-twentieth-century feminists be reduced to fragments of political archaeology before we are even in our graves? This time, we want to be sure that history doesn't repeat itself.

Let's begin by drawing a link between the Burning Pillar-Box and the Burning Bra. The first is real, a part of women's history; the second is unreal, a part of male mythology.

In 1905 a young woman called Jessie Stephen was employed as a domestic servant in Glasgow. A member of the Women's Social and Political Union, she took part in the militant campaign which began, she explained, 'because the politicians treated the movement with contempt, as being run by eccentrics — which only goes to show how stupid politicians can be sometimes!' Throughout Britain, there was a series of highly organized raids on property ('the thing authority regards as more sacred than human life'). Castles were burned, plate-glass windows were smashed and, in particular, Jessie Stephen remembered the occasion when every pillar-box in Glasgow was set on fire, without a single arrest:

> Scores of us were involved and the timing meticulously set for every section. I know I walked from my place of service in my uniform and dropped the acid container in the pillar-box and made my way without interruption by anyone. A few minutes later the contents were aflame . . .

A maid fire-bombed a pillar-box in Glasgow. One incident among many thousands, it was part of a major political development, a women's uprising. Sixty-four years later, Jessie Stephen's own account of it appeared in one of the first publications of the new women's movement — the magazine of Bristol Women's Liberation, *Enough!*[1] But what had happened to the information in the meantime? Most people had read about the suffragettes, but few (if any) had learned enough to appreciate what they actually did, or what they really stood for. From the meagre information that was readily available, it seemed that women had campaigned for the vote in the early part of the century . . . that some of them were a bit 'extreme', chaining themselves to railings and throwing themselves under horses . . . and that after the war the vote was won, and that was the end of that.

Newcomers to feminism in the 1960s began to refer back to the suffragette era and to re-examine it. It has taken some time for the meanings to sink in. Women in the early 1900s were not fighting for the vote alone, but for liberation (although they used a different vocabulary). They saw the vote as one step on the way to getting what they wanted. Feminists at that time were no less vigorous or resourceful than we have been, and it was a women's movement every bit as large and strong as ours: complex and multifaceted, combining those for whom hope lay in constitutional reform with others who believed in the necessity of revolution. It did not die simply because the vote was won. It lost momentum as social and economic conditions changed, and because women had not developed a firm strategy for the future. Moreover they lacked the means to transmit their politics to a new generation and so to consolidate their gains. We are now beginning to understand these facts, *in spite* of their being consistently misrepresented by those who have power to construct our sense of history.

And what has all that to do with the Burning Bra? In 1968, the Miss America pageant in Atlantic City, USA, was the scene of the first public manifestation of a new wave of feminism. For about two years before that, small numbers of women in the United States had begun to meet and talk to each other, to organize and to develop their own political theory. They took the view that the Miss America pageant degraded *all* women, contestants and viewers alike; its fake standards of beauty forced women to push and pull their bodies into alien, uncomfortable shapes, merely for the pleasure of men. They decided to stage a protest — and to illustrate their point they dumped bras and girdles into a 'freedom trash bucket'. Imaginary flames were added later by a news agency reporter, and the idea caught on in a big way. The media loved it. Sexy and absurd, it neatly disposed of a phenomenon which would otherwise have proved rather awkward to explain.

'Bra-burning' became an international byword for women's liberation. Well into the 1970s, on both sides of the Atlantic, this remained the image which was most widely associated with feminism. So farcical did it seem that it put paid to any serious questions being asked (outside the movement) about *why* women wore bras, or why some women now chose to stop wearing them. Even the original connection with the Miss America protest was forgotten.

Just as the scale and coherence of suffragette militancy had been hidden from view, so the smokescreen of the 'burning bra' helped to obscure the real nature of the women's liberation movement. It wasn't a result of a deliberate conspiracy; it was simply an example of what happened as the dominant sex went about its daily business of managing information and opinion.

A 'strange stirring'

If the new wave of feminism was not just an outbreak of underwear arson, what was it? And why did it happen at that time?

In one respect, it was a reaction to the fetishized femininity of the previous decade. After the Second World War, accepted notions about what women should be and what they should do changed quite rapidly.

Their work in the home as wives and mothers was emphasized, as men came back from the war to reclaim their jobs. As the shops filled up with food and clothes and domestic appliances, women were designated a key role, as shoppers-in-chief, in the new consumer economy. They weren't altogether unwilling participants — it made a change from the austerity of the 1940s — but in the process they developed a new, restricting sense of what femaleness entailed. 'The fifties was an era of elaborate hairdos, and constraining clothes and Dr. Spock,' records the feminist historian Sheila Rowbotham. 'The child psychologists stressed breast-feeding. Women with husbands who had been in the war went through paroxysms of guilt at the thought of leaving their small children. The bogey of mother deprivation was let loose. The nurseries closed. . . . In England the young Queen and her family reinforced the idyll of love and marriage.'[2]

At the same time, women had more potential choice and freedom than ever before. The Pill had arrived: an imperfect drug, which brought with it a range of unpleasant side effects, it nevertheless enabled women to choose with some certainty when to have children. There were more jobs for women than ever before — assembly-line jobs in new manufacturing industries, cleaning and catering jobs in fast-growing service industries, professional and para-professional jobs in Britain's developing welfare state, and a constantly expanding supply of office jobs.

There was bound to be a conflict between these new opportunities and the powerful propaganda of post-war 'femininity'. Women were not expected to combine employment and motherhood. Some did, out of preference or necessity, yet this was never recognized as something that 'real' women did; the two had to be combined almost covertly, and at the individual's own peril. Many others stayed at home — sensing, perhaps, that there was more to life than that, but unable to articulate their discontent. Isolated within their increasingly privatized families, and knowing they were doing what 'real' women were supposed to do, housewives could only conclude that if they felt unhappy with their lot, then they had only themselves to blame. This was what American social scientist Betty Friedan described, in her book *The Feminine Mystique*, published in 1963, as 'the problem without a name':

> It was a strange stirring, a sense of dissatisfaction, a yearning that women suffered in the middle of the twentieth century in the United States. Each suburban wife struggled with it alone. As she made the beds, shopped for groceries, matched slip cover

material, ate peanut butter sandwiches, chauffeured Cub Scouts and Brownies, lay beside her husband at night she was afraid to ask even of herself the silent question: 'is this all?'[3]

Betty Friedan exposed the fraud of the fifties and provided the beginnings of a vocabulary for women's liberation. In 1966 she founded the National Organization for Women (NOW), to campaign for equal rights and opportunities. It was a middle-class initiative, with a programme which many feminists today would describe as 'reformist' — but at the time, and when combined with the newly felt anger of radical women emerging from the civil rights and anti-war protests, its implications were revolutionary.

Radical politics in the 1960s provided an excellent breeding ground for feminism. Men led the marches and made the speeches and expected their female comrades to lick envelopes and listen. Women who were participating in the struggles to liberate Blacks and Vietnamese began to recognize that they themselves needed liberating — and they needed it now, not 'after the revolution'. Black leader Stokely Carmichael was heard to say that in the SNCC (Student Non-Violent Coordinating Committee) the only place for a woman was 'prone'. Here was the front-line hero of the radical left, who seemed to favour not simply the *deferral* of liberation for women, but their continued subordination. Judging by the number of times that remark has been quoted since, it did as much to fuel the fire for a new women's movement as the publication of *The Feminine Mystique*.

The personal is political

Small groups of women began to get together. They began to talk to each other in a way they had not done before. They discussed their day-to-day experiences, and their feelings about themselves, their jobs, their husbands, their lovers, their children and their parents. Of course, women had been doing this since language was invented — but what was new was that they were now drawing political conclusions from their personal experiences. They began to see that it was both necessary and possible to change their lives, and they realized that this would require a fundamental shift in the social order. It was not they who were at fault after all, but the men who organized and controlled their lives. They began to value each other and to be proud of being women. As one of them later recalled, 'It was like that old cliché of the light bulb going on over my head.' None of it was organized or orchestrated, but the news got around — by word of mouth, through the bush telegraph, it seemed to spread like pollen in the wind, to towns and cities throughout the United States.

New phrases were coined to account for new concepts. 'Consciousness-raising' was what happened when women translated their personal feelings into political awareness. 'Sisterhood is powerful' expressed their new sense of solidarity. They adapted the terminology of Black liberation and anti-imperialism. 'Racism' became 'racism with roses' and then 'sexism'. And 'chauvinism', a term applied to US aggression in South-East Asia, became a useful way to describe men's efforts to subjugate half the world's population.

The new feminists began to publish their ideas — in scores of pamphlets, journals and manifestos. 'We are engaged in a power struggle with men . . . ' declared the New York Radical Feminists in 1969. 'For while we realize that the liberation of women will ultimately mean the liberation of men from their destructive role as oppressor, we have no illusion that men will welcome this liberation without a struggle.' The most influential document was the first manifesto of women's liberation, drawn up by the Redstockings of New York; it deserves to be quoted here at length:

> Women are an oppressed class . . . We are exploited as sex objects, breeders, domestic servants and cheap labour . . . Our prescribed behaviour is enforced by threat of physical violence.
>
> Because we have lived so intimately with our oppressors, in isolation from each other, we have been kept from seeing our personal suffering as a political condition. This creates the illusion that a woman's relationship with her man is a matter of interplay between two unique personalities, and can be worked out individually. In reality, every such relationship is a *class* relationship, and the conflicts between individual men and women are political conflicts that can only be solved collectively. We regard our personal experience, and our feelings about that experience, as the basis for an analysis of our common situation. We cannot rely on existing ideologies as they are all products of a male supremacist culture. We question every generalization and accept none that is not confirmed by our experience. We identify with all women. We define our best interest as that of the poorest, most brutally exploited woman. In fighting for our liberation we will always take the side of women against their oppressors. We will not ask what is 'revolutionary' or 'reformist', only what is good for women.

By 1969, a few women's groups had appeared in Britain — and they emerged with a similar spontaneity. Many of the thoughts and feelings had been there all along; now there began a process of naming the discontent — and because it was about women's own existence, rather than about society 'out there', there also began a process of self-transformation.

Contrary to popular belief, the new feminists were not footloose and fancy-free; many were freshly acquainted with motherhood. 'I had been at home for about a year after the birth of my first son,' Valerie Charlton recalls. 'I found it impossible to adapt. I had the baby when I was twenty-seven, and in one year I had gone from feeling confident and in charge of myself, earning a living, to being completely collapsed and lonely.'

Many were members of the left-wing intelligentsia — a staunchly masculine society in which women were active and committed, yet felt themselves confined to the periphery. Catherine Hall experienced the political turbulence of 1968 not chiefly as an activist, but as a university wife:

> I was pregnant during the occupation of the university, and I was distanced from it both by being pregnant and by being a woman. The only women who were involved in it were the ones who were having relationships with the men. If you couldn't be part of the university culture you were completely marginalized.

It was this knowledge of radical politics, combined with a sense of exclusion from it, which led many women to feminism — just as it had in the United States. Rosalind Delmar went to her first women's meeting in 1968, at the Revolutionary Students' Federation, which had been set up after another student occupation at the London School of Economics:

> A male trade unionist came in and started telling us what to do. We told him to go away, no one was going to listen to him. There had always been a tendency on the student left to defer to industrial workers because they were felt to be more strategically important than anyone else — certainly more than women. I was very impressed with what we had done.

Once the news was abroad, it travelled at extraordinary speed, and soon reached well beyond the campuses. In Peckham Rye, South London, a group of predominantly working-class women found each other at a 'One O'Clock Club', laid on by the local council, for mothers with small children. They formed themselves into one of the first women's liberation groups in the country. 'I used to push my kids round and round the duck pond, wishing I could push them in it,' Jan Williams remembers:

> Instead, I went straight to the group. It was really good. We talked about the same things again and again — about children, about sex, about being used. I had started a part-time job and my husband had said he would look after the kids, but he didn't. I began to feel that there was something wrong with the unfairness and inequality of it. If you're at home all day and you keep everything together, you feel completely buffeted. Then you're expected to make love and it's just another imposition, another chore.

In 1969, Audrey Battersby had just had two of the most difficult years of her life:

> My marriage broke up in 1967, leaving me with three small children, one of them brain-damaged by whooping cough vaccine, to bring up alone. The feelings of despair, failure, anxiety about the children (how could I cope?) were almost overwhelming.
>   Predictably, I leaned heavily on a few women friends and we spent many, often happy enough, hours looking after each other's children and belly-aching about men, clothes and menstruation, and wondering where it all went wrong . . . but we never made the links between politics and our individual feelings of disillusionment and discontent.[4]

That summer, she and a friend attended a short course at the 'Anti University', which had been organized by radical academics as part of the student protest movement. Run by Juliet Mitchell, the course was entitled 'The Role of Women in Society'; it led her to read *The Feminine Mystique* and other new feminist writings . . .

> Then the bells rang and the connections were made and there was that feeling of militancy that I'd never experienced before despite involvement in various left-wing groups. I was no longer alone, but part of a movement which was primarily political but could be personal to me.[5]

Out of socialism

While women's liberation in Britain drew some considerable inspiration from the United States, it had its own, independent beginnings, too. This is not to make a patriotic point, but to help demonstrate that a women's uprising is bound to be deeply rooted in the cultural and economic life of the country where it takes place: it cannot simply be imported. The first major exponent of socialist feminism was the English academic, Juliet Mitchell, whose essay 'The Longest Revolution', published in *New Left Review* in 1966, began the heavy work of hauling the 'woman question' back into the consciousness of the radical left.

> The problem of the subordination of women and the need for their liberation was recognized by all the great socialist thinkers in the nineteenth century. It is part of the classical heritage of the revolutionary movement. Yet today, the problem has become a subsidiary, if not an invisible element in the preoccupations of socialists. Perhaps no other major issue has been so forgotten.[6]

Continuing the theme, Sheila Rowbotham's brilliant pamphlet *Women's Liberation and the New Politics,* published in 1969, had a profound influence on the development of feminism. Linking housework with unequal rights at work, and placing both in the context of cultural traditions which objectify and silence women, she insisted that such an analysis was crucial to socialist theory:

> Unless the internal process of subjugation is understood, unless the language of silence is experienced from inside and translated into the language of the oppressed communicating themselves, male hegemony will remain. Without such a translation, Marxism will not be really meaningful . . .[7]

This explosion on the left was paralleled by a new mood of militancy within the labour movement, and with an unprecedented wages offensive at the end of the decade. Women trade unionists had launched an equal pay campaign during the 1950s, but it was not until 1968 that they made any real impact on the trade union movement. Women sewing machinists at the Ford motor factory in Dagenham, Essex, came out on strike — shortly followed by their sisters at the Halewood plant in Liverpool. These women wanted to be hoisted from an unskilled grade to the equivalent of semi-skilled production workers (who were predominantly male). Amid national clamour, with the women being entertained to tea by Employment Secretary Barbara Castle, the first equal pay strike to enter the political stage was politely settled. In the tradition of triumphalism, the strike was hailed by the labour movement as a great success. And certainly it was a source of inspiration for other women workers. However, the women had only been conceded 95 per cent of the men's rate, still within their old 'unskilled' grade. Seventeen years later, in the winter of 1984, the Ford machinists went into battle again, claiming 'equal pay for work of equal value' with male workers in Grade C, under the amended Equal Pay Act. At first, an industrial tribunal ruled against them — during the hearing a representative of Ford had declared their work could be done by 'a bunch of bananas'. Incensed, the 270 women went on strike and stayed out for six weeks, once more bringing production to a virtual standstill. They only returned to work when the company agreed to an independent review of their claim. On 25 April 1985, they at last won the right to be moved from grade B to grade C, gaining parity with welders, metal finishers and body repair workers, and earning an extra £7 per week.

Soon after the Ford machinists' first 'victory' in 1968, a group of trade unionists formed themselves into the National Joint Action Campaign for Women's Equal Rights (NJACWER). They adopted a five-point charter which included a call on the Trades Union Congress to lead a campaign for equal pay and opportunity; and in May 1969, they held a rally in Trafalgar Square. Not unnaturally, these events had a formative influence on the newly emerging women's liberation movement. Ellen Malos of Bristol remembers trying to organize a coach to take women to London for the Trafalgar Square rally. They didn't make it to the rally, but as a result a small group began to meet on a regular basis — and Bristol Women's Liberation was born.

The factory dispute and the physical discovery

We asked a large number of women what they remember as being most influential in leading them to feminism in that early stage of the movement. We were struck by how many mentioned in almost the same breath the Ford strike and a paper written by an American, Anne Koedt, which had begun to circulate on ill-typed roneoed sheets among British women in 1969. Entitled 'The Myth of the Vaginal Orgasm',[8] it pointed out that the clitoris, not the vagina, was the centre for sexual pleasure for women, and it drew attention to the manner in which this potent little fact had been suppressed.

The startling disparity between the two catalysts — the factory

dispute and the physical discovery — is more apparent than real.
Women clearly sensed that the two were part of the same problem,
although few would have consciously spelt out the connection at the
time. In a sense they symbolize the link between 'the personal and the
political' which has been the essence of women's liberation. Not only
do they express the range and complexity of female oppression, but
they also measure the breadth of the stage on which women were
beginning to create a political movement of their own.

Anne Koedt cited research by the sexologists Kinsey, and Masters
and Johnson, who had established that the clitoris was the centre of
women's sexual sensitivity (with no other function than pleasure,
which often rippled throughout the pelvic region) while the vagina
was largely devoid of feeling. 'Today, with anatomy, and Kinsey, and
Masters and Johnson, to mention but a few sources, there is no
ignorance on the subject,' she wrote. 'There are, however, social
reasons why this knowledge has not been accepted.' She observed that
men failed to see women as total, separate human beings, defining
them only in terms of how they benefited themselves; for men,
penetration was the most effective way of reaching orgasm; and they
feared that they could become sexually expendable if the word got
around that the penis was not, after all, the key to female ecstasy.

> The position of the penis inside the vagina, while perfect for
> reproduction, does not usually stimulate orgasm in women . . .
> women must therefore rely on indirect stimulation in 'normal'
> positions.

Many have described the impact of Koedt's paper as 'revolutionary'.
It didn't tally with every woman's experience, nor did it lead to
wholescale abandonment of heterosexuality. But it did enable women
to talk about their sexuality in their own terms, to escape from male
definitions of 'normality' and 'frigidity', to feel they had a right to
make demands, and to perceive what had previously seemed to be
their own individual 'problems' as part of a pattern which was
essentially political.

It was a necessary antidote to the 'permissive society' of the 1960s
which, far from permitting women to do anything, had kidnapped
them and carried them off as trophies, in the name of sexual freedom.
In the era of flower-power and love-ins, of doing-your-own-thing and
not being hung up (especially about sex), 'girls' were expected to *do it*,
and impose no conditions. The more they did it, the more 'liberated'
they were deemed to be. It is true that the sixties' counter-culture
challenged a lot of old ideas and allowed new ones to blossom; thus

far, it nourished the roots of emergent feminism. But at the same time it added a new dimension to the oppression of women — setting them up, in their mini-skirts and mascara, alongside the whole-foods and hippy beads and hallucinogens, in a gallery of new toys with which men were now free to play.

Germaine Greer's *The Female Eunuch*, published in 1970, gave a perspective on patriarchy from within that culture. She poured scorn on many of the new feminist writers, including Anne Koedt, and wagged a finger at faint-hearted women, whom she saw as partly to blame for their own subordination:

> It would be a genuine revolution if women would suddenly stop loving the victors in violent encounters. Why do they admire the image of the brutal man?[9]

Women had to pull themselves together, give up their bad habits, reassert their potency and, above all, have a good time: 'The chief means of liberating women is by replacing compulsiveness and compulsion by the pleasure principle . . .' (We examine her views on sexuality in more detail later on, p. 240.)

Greer sought neither to blame nor to diminish men; nor did she meddle in economics. But *The Female Eunuch* was powerfully written and often wise; it was widely publicized and wildly popular. It dug a channel through to the women's movement from the Love Generation, and introduced many thousands of women to a new sense of themselves.

The Ruskin conference

In February 1970 the first National Women's Liberation Conference was held at Ruskin College, Oxford. Like so many events at that stage of the movement, it happened almost by accident, taking everyone by surprise. A handful of women had attended one of the Ruskin history workshops, organized by the college to bring worker historians and academics together. As usual, it was entirely dominated by men and the work proceeded as though the female sex had no part in history at all. But this time, the women historians would not stand for it. They held a separate meeting to discuss the problem. At first, they resolved that the next history workshop should be about women, but as they went on talking they grew bolder and decided that it would be not just a history workshop, but a national women's liberation conference. 'I remember the Saturday morning it began, sitting in the pub and getting rather pissed, amazed it was actually happening,' says Sally Alexander, one of the organizers. They expected three hundred, but nearer six hundred came. Most were from the new women's liberation groups which had sprung up in London and a few other cities and campuses. Some were from NJACWER, some from political groups on the Maoist and Trotskyist left. There were even a few from organizations which dated back to the suffragette era — like veteran resistance figures who'd heard the good news and come down out of the hills. There was a crèche for children and it was run by men — a revolution which was to set the pattern for future women's conferences.

There were bound to be passionate disagreements at such a diverse gathering. But there was also a great sense of exhilaration. The women knew they were in at the start of something big. They discussed proposals to lobby for a Sex Discrimination Act; to research into women's history; to campaign for free contraception and abortion on demand; and to study alternatives to the nuclear family and conventional ways of bringing up children. Sally Alexander recalls a speech by a woman from the shopworkers' union, USDAW, whose name was Audrey Wise:

She said: 'When we run out of toilet paper in our house, *either* my husband *or* I go out and buy some more. We both work, we both bring up the children and we both share the shopping and the cooking and the cleaning.' I sat there open-mouthed — I'm sure many others did too. She spoke intensely about being a socialist and a feminist and a working-class woman.

In 1970, it was an entirely novel experience to hear someone talk in those terms. But then, everything about the conference seemed new. It was the first time most of them had seen a woman chairing a political discussion and — more important — the first time they had been together in such numbers. As Sally Alexander puts it: 'All those women! Women I've become very close friends with since . . . we just spent a lot of time talking, talking about our kids and laughing. And walking round Oxford in gangs of women. It was wonderful!'

For the average Ruskin student, it was a traumatic occasion, especially on the Sunday, waking to find slogans daubed all over the walls. ('Sisterhood is powerful!') Two of the conference organizers spent a couple of fraught hours in the morning, scrubbing the walls to spare the college cleaners — only to find later that the town was full of slogans too.

Ellen Malos, who was there, was struck by the way in which the women's discontent, once articulated, swept inevitably towards radical conclusions. In the face of a feminist critique, it seemed that no part of the patriarchal house-of-cards could remain standing.

> The most strongly expressed wish was for a total transformation of society from the bottom up, not only a change in economic and political organization, but in the organization of the family and personal relationships.

She remembers there was also a 'deep disillusionment with traditional forms of political activity'. The conference challenged the orthodoxy of left-wing groups, whose passionate commitment to the struggle against capitalism and imperialism had never been examined from this perspective. 'I'm absolutely bored with hearing these series of accounts of the war in Vietnam,' complained one woman. Someone else retorted that it was 'anti-liberating' to go on talking about housework because such discussions emphasized 'the negative reasons for fighting'. 'Our main task is to overthrow capitalism,' another speaker said helpfully, but that was missing the point. The women were not less committed than others to the class struggle and the liberation of Vietnam, but they were determined to assert their own political place.

It was a terrible test for women who had been brought up on a theoretical diet which specified one absolutely determining contradiction in society — that between classes. There was nothing in the history of revolutionary socialism which allowed even the possibility of the sexual contradiction being instrumental to the organization of human society. The same history was charged with disdain for so-called 'bourgeois feminism'. So it was not lightly that a speaker from the London women's liberation workshop declared: 'We want women to be in charge of their own lives, therefore we must be in control of our own movement directly.' And the words of one of the conference organizers, who pointed out that 'the relation of men to women is the missing gap in the discussion', were momentous at that time.

The first formal act of the conference, the setting-up of a National Women's Coordinating Committee, celebrated variety, not vanguards. They adopted a structure of small autonomous groups based on localities or special interests, each with equal status, loosely coordinated through national meetings, to which each group could send two delegates.

From this beginning, women's liberation developed into an autonomous political movement. It was self-starting, self-regulating and self-directing, owing no allegiance to any other organization or set of beliefs. Women recognized that the form and practice of their politics were crucially important. In the magazine *Shrew*, which the new women's liberation groups took turns to produce, the Tufnell Park (North London) group explained in October 1969 why they emphasized the need for 'small group discussions':

> Our first priority isn't to get over information, but to know what everyone in the room thinks. We believe in getting people to interact, not to listen to experts. We want them to *themselves* make an analysis of their situation, which will lead them to action . . .

There would be no hierarchies, no lines of authority, no leaders, no stars — and by implication, there would be no purgings or palace *coups*.

Miss World and the first march

Nine months after the Ruskin conference, in November 1970, came the first experiment with civil disobedience. In a carefully organized operation, about one hundred feminists infiltrated and then disrupted the Miss World competition, put on by Mecca at the Albert Hall and compèred by American comedian Bob Hope.

> We were all dressed up to the nines and terrified. When the rattle went, that was the signal, we rushed down the aisles, throwing out leaflets and mice. Why on earth did we have *mice*? At the planning meeting people had talked about letting off white mice and somehow that got transformed into plastic mice. We were charged with riotous behaviour and throwing dangerous weapons — you know, leaflets and mice . . .

Smoke bombs, bags of flour and stink bombs were hurled towards the stage as well. It wasn't a protest against the contestants, but against the contest. 'We've been in the Miss World contest all our lives . . . judging ourselves as the judges judge us,' they wrote later in a pamphlet assessing the event. In protesting against women's 'narrow destiny', they were striking a blow against the passivity of both the contestants and themselves. Later, at their trial, most of them insisted on conducting their own defence and having their friends around to consult while they were in the dock. Their action also expressed the movement's desperation to communicate with other women. Having no means of access to the media, they chose 'propaganda by deed' and found themselves suddenly on the screen before millions. But their fears that the media would distort their message were soon justified — especially as they had no experience of handling reporters and there seemed no alternative but to race back into seclusion. The protest attracted a lot of publicity; much of it was hostile. It nevertheless helped put the movement on the map.

The first women's marches took place in London and Liverpool on International Women's Day, March 1971. The Women's National Coordinating Committee had worked out four basic demands, to be carried on banners: equal pay now, equal education and job opportunities; free contraception and abortion on demand; and free 24-hour nurseries. The first three speak for themselves, but the latter has been widely misunderstood as the expression of some heartless desire to dump children in institutions and leave them there around the clock. Clumsily worded, perhaps, it was the most sophisticated of all the demands and focussed on the importance of high-quality, flexible child care available to all families. As one of the originators later explained: 'The emphasis was on the child and the child's needs. I remember thinking it was the only demand which was really worth having. You had to combine the idea that there should be proper child care with the idea that women worked, and that many of them worked unsocial hours. It was all argued through. Women with children were the main protagonists.'

The four demands were not intended to represent the politics of women's liberation; they were designed simply to unite as many women as possible around the new campaigns. If anything, it was the atmosphere of the first women's march which best summed up the movement. It was an optimistic, iconoclastic piece of theatre. There were plenty of kids and a fair smattering of men. One women's group brought along a wind-up gramophone on a set of wheels and danced through the snow (yes, snow) to the refrain of Eddie Cantor's 'Keep Young and Beautiful'. A group of child care campaigners brought a twelve-foot-high Old Woman's Shoe, with the nursery rhyme suitably rephrased and written out in giant letters. Others rigged up an irreverent simulation of child-birth, on a float bedecked with strings of cardboard cut-out babies and sanitary towels. There was a caged woman displayed as 'Misrepresented' and banners appropriating the admen's appropriation of the movement. One carried an ad showing three women striding across the desert, clad only in bras and corsetry, under the slogan 'Freedom'. 'We want freedom not corsets,' said the feminist banner. Names were collected of women who wanted to meet again, and in London alone more than fifty new groups were formed after the march.

There is a remarkable similarity in the descriptions women give of the moment of recognition, the sudden, excited discovery of . . . of what exactly? Of themselves, of the value of women and the pure pleasure of their company, of a new sense of identification and a new intimation of power. Nan Fromer recalls her first encounter with a women's group: 'Fifteen minutes after my arrival I was aware I would not miss another of these meetings if I could help it. So many of the women in that small sitting-room, despite their surface differences, seemed to share what for so long I believed to be my own, idiosyncratic suffering.' And in another city at about the same time, the same sort of thing happened to Catherine Hall: 'It was like a Christian conversion, suddenly we found these friendships. They completely changed my life.'

The elation of sisterhood did not mitigate the pain, however, of coming confrontation. This could be uncomfortable and frightening — whether it meant starting an argument at home about who did the housework, or finding things suddenly intolerable at work and having to strike out in a new direction, or ending an affair or marriage which could not be transformed. Mary Barnes, a young married woman, remembers being lent a copy of Anne Koedt's paper, 'The Myth of the Vaginal Orgasm':

> I don't know why I felt so upset by it, but I do remember just flinging it across the room in an incoherent rage. Maybe it was because it showed me that I didn't know my body, but beginning to find out about my body was too dangerous, it was like I knew what it would mean — I would have to take steps to change a relationship in which *I* had always been seen as the problem. Somehow staying that way was less dangerous than showing my husband that *he* was the problem. I wouldn't have known where to start.

The meeting and talking continued. And since there were no set texts, nor any 'line' to follow, different groups set about producing their own analyses of what was wrong, and what needed to be done. A paper prepared by the Bristol Group in 1971[10] gives a picture of how these early discussions were conducted:

> We went around the room trying to establish when each of us

first discovered that it was a disadvantage to be a woman, and in what context. It was quite clear that in important ways all the things which seemed disadvantageous related to the family set-up . . .

The Bristol women identified the family as the area which 'defines the oppression of *women as a group different from other groups';* they recognized that 'although the oppression of women is related to class oppression, it is not the same thing': and they understood the importance of ideology:

> In order to change the economic structure of society *and* to liberate women it is going to be necessary to change our ideas, and changing the ideas of women towards consciousness of the need for their own liberation . . . will begin a process by which they see the need to change society. So we need to pay attention to consciousness and to *all* the aspects of the oppression of women. To concentrate entirely on the economic basis of oppression, to talk only of class questions is too schematic. We need to work out more carefully the relationship between the oppression of women and class oppression *for our own time* and *place.*

The paper was presented to the second National Women's Liberation Conference, held at Skegness in 1971, where it met with broad agreement. The ideas and strategies of the movement were gradually devised and accumulated in this manner, as the years passed.

Later, three further demands were added to the original four: in 1975, 'financial and legal independence', and 'an end to all discrimination against lesbians and a woman's right to define her own sexuality', and in 1978, at the last national conference of the decade, 'freedom from intimidation by threat or use of violence or sexual coercion, regardless of marital status; and an end to all laws, assumptions and institutions which perpetuate male dominance and men's aggression towards women'.

Radical feminism

The 1978 conference, like most others before it, was dominated by a split between what appeared to be two divergent schools of thought. After the early 1970s, many feminists within the women's liberation movement identified themselves as 'radical feminists' or as 'socialist feminists' and the gap between the two seemed increasingly wide and unbridgeable. Both sides had complex political analyses which continued to develop. From an early stage, each had different pre-occupations, different analytical approaches and different strategic priorities. Between their further fringes, there was little in common. However, when it came to their understanding of the forces which perpetuate female subordination, the majorities on both sides held strikingly similar positions.

As we have seen, the original radical feminist groups of New York City were responsible for the first policy statements of the women's liberation movement. Their most important contributions to feminist thinking, and the foundation stones of their own politics, were their designation of women as an oppressed *class* and their formulation of the 'pro-woman line'.

The sex-class analysis was expressed (in a rudimentary form) in the Redstockings' manifesto of 1969. It was a bold initiative, aimed at constructing a theory of a dynamic of power, rather than of an unequal relationship arising out of a fixed distinction. It was spelt out in more detail by Shulamith Firestone, a founder-member of the Redstockings, in her highly contentious and influential book, *The Dialectic of Sex*, published in the UK in 1971. In this, she inverted the analytical methods of Marx and Engels in order to identify the primary cause of conflict between women and men — which she located in the relations of reproduction. She argued that pregnancy and the dependence of small children upon their mothers put women at a disadvantage from the start of human society and made it possible for men to wield power over them. Since then, she said, those first causes of inequality had been overcome. We had learnt to regulate pregnancy, and we had created an environment (in parts of the world at least) where survival did not depend on physical strength and where children were routinely sheltered from most natural hazards. Yet men had maintained their supremacy by developing ideas and customs which enhanced the dependence of children upon adults as well as that of women upon men. She pointed to the fact that 'childhood' as we know it scarcely existed two centuries ago; it had since been constructed — by treating children not as young adults, but as an almost separate species, with special pastimes, playthings, clothes and language. Similarly, the economics of family life and the notions and trappings of 'femininity' and romantic love had served to keep women financially and psychologically in the thrall of men.

For women to free themselves, Firestone argued, they would have to seize control of reproduction, just as the working classes must seize control of production to free themselves from economic oppression.

She quoted approvingly Simone de Beauvoir's observation that 'human society . . . does not passively submit to the presence of nature but rather takes over the control of nature on its own behalf'.

She was at her most controversial, however, when she came to recommending a course of action. For although she noted that the biological basis of male power had been undermined (by the regulation of pregnancy, etc.) and that men had adopted cultural and socio-economic strategies to defend their supremacy, she nevertheless recommended that women should fight back *at a biological level*. She advocated 'not just the elimination of male privilege, but of the sex *distinction* itself'. And finally she proposed the development of artificial means of reproduction, together with a form of communism described as 'cybernetic', in which human labour was replaced by machine labour, so that women and children could be fully integrated as equal social beings.[11]

But Firestone's thesis cannot be taken as entirely representative. Her views on cybernetics were dismissed by most radical feminists as an extravagant footnote. Many disagreed with her biological formula for 'seizing control of reproduction', while agreeing — broadly — with her sex-class analysis. They proposed other measures for controlling reproduction — by women gaining power to determine for themselves when to have children, with whom and in what context, and being able to give birth and raise their young in conditions which were neither economically dependent on men nor socially subordinate to them.

Since *The Dialectic of Sex* was published, a range of philosophical and strategic ideas developed out of the 'radical feminist' current. Some took the view that it was not the biological base of male power that needed to be destroyed, so much as the social, cultural and economic structures which had developed out of the biological difference between women and men, and which constituted the patriarchal system that now held women in subordination. (This comes close to the socialist-feminist position on patriarchy, which we examine later on.)

A precept which united all radical feminists was the fight for women's liberation was primarily *against men*: they saw it as overriding all other struggles and were deeply suspicious of any attempt to link it to a wider political strategy. The question then was whether one was fighting in order to destroy *masculinity* as a social construct, and so transform men as human beings, with a view to developing a harmonious relationship in which they wielded no power over women; or whether one sought to end the necessity of the biological distinction by establishing ways of living and reproducing which were entirely independent of men. There were radical feminists who took the former position, and others who took Firestone's biological determinism to its logical conclusion, insisting that women must live separately from men, repudiating not only heterosexual intercourse, but boy children as well. For others, a degree of separatism was necessary, but as a strategy — in order to make the fight for women's liberation more effective — rather than as an end in itself.

The first major statement by British radical feminists was a paper presented to the National Women's Liberation Conference in November 1972. They pointed out that a change in the political system would not necessarily change the way men behaved 'in pubs, in the home, in the bedroom, in the office, or on a darkened street at night'. They insisted that women's personal and political autonomy could be safeguarded only if women's relationships with men were severely curtailed: 'As long as women's sights are fixed on closeness to men, the ideology of male supremacy is safe.' As for sex, they concluded that 'liberation for women is not possible as long as vaginal sex is accepted as the norm rather than as a possible variation'. Separatism for them seemed to be a strategic necessity rather than a political goal. 'We hope to show,' they said, 'that we are not anti-man but pro-woman.'

This was a reference to the founding principle of the Redstockings. In formulating it, the New York feminists were influenced by the politics of American Blacks, who had developed out of the Civil Rights movement a new sense of the validity and significance of Black experience. ('Black is beautiful' was a slogan which tried to express it; the Black Consciousness movement which emerged in South Africa in the late 1970s was based on the same concept.)

The pro-woman line was a way of recognizing and affirming female experience, as well as the strategies women adopted to cope with their subordination and their manoeuvres within it. In an interview published in the British feminist magazine *Spare Rib* in 1979, two of the founding Redstockings, Kathie Sarachild and Collette Price, explained what it meant to them:

> Women were OK, we weren't damaged, we weren't inferior; if we were honest and paid attention to our feelings, we could come to a correct evaluation of our situation . . . It gave a certain authenticity to what we were feeling and going through, and it prompted a certain kind of honesty . . .
> The pro-woman line was essentially against the 'it's-all-in-your-head' analysis of women's oppression . . . [it said] that oppression was real, our behaviour was based on real options or

lack of options, and changing our head was not going to free us . . .
You have to find out what the truth is when you're fed lies, you
have to study things that *men* weren't studying about
oppression . . .[12]

It didn't necessarily mean that everything women did was always in
their best interests:

The pro-woman line was that everything women do is an *effort* to
be in their interests. It has a rational basis. It doesn't mean you
can't make mistakes.[13]

So thoroughly had women in the 1960s been programmed to
undervalue, despise or psychoanalyse-away their experience that the
importance of the pro-woman line as a starting point for female
liberation cannot be underestimated.

Later expressions of radical feminism were more determinedly
separatist than the Redstockings' manifesto or the 1972 statement of
UK radical feminists. In a paper entitled *The Need for Revolutionary
Feminism*, which began to circulate in Britain in 1977, Sheila Jeffreys
set out to translate the political theory of radical feminism into a
revolutionary strategy. This would involve, she said,

the determination to wrest power from the ruling group and to
end their domination. It requires the identification of the ruling
group, its power base, its methods of control, its interests, its
historical development, its weaknesses and the best methods to
destroy its power . . .

She and other women who identified themselves as 'revolutionary
feminists' were in no doubt that men were the 'ruling group' and,
accordingly, women who lived with men, had sex with men or worked
alongside men politically were regarded as being in danger of
collaborating with the enemy. In a 1979 statement, the Leeds
Revolutionary Feminist Group declared: 'We do think that all
feminists can and should be political lesbians.' (We examine feminist
debates on sexuality in more detail in a later chapter, p. 230.) This
position seemed at odds with the pro-woman line and was criticized by
many who identified as radical feminists, as well as by those who
called themselves socialist feminists.

It is a common misconception that the radical-socialist divide
reflected a split between lesbians and heterosexuals. This was not so.
As we will reiterate in chapter 8, the women's liberation movement

encouraged love between women, it celebrated active female sexuality, and it enabled women to discover how their bodies worked and what gave them pleasure. This led no small number of women into bed with each other; for some it was a brief adventure; for others it became a continuing option; and for some it coincided with a permanent change in their sexual relations. However, lesbians did not all think that men were the enemy, any more than heterosexual women all thought men were ideal comrades and life partners. A considerable number of heterosexuals espoused the radical feminist cause, while many lesbians were committed socialist feminists.

Socialist feminism

The development of socialist feminism as a distinct political current within women's liberation began as a response to the challenge of radical feminism. For the most part, it was made up of women who were determined not to abandon their association with left-wing politics. They belonged, variously, to the Labour Party, the Communist Party, the International Socialists (later the Socialist Workers' Party) and the International Marxist Group; the majority, though, were non-aligned feminists.

One characteristic which distinguished the British from the American women's movement was the strength of the organized left. In Britain there was a mass-based Labour Party in government and a trade union movement which constituted the biggest working-class assembly in the country. British feminism was always more socialist than its counterpart in the United States.

Socialist feminists saw their feminism as the human face of socialism; it was a critique of the male chauvinism of the left, which would transform much of its conduct and many of its priorities. They knew they would have a job on their hands to make male socialists recognize the importance of feminism, but they did not see it as being essentially a fight against men, or precluding alliances with them.

They were convinced of the importance of understanding economic forces and of Marx's analysis of class conflict. For the committed Marxists especially, the radical feminists' sex-class analysis, with its inversion of Marx's analytical methods and rejection of Marx's own prognosis, was unacceptable. In their view, the pro-woman line raised awkward questions about the role of women who reaped the privileges of capital and strove to uphold its power. They rejected separatism both as a strategy and as an end in itself, for a range of reasons — from a commitment to class unity and a common struggle with men, to alienation from a political creed which cited husbands, lovers, fathers, sons, brothers, comrades and friends as 'the enemy'.

There was also the consideration of building popular support. They wanted to draw as many women as possible, especially working-class women, into the women's liberation movement, and to enlist male support — in the trade union movement and elsewhere — for feminist demands. They guessed, not unreasonably, that radical feminism, with its strong tendency towards separatism, would alienate a great many women and almost all men. It was therefore necessary to make the distinction clear.

Socialist feminists did not issue manifestos. Having begun with a rejection of some aspects of radical feminism and an expression of commitment to the politics of the left, they developed an increasingly detailed and sophisticated analysis of the construction of male power and female subordination. This process was still under way in the mid-1980s. Their ideas can be found in countless magazine articles, conference papers and books, many of which we have drawn on for this book.

They were concerned with understanding the historical development of patriarchy (a term with many interpretations, but which can be taken — broadly — to mean the combination of social, economic and cultural systems which ensures male supremacy), and with unearthing the patriarchal character of economic class relations. They drew on psychoanalysis to examine the specifically sexual dynamic between women and men (which was not necessarily reducible to economic determination), and the construction of masculine and feminine psychologies which again could not be accounted for in Marxist theory of class exploitation. They did not conclude that biology was the root of the evil: in their view men oppressed women not by virtue of their biological maleness but by virtue of their social and economic relations with women. It was these relations which needed to be transformed. The fight to end women's subordination was, in the socialist feminist analysis, inextricably bound up with the class struggle and could not be lifted above it — because capitalism itself was not only grounded in patriarchy, but had changed the shape of it. From this perspective, socialist feminists began to develop an exacting critique of theories of class exploitation. They insisted on the centrality of ideological struggle, which had been all too glibly nudged to the periphery of politics by much of the left. Reproduction and family relations were placed at the heart of social and economic theory and strategy.

At this point, the gap between radical feminism (in its non-biological-determinist form) and socialist feminism was at its narrowest. What distinguished the two was that socialist feminists' politics entailed neither a rejection of men nor a withdrawal from them, but an urgent necessity to fight *both in and against* male dominated power relations; for them, the women's liberation movement was not a sanctuary from male supremacy, but a means of combative engagement with it. They wanted to transform the struggle for socialism and redefine its objectives; they did not want to supersede or reject it.

Inevitably, there were differences among socialist feminists. Some were more sceptical then others about the commitment of male socialists to feminist objectives and the degree to which men would allow women to make gains that conflicted with their own interests. The experience of the late 1970s and early 1980s tended to swell the ranks of the sceptics.

Arguments between socialist and radical feminists shook the women's liberation movement at times. Yet feminists on both sides saw eye-to-eye and campaigned together on a number of specific issues, and for most of the time, the movement managed to remain a singularly heterogeneous body, in which radical and socialist feminism co-existed.

The problem with men

The debate underpinned another controversy which loomed large within the UK movement in the early 1970s. This concerned the participation of men in the politics of women's liberation. It was not clear in the early days that the movement was to be for women alone, and a number of groups included men — as did the first two national conferences. A few women (notably two small groups of Maoists) insisted that it was politically correct to include men in what was, after all, a mere colony in the empire of class struggle. Most didn't care, or definitely didn't want them there because their presence disrupted discourse between women. It seemed impossible to create the conditions in which men could cooperate. 'We met with the husbands at first,' says Hazel Galbraith of the Peckham Rye group, 'but they took over, so we had to stop.' Invariably, women found that the presence of men altered the *quality* of their conversation and diluted its potency, absorbing their attention and stilling their imagination. Either too little was said — or too much. Jean Hart remembers what happened when her group in North London decided to admit men, after some of the husbands had asked to come along:

> The women whose husbands came were very deferential at first, trying desperately to negotiate the two worlds. They wanted the

women to be seen as jolly decent people. But people were goaded into honesty by the group. One couple ended in a slanging match, with the man shouting things like 'I can't look after the kids because I go to work' (as if the roles were made in heaven!). One woman confessed that she didn't have orgasms with her husband. He yelled back, obviously pushed to extremity, 'You don't because you're frigid!' My husband didn't come to the meeting. I didn't want him to. I was fighting a gentle battle at home, I was cautious about expressing my worries. In the group I was fiery and opinionated, and I couldn't bring these two selves together . . .

Women's experience of getting together on their own, and the political imagination generated by their mutual understanding and sense of solidarity, were too precious to forfeit.

At the second national conference at Skegness in 1971, a small but symbolic incident put an end to the permissive line on men's attendance. Conference proceedings have not always been 'ladylike' in the traditional sense of the word. At a certain point on that occasion two women became involved in a wrangle over the microphones, and the husband of one of them rushed to her aid. At the sight of a man intervening in a physical confrontation, row upon row of women surged forward, cables were pulled from sockets — and men were barred from all but the post-conference discothèque. But at the next conference, in Manchester, there was another punch-up between a man and a woman at the disco, and henceforth these, too, were an all-female affair.

There was a long argument among London feminists in 1973 over whether or not men should be admitted to any part of the new women's liberation workshop, about to be opened in Covent Garden. Affiliated groups sent delegates to a series of meetings that autumn, and on 17 November they voted for exclusion by 117 votes to 30, with 20 abstentions. Most socialist feminists voted for exclusion along with the radical feminists — if only on the ground that it was better for the cause of female solidarity to keep men out if some women objected to their presence. However, since the dispute was no longer over whether men should attend meetings, but whether they should be allowed across the threshold of a women's centre, it raised questions about just how separatist the character of the movement should be. It seemed to many that the radical feminists had seized the strategic initiative. The wrangling was bitter and it demoralized many of the stalwarts of the movement, who began voting with their feet. For the argument about men seemed to have become an argument against categories of women.

In truth, the majority of feminists didn't much care about the exclusion of men, but were appalled by the prospect of women feeling excluded by their relation to men. What they wanted above all was *autonomy*. They wanted their movement not to reject men so much as to be independent from them.

It was this same determination to preserve the movement's independence which led to the dissolution of the Women's National Coordinating Committee in 1971. Although the committee had been devised initially to avoid any take-over, its meetings had become a sectarian battleground, with the Maoists, in particular, trying to capture it. What the Maoists could do today, the Trotskyists, or liberal reformists, or any other group could no doubt do tomorrow — and so it was decided at the Skegness conference that it was best to have no committee at all. (The disgruntled Maoist at the conference door, handing out boycott leaflets, was to become a familiar sight: 'SHAM SOCIALISTS HELP BRITISH IMPERIALISM DIVERT THE WOMEN'S MOVEMENT . . .')

Most women were confident that the movement would hang together without a coordinating committee — and it has remained a loose federation of small groups, linked chiefly by a sense of involvement and a common cause. That it survived nearly two decades was a measure of the strength of the *idea* that held it together. It was also due to the fact that the movement's lack of formal structure was a positive, not a negative feature, and one to which feminists gave careful and critical consideration. A paper entitled 'The Tyranny of Structurelessness'[14] began to circulate among women's groups in the early 1970s and became one of the key documents of the movement. The author, American feminist Jo Freeman ('Joreen'), described how an absence of leadership and organization could encourage informal élites with vested interests, allow 'stars' to emerge, and lead to undemocratic decision-making and political impotence. She set out principles for democratic structuring, stressing the importance of such things as wide distribution of authority, accountability, rotation of tasks, and equal access to information and resources. 'The group of people in positions of authority will be diffuse, flexible, open and temporary,' she explained. 'They will not be in such an easy position to institutionalize their power, because ultimate decisions will be made by the group at large. The group will have the power to determine who shall exercise authority within it.'

Most of these ideas were tried out in various ways and some became standard practice. Efforts to be genuinely democratic absorbed a lot of energy and they often caused anger and frustration, especially when there seemed a need for swift, effective action. But the process was a creative one, which played a vital part in the development of feminism and even determined the nature of women's demands. (To give just one example, a feminist campaign to set up a nursery might include a demand that it be organized along democratic lines, with parents and workers being involved in decision-making.)

Black women

In the late 1970s and early 1980s, Afro-Caribbean and Asian feminists developed their own political movement, with their own groupings, campaigns and objectives. They saw the existing women's liberation movement as a white women's affair, which neither took account of their experience in a racially divided society, nor took responsibility for its own inherent racism.

In their book. *The Heart of the Race,* Beverley Bryan, Stella Dadzie and Suzanne Scafe described this development from the point of view of Afro-Caribbean women in Brixton, South London. It grew out of a long tradition of women organizing to defend the Black community — from poverty and abominable housing conditions; from the crisis over child care suffered by immigrant workers cut off from the support of extended families; from the escalating racism of white neighbours; from the injustice of new immigration laws, and from increasing harassment by the police. Women were mobilized alongside men in the new Black Power Movement of the late 1960s, which celebrated Black pride, drew inspiration from Malcolm X, Stokely Carmichael and other militant leaders in the United States, and identified with revolutionary struggles in Africa.

> By the beginning of the seventies, Black nationalism had given birth to organisations and pressure groups in Black communities up and down the country. Their common purpose — to organise and agitate for the rights we had so long been denied — was pursued with a new militancy. Demonstrations, boycotts, sit-ins, pickets, study circles, supplementary schools, day conferences, campaign and support groups — all had become commonplace activities, exposing both young and old to their politicising influence.[15]

Black women found their part in all this was constrained. Their account finds a clear echo in those of white women caught up in left-wing politics during the 1960s:

We could not realise our full organisational potential in a situation where we were constantly regarded as sexual prey. Although we worked tirelessly, the significance of our contribution to the mass mobilisation of the Black Power era was undermined and overshadowed by the men. They both set the agenda and stole the show.[16]

The first Black women's caucuses were formed during the early 1970s. They began to discuss their common experience of racial and sexual oppression, and to organize around issues of particular concern to Black women — like women's work, their economic dependence on men, and child care.

They felt themselves to be influenced less by the existing women's movement in Britain than by African women engaged in revolutionary movements in Mozambique and Zimbabwe. 'And those sisters weren't just picking up a gun and fighting — they were making demands as women, letting it be known that they weren't about to make all those sacrifices just so that they could be left behind when it came to seizing power.'[17]

They organized autonomously, rather than jointly with white feminists, partly because their priorities seemed so different. They felt they couldn't afford to worry about changing lifestyles and attitudes when their very survival depended on fighting for decent housing and education, and against police brutality. White women were campaigning for the right to abortion; Black women often found themselves under pressure from a white-dominated health and welfare system to terminate pregnancies they wished to continue. Nor did the 'Wages for Housework' campaign make much sense to them: 'We were more interested in getting properly paid for the work we were doing outside the home as nightcleaners and in campaigning for more childcare facilities for Black women workers.'[18]

Black women needed to organize as women, but in a way that didn't rupture the solidarity of the Black community. They saw how Black men — their own brothers, sons, husbands, fathers, lovers — were being criminalized by oppressive laws and racist policing methods. Their struggle against the sexism and violence of these same men had to be carried on with backs turned against a white state, which might otherwise exploit divisions between them. White women who were beaten up at home might sometimes feel they could call on the police for protection; for Black women, this would mean handing over their menfolk to a force that represented a worse form of violence.

The Brixton Black Women's Group was formed in 1973, the first of its kind.

> There were no models for us to follow . . . We just had to work it out as we went along. We were very wary of charges that we might be 'splitting the black struggle' or mobilizing in a vacuum, or imitating middle-class white women. These were the kinds of criticism Black men were making . . . But it was so good to be in a group which wasn't hostile and didn't fight all the time. The sense of autonomy, of woman-purpose was something everybody felt . . .[19]

This group and others formed in the same period mobilized around Black women's needs, and at the same time were in the forefront of struggles involving the whole community — for instance, against the notorious *'sus'* law, which gave police power to arrest and search anybody they merely suspected of being likely to commit a crime, and which was used mainly against young Black men. The Brixton women also made links with women's groups in Africa and with Asian women in Britain.

Inevitably, there were (and are) differences between Asian and Afro-Caribbean women. They had profoundly different backgrounds, as well as different needs and priorities. Most Asian women, for example, were heavily constrained by family and religious traditions. Their parents arranged marriages for them. Many Muslim girls and women would not be allowed out of their homes, except for school or paid employment, so they had little or no freedom to organize politically. Asian communities tended towards a different kind of economic organization, based on small businesses and private housing, so they would encounter different forms of institutionalized racism. They were more likely to suffer from the racism of Britain's immigration laws.

Awaz was one of the first Asian women's groups in Britain. In her book *Finding a Voice*, Amrit Wilson described its activities:

> 1978—1980 was perhaps the peak of our activity. We took up and campaigned over immigration cases. We organized pickets over the issue of sexual harassment of Asian women at airports (virginity testing as it was called). We also organized a major national demonstration against state racism, and we supported women in struggles at work and were involved in setting up an Asian women's refuge. But in most of these things we worked

with other groups — long-established ones like the Indian Workers' Association of Great Britain, black women's groups and the then newly-formed and very male dominated Asian youth movements.[20]

Afro-Caribbean as well as Asian communities were familiar with racial abuse and police harassment, with discrimination on the job market, and with the injustices of immigration and nationality laws. Asian and Afro-Caribbean women shared many experiences: low wages, abject working conditions, discrimination in the education system; subordination within the family, domestic violence. They shared the need to fight sexism within a broader struggle against racism and imperialism.

In 1978, OWAAD was formed: the Organisation of Women of Asian and African Descent. Three hundred attended its first conference in 1979 and there was soon a network of groups, projects and campaigns, liaising through a newsletter, *FOWAAD*. It was non-hierarchical and self-determining. For five years until its demise in 1982 it enabled Afro-Caribbean and Asian women to present a united front on a range of issues and campaigns.

There were some marked similarities between the politics of Black women and those of white socialist feminists. Neither group saw men as 'the enemy'. Both recognized a broader struggle which women shared with men and which women had to transform if it were not to carry within it the seeds of conflict and oppression. Both were fighting on two fronts — to free themselves and to free their people. Both recognized that women shared experience across the divides of race and class but that women could also be divided from each other by the interests of race and class. And here was the critical difference between them. Many Black women felt that white women (even working-class socialist feminists) enjoyed racial privilege alongside white men; unless white women's politics were organized around eliminating that privilege, they remained part of the problem Black women faced.

From the early 1980s, Black women presented an increasingly confident challenge to white feminism. The effect was mixed. There was a lot of rather unproductive guilt, as well as bitter recrimination. There was also an important shift of perspective in some parts of the women's movement, as white women started to explore the relationship between race-, class- and sex-based oppression, and to place their struggle in the context of a broad movement of women across the world. Black women in Britain, meanwhile, continued to build their part of it.

Early campaigns

While women's liberation can't be understood without appreciating the quest for analysis and democratic forms, nor can the movement be understood without its campaigns. One of the first arose in the early 1970s, when the Conservative government under Edward Heath was planning to abolish family allowances (a sum paid to mothers for each child — the precursor of child benefit) and replace them with a tax rebate or 'credit' for the family breadwinner: in most families this would have meant transferring resources for child support from the mother to the father. The same government intended to introduce a new pension scheme which offered women inferior benefits. And meanwhile the Society for the Protection of the Unborn Child had begun its attack on the liberal 1967 Abortion Act. Defensive campaigns on these fronts, combined with a new offensive for a law against sex discrimination, were major items on the agenda. The first edition of the feminist newsletter *Women's Report*, launched in the winter of 1972–3, tells us that a group in Southampton was organizing a petition to retain family allowances, while one in Watford was organizing a petition in favour of the (then) Anti-Discrimination Bill, and another in Hemel Hempstead was carrying out a survey on women's reaction to the government's tax credit scheme. At the same time, the Women's Abortion and Contraception Campaign was working towards 'free contraception and abortion on the National Health Service as every woman's right, and an end to forced sterilization', while a group called 'Mothers in Action' were campaigning for paid maternity leave.

Alongside operations such as these were others focussed more directly on the workplace. For example, a major campaign of the early 1970s was one which aimed to persuade office cleaners to join a union. Office cleaning was — and still is — a job done mainly by women and at night. May Hobbs, the outspoken East Londoner who set the campaign going, pointed out that women do night work because their family responsibilities make it impossible for them to work during the day, and they need money 'for little luxuries like food, rent and clothes for their kids'. It's tough, dirty work. 'And because these women need the money so desperately they will bow to anything, and that is the reason why you have to get this industry organized.'[21] Her aim was to get the cleaners to join the Transport and General Workers' Union as a first step towards negotiating better pay and conditions. She drew support from London women's liberation groups, who turned out in considerable numbers to leaflet office buildings as the night cleaners came into work. Further north, a women's liberation group in Rochdale, Yorkshire, exposed the scandal of young Filipino women working in a local mill, held in near slavery on low wages and in dismal, overcrowded conditions.[22]

Campaigns to achieve equal rights at work increasingly brought the women's liberation movement into contact with the trade unions. On 16 February 1974, shortly before the fall of the Heath government, the feminist Women's Rights Unit of the National Council for Civil Liberties held a women's rights conference at the headquarters of the Trades Union Congress, to which delegates were invited from the unions and from women's groups. Five hundred and fifty attended. It was the first time that feminists and trade unionists had met together in any substantial numbers, and the first occasion on which representatives of the two movements explicitly recognized each other's strategic importance. Proceedings were opened by Betty Harrison, veteran organizer of the Tobacco Workers' Union:

> This Conference is a real breakthrough. Here we have industrial workers, professional workers, women from the new women's liberation movement, who are to discuss and decide what we must do in the future to fight for equality . . . I have the highest respect for the women's liberation movement. The propaganda they've done has raised the cause of women's rights in a way that it hasn't been raised for a generation . . .[23]

The following month, the London Trades Council launched a ten-point charter for working women, which was drawn up by feminists in the Communist Party. It called for eighteen weeks' maternity leave on full pay, free contraception and abortion on demand, free day nurseries, a big increase in family allowances and a national minimum wage — as well as for equal pay and opportunity and an end to discrimination in tax and social security. It led to the development of a large campaign, with a network of Working Women's Charter groups around the country. The campaign made contact with the unions mainly through unofficial channels and tended to be viewed with suspicion in higher quarters. It helped raise awareness among female members and eventually nudged the TUC into publishing a similar list of demands (see p. 156).

Child care

Child care was a major preoccupation of the women's liberation

movement. From the early 1970s, groups formed all over the country
to try to organize nurseries and playgroups. Some operated on a self-
help basis; some tried to get funds from their local councils. Others
negotiated for workplace nurseries with funding from employers.

Valerie Charlton remembers her initial approach when she first
became involved in a women's liberation group: 'We thought the
problem was women at home, kids; the key issue is to get into nurseries.
We thought that was all you had to do.' After almost two years'
campaigning, she and half a dozen others persuaded the council to
give them a small grant and a short-life property in Dartmouth Park
Hill, where they set up the Children's Community Centre — a full-
time, free, parent-controlled, non-sexist nursery for children aged
two-and-a-half to five. Some half-dozen London feminist groups set up
nurseries during the same period.

The Birmingham women's liberation group tried to raise money
from the council to start a nursery but failed, and so started a women's
liberation playgroup, which aimed 'to counter positively the
conditioning of children into restricting sex roles, and to encourage
the formation of strong friendships among the children, and between
the children and adults other than their own parents'. In 1977, a group
of women employed at the TUC headquarters in London, together
with other women at nearby workplaces, set up the Kingsway
Children's Centre, with up to thirty places: two-thirds of the cost of
each place was to be met by employers, one-third by parents.

Interwoven with the planning and negotiation that went into setting
up and running child care facilities were some difficult problems of
principle. Feminists who launched such campaigns were predominantly middle-class but were keen to provide places for working-class
children, and to involve all parents in running the facilities. However,
working-class mothers were usually out at work all day, and did not
have time to get involved; sometimes, too, they were put off by the
intellectual language of the middle-class women, and stayed away
from meetings, leaving the rest to carry responsibility.

If sufficient funds to pay nursery staff were not forthcoming from
outside sources, women could either organize voluntary rotas or plan
to employ staff on lower wages; yet they firmly believed in paying
decent wages, and in not using unpaid labour to undercut the jobs of
those (largely working-class) women who were qualified nursery
nurses. If employers could be persuaded to pay for workplace
nurseries, there was a danger that they would have undue control
over their female employees: women who had nowhere else to leave
their kids might be forced to put up with rotten pay and conditions. If
parents themselves were to bear the full costs of a nursery, they might

expect to have full control over it; but without any subsidy, costs would be very high indeed, and that would contradict the objective of child care being available to all, regardless of income.

By the mid-1970s, it was becoming harder than ever to raise money for nurseries. There seemed to be a choice between self-help, or no nurseries at all. Did feminist-inspired child care have to be an *alternative* to the welfare state? Feminists were not content to slot meekly into the 'voluntary sector'. They wanted to make claims on the state *and* to change it, as well as to maintain the integrity of their own ventures. (We return to this in chapter 3.) Assessing four years' experience of the Camden Children's Community Centre, Valerie Charlton commented in 1975 that women now knew what kind of nurseries they wanted, but these were still a long way off:

We know a great deal about the needs of women and children. We know what changes we want in the working conditions of nursery workers and we know that men must take up their responsibility in the care and education of their own and all children. We talk of the millions of working mothers for whom lack of nurseries is a problem; but the millions of working fathers also have to see this as their problem, which it most certainly is. But the missing component as yet is the organized power to force the government and local councils to provide what we want and need.[24]

By the end of the decade, the importance of comprehensive child care for all under-fives was recognized (on paper, at least) by the TUC, by many individual unions, by the Labour Party and by the Equal Opportunities Commission. Yet many nurseries were being closed down under pressure of public expenditure cuts. In July 1980, groups from all over the country got together to form the National Child Care Campaign. This co-ordinated local campaigns, collected and published research data and kept up the pressure for 'comprehensive, flexible, free and democratically controlled childcare facilities funded by the State'. It lobbied Parliament and gave advice to groups on how to set up nurseries. It saw some of its aims being realized in the London area, while the Greater London Council actively pursued a policy of meeting the child care needs of women in London, funding more that 220 projects and creating 3,000 child care places, until it was abolished in April 1986. The work of the National Childcare Campaign continued.

Women's Aid

It is interesting to compare the National Childcare Campaign with the relative success of the Women's Aid Federation. In 1972 Erin Pizzey set up the first refuge for battered women, in Chiswick, West London. A skilled publicist, she succeeded in attracting considerable attention from the media — even a spot on the *Jimmy Young Show*. Hitherto, the fact that men regularly beat up women in the privacy of their homes had been unmentioned and unmentionable. Suddenly it was news — and the public had to face the fact that domestic violence was widespread and often severe. (It has taken longer to dispel the myth that it is a purely working-class phenomenon. In 1974 a judge remarked on the case of a 'gentleman' who was found guilty of beating his wife: 'If he had been a miner in South Wales I might have overlooked it . . . There are some sections of the community where beatings of one's wife are not the same as others.'[25])

Unlike the child care campaign, Women's Aid attracted funds from government, from charitable trusts and from individual donors. People (usually men) who had money at their disposal were evidently unmoved at the thought of mothers and children needing nurseries. But wife-battering was different. Perhaps it pricked their consciences, or perhaps it genuinely shocked them. It was certainly more sensational. And refuges were a lot cheaper than nurseries. *Women's Report* commented: 'Too bad women have to be beaten senseless by their husbands before the rest of society will take their cause seriously.'[26]

In towns and cities throughout the country women began to form groups with a view to setting up local refuges. In 1974, twenty-seven groups from as far afield as Dublin and the north of Scotland gathered at a national conference organized by Chiswick Women's Aid. Pizzey herself eventually alienated many of the others, who felt that she was monopolizing the publicity, keeping too much of the money for her own refuge and wanting too much personal control. At a second national conference in 1975 (attended by twenty-eight groups who had already set up refuges and eighty-three more who were working at it) Pizzey stormed out after a row and went her own way thereafter. She continued to be identified as a leading authority on domestic violence, but her own views diverged sharply from those of other Women's Aid groups. She saw wife-battering essentially as a psychological problem and claimed that certain kinds of women were 'violence prone' and invited assault. To feminists, this was dangerous nonsense: they saw domestic violence as an expression of the power that men wielded over women, in a society where female dependence was built into the structure of everyday life. From their own extensive experience of working in refuges they concluded that wife-battering was not the practice of a deviant few, but something which could emerge in the 'normal' course of marital relations.

Since 1975, the growth of the Women's Aid movement — to 179 refuges in England alone by 1986 — was largely the work of feminists, although in some towns refuges were initially opened by social workers and other professional people who did not associate themselves with women's liberation. The Women's Aid Federation, to which almost all groups who ran refuges belonged, operated quite separately from Erin Pizzey's Chiswick outfit. It had its own headquarters, its own non-hierarchical structure and explicitly feminist objectives. Its aims included the demands of the women's liberation movement, as well as an insistence that each group within the Federation be autonomous; that refuges maintain an 'open-door' policy so that no woman was turned away; and that women in each refuge had a right to 'self-determination'.

The campaign bore fruit in Parliament too when the Domestic Violence Act was passed in 1976. Introduced as a Private Member's Bill by Labour MP Jo Richardson, it aimed to simplify and strengthen the procedure whereby a woman could obtain a court injunction to restrain a violent husband or cohabitee. The law remained a clumsy and ineffective means of dealing with the problem, but at least this new Act represented a shift in official thinking. Hitherto, it had generally been assumed that wife-battering was a private affair in which the forces of law and order should not intervene. In 1986, the Women's Aid Federation (in England) recommended that there should be enough refuges to house 10,000 women and their children — that is, 982. Though still a long way from that objective, Women's Aid remained one of the most productive and enduring of all campaigns within the women's liberation movement.

Health and reproductive rights

'Free contraception and abortion on demand', one of the four basic demands of the women's liberation movement, signalled a much broader concern with health and reproductive rights in general. This was manifested in specific campaigns, as well as in a developing feminist critique of the medical profession, the health service and reproductive technologies.

There had been campaigns for better health care for women since (at least) the 1920s, just as campaigns for birth control went back several generations. The women's liberation movement took up these campaigns and gave them a new lease of life. From the early 1970s, women's groups were involved in questioning the way men had usurped health care from women and made moves to reclaim control. Some took up gynaecological self-examination, using mirrors and specula — to overcome fear and ignorance encouraged by a male-dominated medical profession. Some joined campaigns for Well Women Clinics or Centres, which were set up in towns and cities in the late 1970s and early 1980s. Feminists carried on a long tradition among women of lobbying for more control over childbirth, as well as calling for improved cancer screening services. When consultant obstetrician Wendy Savage was suspended from her job at the London Hospital in 1985, her campaign for reinstatement became a national *cause célèbre*: she had been accused of 'professional incompetence' by her male colleagues but was able to show in her defence that she had a better record than they had. The row was really about Wendy Savage's commitment to giving women a say in how they gave birth, and her reluctance to perform Caesareans unless absolutely necessary. She was vindicated by an independent inquiry and reinstated in 1986.

The first major campaign in the area of reproductive rights was the National Abortion Campaign, launched in 1975 with the single aim of defending the 1967 Abortion Act. Opposition to the Act had by that time built up formidably, headed by the Society for the Protection of the Unborn Child and a similar body called Life. Both were supported by the Catholic Church (as well as by numerous individual Anglican clergy) who provided money and facilities, and helped to organize demonstrations and letter-writing campaigns to MPs. They sought not only to make it more difficult for women to get legal consent for abortion, but also to make safe, legal abortion much harder to obtain, by undermining the charitable abortion agencies.

A number of groups were working to defend the Act and these were linked by the umbrella organization Co-ord (Coordinating Committee in Defence of the 1967 Abortion Act). Among them, NAC was chiefly responsible for providing a radical impetus for the campaign, and mass support for a woman's right to choose. It was a specifically feminist initiative, with a non-hierarchical, federated structure linking NAC groups in most major towns and cities. Together with Co-ord and a remarkably determined group of women MPs, NAC succeeded in defeating a series of Private Members' Bills which embodied some of the aims of SPUC and Life. One of its greatest achievements was to spur the trade unions and the TUC into taking action in defence of the 1967 Act. (More of this later, p. 157.)

Beyond the campaign for abortion rights was the complex struggle for a woman's right to control her own fertility. It seemed at first that what women needed most was access to reliable contraception, to prevent unwanted pregnancies. In the late 1960s and early 1970s, the Pill and a range of new intra-uterine devices appeared to meet this need — provided they could be made available to all women on an equal basis — hence the early campaign for free contraception on demand. However, the question of access was quickly overshadowed by the question of safety. New data were casting doubt on an increasingly wide range of contraceptives, and feminists found themselves involved in campaigns to publicize the hazards, and to prevent distribution. It also became clear that women had to fight not only *against* conception, but also *for* conception, as and when they wanted it: there were campaigns against forced sterilization of Black and working-class women, and against the use of Depo Provera, a three-monthly contraceptive injection, which had been found to produce unpleasant side-effects, which was used extensively among Third World women, and which was licensed for use in the UK in 1984.

Yet it remained necessary to defend the right of access to contraception. Women had to be able to make choices, knowing what the hazards were — and to resist pressures from the anti-choice lobby, who would try to turn to their own advantage any adverse publicity about the Pill or other contraceptive devices. In 1981 Victoria Gillick began her long campaign to stop doctors giving contraceptive advice or treatment to girls under 16 without their parents' consent. She took her Area Health Authority to court and won in the Court of Appeal in 1984. Her campaign drew enthusiastic support from the authoritarian right, but it also attracted considerable opposition — from feminist groups as well as from doctors and the established birth control lobby. The DHSS appealed to the House of Lords, where Victoria Gillick was finally defeated in 1985.

Reproductive technologies became increasingly diverse and sophisticated. Scientists found ways of extracting an egg from a woman, fertilizing it and then putting it back into her (or another woman's) womb. This was known as *in vitro* fertilization (IVF). They also developed techniques for freezing and storing eggs and sperm, as well as embryos. Artificial insemination by donor (AID) became available as a means for women to conceive independently of a male sexual partner: it was used by women whose husbands were infertile, by lesbians and by single women. Surrogate motherhood was another practice which loosened the links between marriage, heterosexual intercourse and childbirth: a woman would make an arrangement with a couple who could not themselves have children, to conceive and give birth for them, usually with the husband's sperm donated artificially, and usually in exchange for a sum of money; commercial agencies were set up in the United States to arrange surrogate births and at least one of them opened a branch in the UK in the early 1980s.

All of this was highly controversial, not only for the moralists of the Conservative right, but also for feminists. The moralists were concerned that AID and surrogacy threatened to undermine marriage and conventional family life; they were outraged at AID facilitating lesbian parenthood and at childbirth becoming an explicitly commercial transaction. IVF raised urgent questions for them about the status and rights of the embryo: when eggs were extracted and fertilized *in vitro,* only one was usually put back into the womb.

Feminists were concerned that surrogacy was a means of exploiting poor women and that commercial agencies should not profit from it. Some opposed it altogether. Some were reluctant to extend the power of the state over women. Others saw it as an acceptable way of women helping each other (but felt that money should not change hands), and yet others took the view that the surrogate mother should be paid appropriately for doing a valuable job. AID was welcomed for the opportunities it gave women who could not or did not want to conceive through sexual intercourse: it represented an important — and potentially liberating — extension of choice, as well as a radical challenge to heterosexuality. There were fears, though, that AID could be a means of encouraging selective breeding — with a premium on sperm produced by certain types of men. Most felt that women themselves should control the process and that doctors should not have power to decide who had access to artificial insemination.

As for *in vitro* fertilization, it was, like AID, a useful opportunity for women who could not otherwise conceive. But it could be painful and it carried risks (eggs were extracted surgically, while the woman was under general anaesthetic). It was also commonly used as a way of overcoming the sub-fertility of the male partner — which raised the question of whether it was really in the woman's interest to suffer pain and endanger her health in order to ensure her partner's paternity, when AID or adoption could provide alternatives. Feminists also questioned whether fewer women would want IVF if they were under less social and psychological pressure to produce children; and whether scarce resources should be devoted to expensive technologies when money was needed to improve health care for all women.

In response to a growing public debate about 'test tube babies' and related matters, the Conservative government set up in 1982 a Committee of Inquiry into Human Fertilization and Embryology, chaired by Dame Mary (later Baroness) Warnock. The Committee sought to address 'fundamental questions' of infertility treatment and research as moral issues and matters of public concern. It produced a report in 1984, recommending, among other things, that there should be a statutory, independent licensing body to regulate infertility services and research. Neither AID nor IVF should be provided without a licence; only stable heterosexual couples should be eligible for them — and then only if the doctor deemed it appropriate. The arrangement of a surrogate pregnancy should be criminalized. Research on human embryos should be restricted to the first 14 days after fertilization.

A law banning commercial surrogacy agencies was passed by Parliament shortly afterwards. At the time of writing there had been no statutory move to restrict AID or IVF (the latter was already much more heavily restricted than the former; since it could not be self-administered, it was extremely expensive and was available to very few women under the National Health Service). Attempts were made by MPs Enoch Powell and Kenneth Hargreaves to get a Private Member's Bill through Parliament to ban all research using human embryos. They spearheaded a new campaign by the anti-abortion lobby, aimed at establishing a legal 'right to life' from the moment of conception. If successful, it would threaten not only a range of valuable research projects, but also women's right to choose abortion, as well as the use of some kinds of contraceptive pill and intra-uterine device, which worked by preventing fertilized eggs implanting in the uterus. These attempts at legislation failed, but the 'right to life' campaign continued.

By the mid-1980s, women's reproductive rights had become a significant focus of research, debate and campaign by feminists. The Women's Reproductive Rights Information Centre was set up in 1983 with funds from the GLC Women's Committee. In March 1984 100 women attended the first national conference on the new reproductive technologies, organized by the Leeds Reproductive Rights Campaign. One objective of these and other feminist initiatives was to get practical information to women about different means of preventing and facilitating conception and childbirth. Another was to investigate the impact of scientific developments on women's health and well-being. Overarching both these aims was the need to assert and defend women's *control* over the reproductive process. New technologies should not be allowed to reduce women to 'egg farms' or rentable wombs; neither doctors nor judges should decide how women conceived, or in what circumstances; nor should women's reproductive choices be distorted by patriarchal values, by class bias or by racism.

Women against violence

Male violence was the focus of much feminist activity in the later 1970s. In March 1976 a group of women opened Britain's first Rape Crisis Centre in North London, with a short-life property from the Department of the Environment and funds from two charitable trusts. Working as a collective, with two paid employees and a large number of volunteers, they aimed to provide practical advice, counselling and a sympathetic environment, to help women cope with the experience of rape. Evidently, they answered a need. By 1985, there were 45 similar centres throughout Britain, and more were opening. At the time the first one opened, many women were outraged at the way rape trials were conducted, with the victim herself effectively put 'on trial' as defence lawyers attempted to prove that she had 'asked for it'. Largely as a result of feminist lobbying, another Private Member's Bill was passed in 1976, the Sexual Offences (Amendment) Act, which provided better safeguards for the privacy of the victim during the trial. However, as with the Women's Aid movement, the chief aim of the Rape Crisis Centres has been to provide a woman-centred framework of support, rather than just to win legal concessions from the state. Women set out to help each other, knowing that the cause of the problem was deeply embedded in the social fabric, and could not be solved by piecemeal reforms.

This same knowledge erupted into open protest with the first of the 'Reclaim the Night' demonstrations on 12 November 1977. *Spare Rib* recorded that on that night, 130 women joined hands and sang protest songs in a huge circle in City Square, Leeds; 400 took to the streets in Manchester; 100 marched with torches through Newcastle; 80 sang and danced their way around York. In London, several hundred women invaded Soho, chanting, singing and slapping stickers on windows, greatly discomfiting the male clientele of massage parlours, porn shops and strip joints. A banner proclaimed: 'We are walking for *all* women — all women should be free to walk down any street, night or day, without fear.'[27] At the end of the decade this developed into a large and more explicitly political campaign, 'Women Against Violence Against Women', which we describe in chapter 7.

Component parts of a revolution

Parallel with these action-based campaigns ran a multitude of other activities. Women's health groups learned the art of self-examination.

A group called 'She Can Do It' operated as a work-exchange for women doing traditionally male craft jobs, and later Women in Manual Trades emerged as a pressure group to encourage women to train as plumbers, electricians, carpenters, bricklayers and mechanics. 'Women in Media' campaigned for better jobs for women in the press and broadcasting, and against sexist bias in the content of the media. Women in rural areas set up their own support network. Film-makers organized a women and film collective; artists a woman's art alliance; writers a feminist writers' workshop.

In the early 1970s there was a move into theory — reading groups were started where women read together the work of Marx, the Italian revolutionary Gramsci, the French philosopher Althusser, and the work of feminist theorists like Juliet Mitchell and Simone de Beauvoir. There was a feminist history workshop, a literature collective, a women and psychology group, and several groups concerned with education. A group of teachers and academics set up the Women's Research and Resources Centre. In the mid-1970s, women teachers in colleges and universities began to set up 'women's studies' courses. These appeared at all levels of further and higher education — often as options tacked on to existing courses. The first official MA course was launched at Kent University in 1980, followed by Bradford University in 1982 and Sheffield Polytechnic in 1983. The rapid growth of 'women's studies' spread ideas pioneered by the women's movement. For many who had not joined women's liberation groups in the early 1970s, 'women's studies' courses provided a first point of access to feminist politics; as such they played an important part in the development of the movement itself. Inevitably, too, they helped develop a critique of established academic disciplines, all of which had been constructed and controlled by men.

Information about the women's liberation movement was pooled and dispersed by a collective known as WIRES (Women's Information, Referral and Enquiry Service), who produced a regular newsletter. The magazine *Spare Rib*, launched in July 1972 to compete with traditional glossies such as *Honey* and *19*, has been produced by a feminist collective since late 1973, and has held its own in the market. *Outwrite* was launched in 1982, an anti-racist, anti-imperialist newspaper produced by Black women. In 1985, women's collectives produced two new publications: *Everywoman*, a feminist news and current affairs magazine, and *Women's Review*, on books, arts and cultural matters.

The first feminist publishing imprint, Virago, was launched in 1975 and has flourished since, producing more than three hundred titles. By the end of the 1970s there were more feminist publishers, including the Women's Press, Onlywomen Press and Sheba. All survived when the economic recession sent the book trade into a nosedive in the early 1980s. Mainstream publishers cottoned on to the fact that women's books were good for business and several of them started up special imprints or lists.

There were socialist feminist conferences and radical feminist conferences and lesbian conferences . . . all these and countless other activities, which we cannot do justice to here, comprised the women's liberation movement. These were the component parts of the revolution which sought (as Ellen Malos said in 1970) 'a total transformation of society from the bottom up'. They were the core of a broad alliance of women, who did not all necessarily identify with 'women's liberation', but who supported feminist demands and participated in the struggle to achieve them. Some were based in trade unions, in political parties and in conventional women's organizations; some were individuals who didn't belong to anything at all. Their numbers grew at a phenomenal rate from the early 1970s.

The second major phase of the modern women's movement, which evolved in the early 1980s (described on pp. 174, 254), brought with it a shift in the way campaigns developed. Ideas that had been born and nurtured within women's liberation groups had grown up and left home, spreading out into society at large, and into the political mainstream. Trade unions and local authorities began to initiate campaigns which were inspired by feminist ideas but were not the product of autonomous women's actions. The work of women's committees on local and metropolitan councils is one example of this new development, which we look at in more detail on p. 105. Another example is the campaign against sexual harassment.

Sexual harassment

This phenomenon had been unrecognized and implicitly accepted as 'normal' male behaviour — much as domestic violence had been before it was taken up by the women's movement. It didn't even have a name: the phrase 'sexual harassment' was coined in the United States and crossed the Atlantic around 1981, with the first books on the subject and news of test cases fought in US courts.

The NCCL report on sexual harassment describes one way in which men oppress and discriminate against women at work:

Repeated, unreciprocated and unwelcome comments, looks, jokes, suggestions or physical contact, that might threaten a woman's job security, or create a stressful or intimidating working environment. Physical contact can range from touching to pinching through to rape.[28]

Women who suffered it usually bore it in silence, or left their jobs to avoid it. It could take a heavy toll on their health and on their capacity to earn a living. As long as it was unnamed, it remained something women perceived as their own individual problem, which they often felt they brought upon themselves. Had they done something to provoke sexual attention? Was it a personal weakness that they could not deal with it satisfactorily?

Studies in the States revealed that sexual harassment was endemic in the workplace. A readers' survey carried out by a national women's magazine in 1976 found that 90 per cent of respondents had experienced it in various forms. An investigation in Canada put the figure at 82 per cent. It became a major campaigning issue among feminists in the States. One of the first major test cases was won in 1977 by Paulette Barnes who was made redundant after refusing to sleep with her boss. She won $18,000 in compensation. In 1981, the US Equal Employment Opportunity Commission published guidelines which confirmed that sexual harassment was a violation of women's right to equal employment opportunity under the 1964 Civil Rights Act.

As news of all this filtered through to Britain, the issue was taken up not by women's groups as such, but by trade unions and by the National Council for Civil Liberties, as a result of pressure from feminists. It was also taken up by some feminist academics, and women's magazines such as *Cosmopolitan*.

The first step was to identify the scale on which sexual harassment occurred, so that it could be seen as part of a pattern of male behaviour, rather than a private problem of individual women. The white-collar public sector union Nalgo conducted a survey among 504 workers in Liverpool, which found that a third had experienced some form of sexual harassment. A survey of women managers conducted by the University of Manchester Institute of Science and Technology found that 52 per cent had experienced unwanted sexual attention. The difference in scale could have been due to the way questions were put and what kinds of behaviour were identified as harassment. In 1980, the European Commission had asked 3,000 women whether they had ever found themselves 'the object of sexual advances or propositions which are more or less a kind of blackmail'. Only 6 per cent said yes. Blackmail is a strong term, which would not have covered all forms of harassment identified by women in the Nalgo survey. These included staring, leering, sexual innuendo, touching and grabbing; 13 per cent said they had been directly propositioned with sexual intercourse.

Awareness of sexual harassment was spread through the media. Press and TV took an interest because it was a 'sexy' topic, and perhaps because it had not been openly politicized by the women's movement. Nalgo and some other unions adopted special policies on it. Nalgo issued guidelines encouraging members to use union procedures to deal with the problem. The TUC recognized it as a source of discrimination against women workers. The NCCL helped individual women gain redress through industrial tribunals, using the laws against unfair dismissal and sex discrimination.

In 1985, a woman-only group, Women against Sexual Harassment

(WASH) opened Britain's first centre to advise women on how to combat sexual harassment. It opened one night a week in London to counsel and advise individuals, helped initiate litigation, and gave talks and training sessions. Similar work was done by groups of women in Sheffield, Leeds and in Scotland.

The Equal Opportunities Commission eventually took up the issue, backing a key test case which went to the Scottish Court of Session in 1986. Jean Porcelli, a laboratory assistant at a Glasgow school had been forced to transfer to another job when two male colleagues had subjected her to a campaign of sexual harassment. She appealed against an industrial tribunal decision that a man in her position could have been treated in an equally unpleasant way. The Law Lords of the Edinburgh Court finally ruled that she had suffered 'a form of unfavourable treatment to which a man would not be vulnerable', making it clear that sexual harassment could amount to unlawful sex discrimination.

The campaign against sexual harassment entered a world where ideas about equality and women's rights were already established. It was conducted mainly through established organizations and through litigation. The campaign was effective, but its political dimension was muted. Sexual harassment at work was an expression of male power over women, which could be compared with domestic violence or rape. Yet, unlike those issues, it did not become a focus of passionate, autonomous political engagement by women, for women. In a sense, it was a measure of the success of the women's movement that women no longer had to fight their battles entirely alone. But it also presented a new kind of challenge: women had to find ways of campaigning in the mainstream without dilution of their politics or their strength.

Peace

Here is another, quite different, example of a women's campaign that developed in the 1980s. It is distinct from the earlier campaigns in that it grew out of a concern that was not exclusive to women, nor was it begun by women who thought of themselves as feminists. Yet it is hard to imagine it happening at all — and impossible to imagine it gaining the strength that it did — if the women's liberation movement had not already come into being, and spread a sense of what women could achieve.

Thirty-six women set out from Cardiff, South Wales, on 27 August 1981, accompanied by four men and a handful of children. They walked 120 miles to a place few people had heard of at the time: Greenham Common, near Newbury in Berkshire. It was, as almost all the world knows now, the planned site of Europe's first Cruise missiles.

The marchers called themselves Women for Life on Earth. A letter they delivered to the Commander of the RAF base at Greenham Common explained that they had undertaken this action because they believed the nuclear arms race constituted 'the greatest threat ever faced by the human race and our living planet'. They pointed out that the British people had never been consulted about the siting of Cruise missiles . . .

> We wish to be neither the initiators nor the targets of a nuclear holocaust. We have had enough of our military and political leaders who squander vast sums of money and human resources on weapons of mass destruction while we can hear in our hearts the millions of human beings throughout the world whose needs cry out to be met . . . We want the arms race to be brought to a halt now — before it is too late to create a peaceful, stable world for our future generations.[29]

Four of the women chained themselves, suffragette-style, to the fence of the air base. The others built a fire and spent the night in sleeping bags under the stars. News of their action spread and supporters arrived, bringing supplies. For three days they kept up a rota of women chained to the fence. At the end of the week, heartened by all the support, they took a momentous decision: to set up a permanent picket at Greenham Common. A 'peace camp'.

So began a movement which was to transform the international campaign for peace and disarmament, and which brought a remarkable new dimension to women's liberation. The women who began it did not do so as a consciously feminist initiative; many would have rejected the label: 'I'm not a feminist. I just want to stop the threat of nuclear war.' Not until February 1982 did the camp at Greenham become a women's camp — and then only after much disagreement and discussion among the women themselves. The decision was taken partly because, as the peace camp planned its first blockade of the base, the women feared men would more readily engage in violent confrontation with the police. It was also taken for a range of reasons similar to those which had led to men being banned from women's liberation meetings in the early 1970s.

As time went by, more and more women came to Greenham; some left, many stayed — through wind, rain and snow, through eviction by the council, multiple arrests and harassment by local vigilantes. They committed themselves to non-violent direct action. They invented an extraordinary repertoire of tactics, both to draw attention to their protest and to disrupt activities at the base. They lay down in front of bulldozers. They formed a human barrier to stop incoming vehicles. They spun webs of coloured wool across the gates and these became an international symbol of women's action for peace. They danced and sang:'You can't kill the spirit/ She is like a mountain/ Old and strong, she goes on and on and on . . .' They used surprise to great effect — first to block the gates when least expected, then to make sudden incursions into the base itself.

In November 1982, 18 women who had been arrested for occupying a sentry box inside the base were taken to Newbury magistrates' court and charged with 'behaviour likely to cause a breach of the peace'. They defended themselves by claiming the right to stop the British and American governments from breaching the 1969 Genocide Act, calling in expert witnesses to show how nuclear war amounted to genocide. They were given the choice of 14 days' imprisonment or being bound over for £100 to 'keep the peace' for a year. They pointed out that it was not they who needed to be told to keep the peace. There developed a pattern of arrests and imprisonment of women, the like of which had not been seen since the notorious 'Cat and Mouse Act' was used against suffragettes nearly eighty years earlier.

Support for the Greenham women spread like wildfire. Peace camps appeared at RAF Molesworth in Cambridgeshire, a second site planned for Cruise, and at other military installations. The Campaign for Nuclear Disarmament took on a whole new lease of life. Spontaneously, a national network of Greenham support groups appeared — much like the sudden mushrooming of women's liberation groups a decade before.

Meanwhile, a wildly ambitious plan was being laid: to encircle the base and link arms. The perimeter was nine miles long and they thought they'd need 16,000 women. Impossible, surely? On 12 December 1982, 30,000 women converged on Greenham Common and formed a human chain around the base. They decorated the fence with webs of wool and banners, children's toys and clothes, photographs of loved ones. One woman, who'd come all the way from Dublin, remembers:

> We joined hands and began to sing . . . for nine miles we formed a living chain to lock in the horrors of war, to stand between them and our world and to say: we will meet your violence with a loving embrace, for it is the surest way of defusing it. How strong I felt when I joined my voice to the waves of voices shouting Freedom and when the echoes from so far away drifted across the base . . .[30]

The Greenham women (a phrase which describes not just the peace campers, but their supporters too) became world-famous. People came to visit them from far and wide. They were deluged with requests to speak at meetings at home and abroad. They were vilified by some of the British tabloids — as dirty lesbians, Soviet stooges, irresponsible wives and mothers — but much of the media coverage they received was grudgingly sympathetic. They seemed, in spite of continuing arrests and imprisonments, on the crest of a wave. On New Year's Day 1983, 44 women climbed over the fence and danced in a ring around the top of a Cruise missile silo. On 1 April, CND organized a human chain of 77,000, linking Greenham to Aldermaston, and the same day 200 women staged their own April Fool's protest, invading the base dressed as furry animals for a Teddy Bears' Picnic. Later that month they padlocked all the gates with indestructible bicycle locks. In June they sewed a four-and-a-half mile dragon, to weave in and out of the base. On Halloween, they took down four miles of the fence with bolt-cutters. They made links with women from the South Pacific who were protesting against nuclear tests, with women struggling to free Namibia and stop uranium mining there, and with Italian women trying to keep out Cruise from the Cosimo base in Sicily . . .

Cruise arrived at Greenham nevertheless — on 14 November 1983. It was not the end of the peace camp, but the start of a new phase. Cruise was supposed to be a mobile weapon, which could be transported around the country in high secrecy. A 'Cruisewatch' network tried to ensure it never moved unnoticed. On 11 December, 50,000 embraced the base, using mirrors to reflect it back on itself. Protests, arrests and imprisonments continued.

Greenham Common and the peace movement became, in the early 1980s, a major focus of feminist activity, drawing together women of different persuasions, from all corners of the women's movement as well as from outside it. Women who had missed the high tide of discovery and invention that launched women's liberation in the seventies made similar connections through working with other women for peace. They found out about the value of sisterhood, the need for women's autonomy, and the importance of non-hierarchical forms of organization. They learned about their own strength and about the political significance of patriarchy. To a certain extent, they plugged into ideas that were already current, but the main force of conscious-ness-raising came from their own actions. At the same time, they were raising awareness among feminists about the urgency of stopping the arms race. They drew the women's liberation movement towards the peace movement and replenished both in the process.

A collective experience

'Women's liberation' cannot be understood as a vanguard leading the masses — that approach would have been quite alien to its politics in any case. The boundaries between the wider women's movement and women's liberation were not fixed in any way and were impossible to distinguish. You could look up 'Women's Liberation' in the London phone book and find a series of addresses and numbers belonging to various enterprises. But it was more than a federation of small groups. It was a collective experience accumulated over nearly 20 years, and it continued to grow and change. It was reformist and revolutionary. It was a source of political energy, a developing body of theory, a battleground, a sisterhood.

In the following chapters we explore the main areas where the women's liberation movement has been politically engaged. We try to assess how much progress has been made towards feminist objectives, to examine the nature of the struggle and the character of the opposition. It is not a matter of simply finding out how close women have come to achieving specific demands. The struggle for women's liberation has taken place on several different levels. It has involved women changing themselves as well as the external world.

On one level, women were demanding justice and equality. They were saying to men: you have closed the door on us, let us in; you have kept us short on rations, give us more. And since they couldn't rely on men being decent enough to say yes, they were trying, on another level, to stop men having the power to say no — the power to oppress them. To this end, they were fighting to change the cultural, social and economic systems which expressed and maintained male supremacy.

However, women are not simply held in place by the force of male oppression. They are subordinate, as men are dominant, and their subordination goes under their skin, below the threshold of consciousness. This is not to say that women's oppression is 'all in the head', but that women have had to recognize and then struggle to transform the social construction of feminine psychology — as well as men's constructed sense of masculinity — as a crucial part of their fight against oppression. In a way, this has been the key to women's liberation.

Notes to chapter 1

1   *Enough!*, no. 1, Bristol Women's Liberation, 1969.
2   Rowbotham, S. *Women's Consciousness, Man's World*, Penguin, 1973.
3   Friedan, B. *The Feminine Mystique*, Penguin, 1976.
4   Quoted in 'Nine Years Together', a history of a women's liberation group, in *Spare Rib* no. 9, April 1978.
5   Ibid.
6   Mitchell, J. 'The Longest Revolution' in *New Left Review*, November — December 1966.
7   Rowbotham, S. *Women's Liberation and the New Politics*, Spokesman pamphlet, no. 17, 1969.
8   Koedt, A. 'The Myth of the Vaginal Orgasm' in *Notes from the Second Year*, 1970.
9   Greer, G. *The Female Eunuch*, Paladin, 1971.
10   *The Oppression of Women in the 1970s*, Bristol Group, 1971.
11   Firestone, S. *The Dialectic of Sex*, Paladin, 1971.
12   *Spare Rib*, no. 79, 1979.
13   Ibid.
14   Freeman, J. (Joreen) 'The Tyranny of Structurelessness' in *The Second Wave*, vol. 2 (1).
15   Bryan, B., Dadzie, S. and Scafe, S. *The Heart of the Race*, Virago, 1985.
16   Ibid.
17   Ibid.
18   Ibid.
19   Ibid.
20   Wilson, A. *Finding a Voice*, Virago, 1985.
21   Hobbs, M. *Born to Struggle*, Quartet, 1973.
22   *Women's Report*, vol. 1 (3), 1973.
23   Hewitt, P. (ed.) *Danger! Women at Work*, National Council for Civil Liberties, 1974.
24   Charlton, V. 'A Lesson in Day Care' in *Women in the Community*, ed. Mayo, M., Routledge & Kegan Paul, 1977.
25   Quoted in *Red Tape*, 1974; reprinted in Gill, T. and Coote, A. *Battered Women and the Law*, Inter-Action & NCCL, 1977.
26   *Women's Report*, vol. 2 (1), 1974.
27   *Spare Rib* no. 5, January 1978.
28   Sedley, A. and Benn, M. *Sexual Harassment at Work*, NCCL, 1984.
29   Harford, B. and Hopkins, S. *Greenham Common: Women at the Wire*, The Women's Press, 1984.
30   Ibid.

2 Work

'Equal pay now' and 'Equal job opportunities' were two of the first four demands of the women's liberation movement. Paid employment has been one of the most conspicuous areas of struggle, involving more women from more walks of life than any other. It has also been the site of many apparent victories and official reforms.

An innocent outsider, reading reports in the press between 1975 and 1985, might be forgiven for thinking women had achieved their early objectives. There were new Acts of Parliament establishing a right to equal pay (not just for equal work, but for work of equal value) and outlawing sex discrimination in employment. Newspapers regularly celebrated female pioneers: the first 'girl' on a building site, the plucky young thing in the stock exchange, the 'lady' in the lorry cab, the first female astronauts, and of course the first woman in Downing Street . . . all living, breathing proof that women were winning equality at work.

But the pioneers could be numbered in their hundreds. For the remaining 10.9 million women in paid employment, the story has been quite different. Far from making progress towards equality, they found it slipping away from them.

Nothing hindered the steady process by which women were eased out of skilled jobs throughout the twentieth century. Between 1911 and 1971, women's share of skilled (higher-paid) manual work dropped by nearly half, from 24 to 13.5 per cent. Over the same span of years, their share of unskilled manual work more than doubled — from 15.5 to 37.2 per cent. This astonishing trend, in which men accomplished a near-monopoly of skilled work, continued through the 1970s and 1980s. (See table 1, p. 80.)

Women's pay was held down with such tenacity that by the mid-1980s, women workers were still taking home 34 per cent less money than men. In 1984, for every £1 in the average man's pay packet, there was only 65.8 pence in the average woman's. The gap had been closed by less than ten pence in ten years. (See tables 2 and 3, p. 81.)

Nor had anything happened to disturb the patterns of paid and unpaid work — in which women had been designated a particular function in the home (as unpaid child-minder, housekeeper, cook, nurse and cleaner) and a corresponding function in the labour market.

Considered in this light, the call for 'equal opportunity' had a hollow ring about it. 'Opportunity' implied 'choice', yet there had never been any real choice for women. Their position as low-paid, part-time, intermittent, secondary wage earners determined their role in the home from the beginning of the industrial revolution. Correspondingly, their role in the home determined their position in the labour market. Both were set in train by the efforts of male workers to defend themselves against a new breed of employers in the early stages of capitalism; they endured as strongly as ever in the 1980s.

There has been, however, a dramatic influx of women into the labour market in more recent years. The numbers of 'economically active' females increased by 45 per cent between 1931 and 1970. In the same period, the number of married women going out to work increased fourfold. The number of male workers, meanwhile, remained stable. In 1984, there were approximately 10.9 million women and 15.5 million men in the working population. This represented a significant change for women: gone were the days when marriage, or the arrival of the first child, was expected to lift them out of the labour market and deposit them at home for good. But when women entered the workforce, they did not do so freely or at random. They were drawn in, and then confined to a handful of industries and occupations.

As Catherine Hakim demonstrated in her research for the Department of Employment,[1] these were not male-dominated occupations, but 'slowly-expanding female-dominated occupations for which the supply of single women became inadequate'.[2] Women worked separately from men, apartheid-style, in low-paid jobs which held out little hope of advancement. And they entered the waged labour force on the strict but unspoken condition that this would not interfere with the unwaged work they performed in their homes.

The efforts of women to win equality at work foundered because their strategies were designed to attack the symptoms, not the causes of the problem. Not until later in the 1970s did women begin to understand more fully how inequality was constructed, and to see it as part of a system in which men had power and women did not.

Moreover, women's early demands were formulated at a time when the economy was relatively healthy. In 1970, there were just over 800,000 registered unemployed and the figure dropped to 556,200 in 1973. Industry was fairly buoyant, the welfare state was burgeoning; it was easier to believe that new jobs could be opened up for women in the higher-paid, skilled areas. While Labour was in government and the social services were still expanding, the prospect of child care and other facilities being provided on a community basis and financed by the state did not seem all that remote. It was possible to imagine women going out to work on the same terms as men, with only minimal disruption to the lives of men themselves. But it was a vision which was unlikely to be realized even in continuing prosperity, and it inhibited the development of more useful strategies.

After the first years of the women's liberation movement, the economic and political weather changed dramatically — from the promise of spring to the bitterness of winter (summer never came). Unemployment rocketed and by the mid-1980s Britain's industrial life and its welfare state had been brought to the point of collapse. There was no immediate prospect of improvement and it was clear that, even with a new Labour government, recovery from the economic recession would be a long, slow, painful business. There would be little or no economic growth and there could be no hope of any prosperous overlay of new 'opportunities' for women.

In the following pages we consider some of the main components of women's subordination as waged workers. How far have women been kept in separate jobs from men, and why has this *segregation* developed? How has the notion of *skill* been constructed, and to whose advantage? How has the idea arisen that there should be one main breadwinner for each family — the ideology of the *family wage* — and what are the implications for women? How far do female and male workers have different relationships to *time*, bearing on their different roles at home, and what effect does this have on their relative positions in the labour market? What are the characteristics of female and male *pay*? What has been the impact of *new technology* and *unemployment*? By examining these issues we hope to show why women have made so little progress towards equality at work, and why we need to develop new approaches to the problem.

Occupational apartheid

The latest studies on job segregation show that women have been concentrated overwhelmingly in the service industries. (These are industries which do not produce goods — such as banking, hair-dressing, cleaning and public administration.) Between 1961 and 1980, more than two million women joined the service industries and more than half a million women left the production industries. As a result, by the mid-1980s more than three-quarters of all female workers were in the non-productive sector.

Women have been confined to specific industries within each sector. For example, by 1980 half of all women in the productive sector were in only four of the nineteen industrial groups: food and drink, clothing and footwear, textiles and electrical engineering. And they were in a very narrow range of occupations. More than half of all women workers were either caterers, cleaners or hairdressers, or were performing 'other personal services', which include nursing and secretarial work.

The concentration of women in lower paid jobs has increased dramatically since the beginning of the century. We have seen that men monopolized skilled manual work. Among non-manual workers women increased their share of managerial and administrative jobs by a tiny margin — from 19.8 to 21.6 per cent — in the course of seventy years; but in the same period they more than tripled their share of clerical work — from 21.4 to 73.2 per cent. Jobs which at the beginning of the century had a balance of male and female workers typical of the economy as a whole were transformed by the 1970s into 'typically feminine' jobs. By that time, ninety-nine per cent of all typists, shorthand writers and secretaries were women, but only 14 per cent of office managers. In other occupational groups, there were deep divisions too. Among electrical and electronic workers, 84 per cent of assembly-line workers were female, but only 1.4 per cent of 'linesmen and cable-jointers'.[3] These patterns did not change significantly during the 1980s.

There has been a staggering degree of total segregation — that is, women and men doing jobs where there are *no* members of the opposite sex doing the same thing at the same workplace. A 1980 study revealed that 45 per cent of women and about 75 per cent of men worked in totally segregated jobs.[4] The likelihood of men doing work which was all-male or nearly all-male increased considerably in the course of the century.

This trend towards greater segregation was occasioned partly by changes in the structure of the labour market. Old jobs disappeared, new ones were created. With the expansion of the public sector after the Second World War, and the rapid growth of administrative work and retail distribution, traditional sources did not yield enough labour — and so new ones had to be tapped. For the first time in peace time, mature women were employed who had hitherto been confined to the home, either because of formal 'marriage bars' against their employment or because of a general consensus that motherhood was a full-time occupation.

But this alone cannot explain why the idea developed that there were 'men's jobs' and 'women's jobs', rigidly divided from each other; or why men's jobs were more skilled and higher-paid, while women's were less skilled and lower-paid; or why both were part of a system in which women worked unpaid at home and men were regarded as the main family breadwinners.

It cannot be explained away as a 'natural' consequence of women's unique capacity to bear and breastfeed children. Why should this dictate the way children are looked after when they are not being breastfed, or how domestic work is done? Why should the bearers of children do unskilled, low-paid jobs? We know from contemporary experience that women/mothers are as capable as men/fathers of doing skilled work, yet only exceptionally do they do it. Caring for children is no more a 'naturally female' pursuit than cleaning kitchen floors or typing letters; nor is it more 'natural' than it is for a man to operate a lathe, or manage a bank or go to the pub on Friday night. These are social roles, social habits, which have developed over time and which are the product of political struggles.

Skilled workers of the world unite

It has been common, even among socialist theoreticians, to accept women's domestic role as *given*, to take it for granted, and to view women's role in the labour market from that basis. Feminist historians and economists have been delving deeper into the structure of inequality. One significant part of this is the relationship between sex, skill and control.

In the nineteenth century, as production became factory-based, the social and economic order was transformed, and the struggle between labour and capital began in earnest. The only established means of resistance for workers were craft-based organizations. These were self-regulating, determining for themselves who should acquire skills and who should gain entry to them. They had their roots in pre-capitalist society, which was patriarchal; women were generally excluded from them. They set a precedent for the development of trade unionism in the later years of the century. Access to skill was associated with access to working-class political organization and self-defence; and together they afforded some measure of control over income. To be outside this axis of skill and organization was to be relatively poor and powerless. Since women were excluded from trade unionism, their bargaining position was weak, and the pay they could command was consequently low. In turn, this meant that they could be accused by men of undercutting them.

Skill was about control over production as well as over income. In some of the staple industries of the new capitalist system, skilled craftsmen contracted work from the factory owner and engaged other workers as sub-contractors, among whom income was unevenly distributed and whose access to new skills was blocked. Soon, employers sought to reduce their dependence on well-organized, higher-paid male workers. Apart from wanting to reduce the cost of labour, they needed to weaken the control which skilled craftsmen exercised over the production process. One strategy was to break down the work of skilled individuals into a series of simplified, routine tasks, to be carried out by cheaper labourers, whose productivity could more easily be measured and controlled; another was to invest in machinery which simplified or replaced human labour. As a result, more and more jobs were created which were neither highly skilled nor heavy, and which could be done as easily by women as by men.

Skilled workers tried to defend their control over production and to stop earning power being undermined by unskilled workers, male and female. As part of their defence, they sought to preserve the patriarchal relations that had prevailed in pre-capitalist society, in which men had authority and control over women and children, based in the family home. Capitalism in its early stages had disrupted family life, forcing women, children and men out of their traditional communities and into towns and factories, where human labour was required, regardless of sex or age. Patriarchal relations were consequently under some threat. In a bid to reassert control in the new economic order, men developed a role for themselves as chief family wage-earner — leaving the rest of the work in the home to be performed, unwaged, by women. Thus the attrition between capital and early craft unionism helped to ensure the survival of patriarchy and served the interests of capital by arranging for labour to continue to be reproduced and sustained without paying the people who were doing the necessary work.

This is not to suggest that women were helpless victims of a male conspiracy. We know that many of them fought for the right to waged work and the right to organize. But they were relatively powerless. Moreover, for many of them it may not have seemed an intolerable arrangement to perform a role which approximated — however tenuously — to that of their mothers and grandmothers before industrialization. The appeal of tradition helped to mould familiar relations in the early days of capitalism, and staved off the resistance of women when there was otherwise a strong possibility of change.

This was the arena in which the character of contemporary wage bargaining was formed. It has been concerned with preserving differentials; it has been shaped by the balance of power between different groups of workers; and it has produced hierarchies within the working class with skilled men at the top and women at the bottom.

As new manufacturing processes were developed in the later part of the nineteenth century, male workers followed the pattern set by craftsmen (whether or not they themselves had originally been trained in craft skills) — carving out areas of work, which were designated skilled or semi-skilled, and defending them against intrusion by the lower-paid. As new trade unions were formed, women were usually excluded from these too, as part of men's defences against the danger of having their wages undercut.

William Lazonick and others pointed out in their study of the textile industry that when the mechanized mule was introduced, it could have been operated by either sex. Instead, men operated the bigger mules and defended their control over the production process:

the persistence of the internal sub-contract system, with its hierarchical divisions of labour, meant that the job of mule-spinner . . . [came to involve] a supervisory as well as an operative function.[5]

The men's union opposed the employment of women as mule-spinners. This had a cumulative effect. By securing the job for themselves and retaining control of skilled and supervisory functions, the men built a basis for stronger trade union organization. And so they were better equipped to fend off threats from female labour, which continued to be low-paid because of women's weak bargaining position. There were similar developments in most manufacturing industries.

The notion of skill in many areas of work eventually had less to do with the content of a job and more to do with the gender and bargaining power of whoever was doing the work, as the history of the English clothing industry illustrates. Throughout the twentieth century, machining in this industry has been done by women and by men. Where it is done by women it is semi-skilled and where it is done by men it is skilled. The two sexes have seldom worked side by side. They have used different machines, usually in separate workshops. However, their respective machining work has not been sufficiently disparate to justify the separate 'skilled' and 'semi-skilled' labels.

The men who worked in the clothing industry at the beginning of this century were engaged in a struggle to preserve dignity, status and control. These attributes relied heavily upon their authority as heads-of-family. The men were forced to take on machine work which was usually done by women and defined as semi-skilled, but they redefined their own machining as skilled labour.

For them, craft status was identified with manhood, and the struggle to maintain their position in the upper level of the labour hierarchy was fuelled by a determination to maintain the traditional balance of power in families where men had always acted as primary breadwinners.[6]

The pattern continued well into the third quarter of the century. A study published in 1980 showed that women were employed in both the paper-box and the cardboard carton industries. They used hand-fed machines to make paper boxes, but the carton-making process was more automated and so required less concentration. However, in the paper-box industry, the work was considered unskilled, while in carton making it was considered semi-skilled. As Ann Phillips and Barbara Taylor observed in their paper on 'Sex and Skill':

It is hard to escape the conclusion that it is because of the similarities between the work of men and women in the carton industry that women in carton production are considered more skilled than box workers. Men and women work in a similar process; men are recognized as semi-skilled rather than unskilled workers; therefore carton production must be semi-skilled. The women producing paper boxes are simply women producing paper boxes, and however much the work itself might seem to qualify for upgrading, it remains unskilled because it is done by typically unskilled workers — women.[7]

When women were drawn into office work in their thousands at the beginning of this century, they acquired a number of skills — typewriting, shorthand, telephoning, office administration. But they were carefully distinguished from male workers, often in segregated offices with separate entrances. Male clerks — the 'black-coated workers' of the nineteenth century — disappeared from office life and re-emerged in new guises, as managers and trainee managers, accountants and trainee accountants, executives and junior executives. In offices, as in the textile factories, men defended their status by retaining control over key jobs which ensured them a degree of power. The jobs of female office workers were designated *less* skilled than those of men, simply because they were performed by women. And their low status was further confirmed as the work itself became 'feminized'. The female secretary looked after her boss as only a woman could. She brought him cups of tea, dusted his desk, dialled his telephone calls, took his suits to the cleaners, bought presents for his relatives . . . became, in short, the office wife. Typists and clerks

were regarded (because of their sex) as junior secretaries rather than
as junior managers or as a separate category of skilled manual workers
— and they, too, found themselves performing wifely duties for the
men in the office. Thus, patriarchal relations were re-created in the
workplace, guaranteeing the superior status of the male.

Something similar happened in the area of health work. Women
were, of course, the original health workers (witches, wise women,
midwives),[8] but were supplanted by men, who tried to turn the whole
business into an exact science and a closed shop. In the nineteenth
century, women re-established themselves in the field by creating
their own profession — largely due to the efforts of Florence
Nightingale — to ensure that they were *paid* workers, not voluntary
aides (an important gain). To do this, they had to win recognition
from the male establishment and the price was to reassure doctors that
the female interlopers would pose no threat to their supremacy. The
nurse, in Nightingale's words, was to be 'the skilled servant of medicine'
who operated 'in strict obedience to the physician's or surgeon's
power'. The need to distinguish men's work (diagnosis-prescription)
from women's work (treatment-observation) determined the assessment
of their respective skills and the very character of health work. And all
was justified by defining the woman's role in the workplace in the
same terms as her role in the home — as though it were her 'natural'
destiny. 'The best nurse is that woman whose maternal instincts are
well developed . . . The connection between mothering and nursing is
very close,' decreed *Hospital* journal in 1897; and in 1902: 'A good
nurse must first be a good housemaid.'[9]

In her book *The Machinery of Dominance*, Cynthia Cockburn
described how, as computers revolutionized work in factories and
offices, overturning traditional definitions of skill, men nevertheless
maintained their monopoly of higher-paid jobs. In the clothing
industry, for example:

> New technology has brought its ambiguous new operator roles
> within reach of women but it has not brought them *technical*
> training or competence. The wave of women into the industry is
> lapping up against twin cliffs of male interest: senior management
> and skilled technical posts.[10]

Men who could no longer claim physical prowess because they worked
with computerized technology had to find ways of explaining why
women could not do the same work. Cockburn recorded some of their
justifications:

'I wouldn't think that a woman could possibly be logical enough in her thinking to do the job we do.' But wait, here is someone else saying that 'women are *too* logical': 'Women don't have the imagination, the flair, to diagnose faults . . . we've come to the conclusion that it is half the time intuitive . . .' *Isn't that supposed to be a woman's quality?* 'Ah well,' this engineer responded quickly, 'Probably it isn't intuition. It's probably just that we know the machine. We've seen it all before.' And so on, in circles. Patience is it, you need? Women haven't got patience enough for engineering, but they have patience for the drudgery of data processing. Dexterity? Not what it takes to repair a sewing machine, only what it takes to sew.

By whatever contortion it takes, in masculine ideology women are represented as non-technological, as incompatible with machinery, except in the controlled, supervised, guided role of operator.[11]

Will the real breadwinner please stand up?

As men guarded 'skilled' work and organization as exclusive male territory, so the working class remained divided, with a gun at the heads of the strongest sector in the form of a weak, cheap and abundant source of alternative (female) labour. The idea which lay behind this development, and which also served as a defence of male pre-eminence, gathered strength towards the end of the nineteenth century: this was the idea that the man was the main breadwinner for the family. The woman's main role is at home, looking after husband and children. In theory, she does not need paid employment because her husband supports her.

In practice, this support has rarely been forthcoming in most families. Working-class women, however demanding their domestic responsibilities, have always had to turn their hand to a bit of cleaning, child minding, sewing or suchlike for somebody else, to eke out the man's wage. But where this has been the case, the woman's employment has been afforded a different status from the man's work, on the ground that it is only a secondary activity, carried on in addition to her real occupation; her wages and her job are regarded as 'extras' — not of primary importance.

In the early nineteenth century, the idea of an individual male breadwinner earning enough to keep a wife and children was not at all familiar, and when factory production began to separate the home from the workplace, initially whole families would go out to work. In agriculture, farmers favoured employing married men, because their wives and children would be available for seasonal work.

Within the middle class, as commercial and professional activities increasingly took place outside the home, married women were transformed, in Ray Strachey's words, 'from partners to parasites' — symbols, in their apparent idleness, of their husbands' prosperity. Hilary Land explained in her paper, *The Family Wage*:

> Some historians of this period have argued that the working-class man believed that by restricting the hours women and children could work in the factory, his hours and conditions would also have to be improved. So too would his pay, for women and children would have less opportunity to undercut his wages, or indeed to replace him. If women and children could be removed altogether, then the labour supply, which throughout much of the nineteenth century was in excess, would be restricted, and at the same time men could argue more forcefully and from increased bargaining strength that they needed wages high enough to support a family, i.e. *a family wage*.[12]

The idea became firmly embedded in trade union philosophy and has continued to exert a robust influence throughout the twentieth century. Clearly, women's increased participation in the labour market has distorted its function in that market. The family wage is dead — but long live the family wage. It lives on in the rules which govern supplementary benefits, it lives on in the minds of men, it lives on as the concept of a 'living wage', and it underpins the determination of male and female pay.

In her essay 'Class Struggle and the Working-Class Family', Jane Humphries quoted a labourer's appeal in the *Trades Newspaper*, 16 October 1825:

> I recommend my fellow labourers, in preference to every other means of limiting the number of those who work for wages, to prevent their wives and children from competing with them in the market . . .[13]

Humphries argued that women's labour was one of the few sources of working-class control over labour supply, and it was one which enjoyed the support of bourgeois ideology.

Almost a century and a half later in 1966, at the annual conference of the Civil Service Clerical Association, a male delegate declared: 'What we want is to give breadwinners throughout the country enough pay to keep their wives at home.'

The National Board for Prices and Incomes (set up by a Labour government with the approval of the TUC) reported in 1971 on the pay and conditions of workers in the contract cleaning industry. This industry had expanded massively since the war, employing some 90,000 general cleaners by the early 1970s; and it was very profitable. Yet, it paid an average hourly rate of 43p, which was 15p less than the median rate for manual workers at that time. The Board maintained that contract cleaning could 'not be seen as a low-paid trade as a whole'. It based its bizarre observation on the fact that it 'set female part-time earnings in the context of their families' income' and, since women's contribution was 'not a major part of the family income', women were therefore 'not in general low paid'.[14]

The Board processed and policed wages and prices; low pay was one of its major targets. It was evident in the early 1970s — as it is now — that the problem with low pay was women's pay and the problem with women's pay was low pay. But the Board managed to camouflage this connection and in doing so it determined the official approach to women's wages which prevailed well into the 1980s. It defined women's pay as being a separate problem from that of low pay — one which might be dealt with by the new Equal Pay Act (passed in 1970 but not enforced until 1975), but which was not to be dealt with on the same terms as men's low pay. The Board was being not a little disingenuous in assuming the Equal Pay Act would solve the problem for women.

When the Board reported on the pay of health service auxiliary workers in 1971, it noted that a third were men, who were 'among the lowest-paid men in the country'. Their full-time women colleagues grossed only two-thirds of the men's average earnings, but they were 'not low-paid by comparison with women in general'. In its next report, on *General Problems of Low Pay*, the Board remarked that it was

> necessary to consider the position of men and women separately; otherwise the problem of low pay could be practically synony- mous with that of low pay among women, and this could ignore the social significance of the fact that men's earnings are normally the main source of family income . . .[15]

This, then, was the triple formula for by-passing the problem of women's pay. First, women's income was not 'a major part of the family income', and although this was *because* they were low-paid, it was also deemed to be the reason why they could not be regarded as

low-paid. Secondly, it was recognized that women were often paid less than men, but this aspect of the problem was discarded as something that would magically disappear under the Equal Pay Act. Thirdly, if all else failed, the problem of unequal pay could be overcome by comparing women's pay not with men's pay but with that of women in general.

In the 1970s and 1980s, the concept of the family wage still occupied an important place in wage determination. The term itself had passed out of use in trade union circles, but negotiators — especially those in the lower-paid, blue-collar sectors — would argue that, in order to maintain living standards, it was essential that their members' wages should not fall below supplementary benefit rates for a 'typical family unit'.

In 1979, when the unions organizing local authority manual workers submitted their claim to the Clegg Commission on pay comparability, they pointed out that 'in 1978 about half of all full-time workers in local authority services were earning less in terms of their net earnings than a typical family would obtain through social security'. More than three-quarters of the members for whom these unions were negotiating were female. Not only did this line of argument bear no relation to the real lives of women (wives were not entitled to claim any supplementary benefit at all), but also, as we shall see (p. 71), it did nothing to help the majority of female workers improve their earnings in relation to those of men.

From about 1978 onwards, feminists began to challenge the concept of the family wage. They pointed out that half of all married women went out to work; and it was absurd to suggest that families were not dependent on female earnings, since it had been estimated that the number of families in poverty would *quadruple* if wives did not take paid jobs. In addition, there were more than a million one-parent families; one in ten of all households was headed by a single mother. Out of the entire 'economically active' population, *only five per cent* could be described as representative of the supposedly typical family unit (i.e. the breadwinning man with a wife and two children to support).[16] The idea that one person's wage should be sufficient to support a family took no account of the number of children; hence, large families were penalized.

The problem of ensuring a proper income for families was never simple, however. Feminists and trade unionists continued to argue about how best to solve it. If child benefit were substantially increased, children could be adequately supported regardless of whether one or both parents worked, or how much they earned. But there was a danger in families becoming too dependent on state support: as the Thatcher government demonstrated, benefits and services could be swiftly undermined.

On the other hand, it was not necessarily safer for families to rely on wages. In pay bargaining, the 'family wage' proposition could be turned against workers. Employers could survey the workforce and use the same formulation to justify maintaining differentials between women and men: 'Wives don't need so much money because they don't have families to support.' And what good was the idea of the 'family wage' to the unemployed?

The crux of the feminist case was that the ideology of the 'family wage' had played a vital part in shaping the labour market and in setting women apart from men in lower-paid jobs; it bore little relation to family needs in the 1980s, yet retained considerable force, perpetuating inequality between women and men. We take up the question of restructuring family income on p. 261.

The time factor

Female workers, as we have seen, have been confined to certain kinds of jobs which are regarded as less skilled and which attract lower pay. Linked with this has been the appropriation by men of the role of chief family breadwinner, and the designation of women as unpaid domestic labourers. Men's superior bargaining strength has left women no choice about this: they have continued to do paid work but, because of their domestic role, they have developed a very different relationship to working time. And this has intensified their unequal position in the labour market.

Women need to work to earn money, but at the same time they have to look after their homes, husbands and children. They cannot work long hours of overtime, or awkward shifts which interfere with cooking family meals or dispatching children to school. There are periods of their lives when they need to work short hours; and there are times when they cannot work at all.

By makeshift means and from necessity, they have reduced their hours of paid employment to what might, in any other time and place, be considered a model schedule for a working week. It has never been viewed as such, and has never been given organized political muscle. For reducing the working week, women have been financially penalized, and made to suffer contractual and professional disadvantage. Men's relationship to working time has expressed their absenteeism from domestic responsibility. The fiction of a full-time working week has depended on long hours being worked by people who are in turn dependent on others to do their domestic work for them. The time-and-motion constraints on motherhood (fatherhood being the passive mode of parenthood) are nowhere more manifest than in the pattern of waged working time.

In the early 1980s, more than half of all married women were working 30 hours or less a week, compared with one in five non-married women and one in 20 men. Of married women 23 per cent were working 16 hours or less, compared with 10 per cent of non-married women and two per cent of men.[17]

Among full-time employees, 80 per cent of women were working between 35 and 40 hours a week, compared with 59.5 per cent of men. Twenty-three per cent of men and only 7.5 per cent of women were working between 41 and 50 hours a week. These figures include overtime: on average, men were working 3.5 hours and women 0.6 hours of overtime a week.[18]

Women's working lifetime has developed a different pattern from men's. Before the Second World War, women most commonly worked in their late teens and early twenties before they got married, and then left the labour market altogether. By 1971, the pattern had changed entirely: most women were now working until their mid-twenties and then returning to employment after a period of child-rearing, in their late thirties and forties. If they worked in between, it tended to be on a casual, intermittent basis.

According to a major survey by *Woman's Own*, 27 per cent of mothers with children under five and 20 per cent of mothers with children aged 5—16 were not employed, but wanted to be. Families with growing children needed more money than young, childless couples, or middle-aged couples whose children have left home. But the *Woman's Own* survey showed that four out of five mothers would still want to go out to work, at least some of the time, 'even in an ideal world where all financial pressures were removed'. The same survey identified a 'lack of suitable child care facilities' as a major stumbling block. Nearly one in five mothers with children under eleven had given up their employment because they couldn't make adequate arrangements for their children.[19]

The uneven distribution of working time between women and men had a bearing on the kind of work that women were obliged to do, and on the degree of protection they enjoyed from exploitative rates of pay and from redundancy. As men defined themselves as the main wage earners for their families, they negotiated with employers (explicitly or implicitly) to reach a definition of a *proper* job, and to agree on an appropriate lifestyle for a *real* worker. A 'proper' job began after school or college and continued without a break until retirement age. It lasted for at least eight hours a day; it might spill over into evenings and weekends; and its most demanding phase tended to be the first twenty years, as training was acquired and vital steps taken towards a higher earning capacity. This coincided with the period when children were young and most in need of parental time. However, a 'real' worker did not have distracting family commitments, and was available for overtime and night work if necessary. A 'real' worker was able to move from one part of the country to another if that was what the employer required.

Jobs that were normally done by men developed along these lines. In some instances, the work itself demanded that jobs were organized in a certain way — for instance, in industries which relied upon continuous processes, or in hospitals, where the work could not cease. But more often than not, the gender of the worker played a large part in determining the structure of the job, just as it helped to determine how far the job was regarded as 'skilled'.

Women were not considered 'real' workers because they could not normally fulfil the necessary conditions (and even if they could it was assumed that they couldn't). Many of the jobs they did were arranged to fit in more easily with their prior commitments at home; but these were not seen as 'proper' jobs. They were casual and peripheral; they had no place in any career structure. Young women were often passed over for training and promotion because they intended (or were expected) to have a break from employment while their children were young. When they returned to the labour market they were thought to have missed (rather than gained) valuable experience; only the lower-paid jobs were available to them.

One example is provided by the teaching profession, where women are in the majority, but men dominate the higher-paid jobs. In 1982, 55 per cent of male teachers were in scale 3 posts or above, compared with only 29.5 per cent of female teachers.[20] A study by the National Union of Teachers and the Equal Opportunities Commission showed that, although women were concentrated in the lower-paid teaching jobs, this could not be explained by their family responsibilities. Many had none, but it did not seem to help their careers. There was a large element of straight discrimination, camouflaged by a general supposition that teachers were mothers of small children.[21]

Laws first passed in the nineteenth century (and later embodied in the 1961 Factories Act) prohibited female factory workers from working long hours of overtime or at night. These 'protective laws' were an expression of men's status as the main family wage earners with only minimal commitments at home. They helped to exclude women from a range of better-paid manual jobs and to confirm their domestic role. But the case against these laws was not a simple one, and was the subject of a long-running controversy. Few women actively desired to work long, unsocial hours (nor, for that matter, did many men).

A government-backed Bill went before Parliament in 1986, seeking to repeal the protective laws, ostensibly to reduce discrimination against women. Many feared that it would lead to more exploitation, not less — forcing women to work at nights, or do jobs involving awkward shift patterns, while they continued to do a second, unpaid job at home.

The impetus for repeal came mainly from the employers' side. Trade unions opposed repeal, usually with support from their female members. However, the unions' motives were not entirely above suspicion, since they had a long history of keeping women out of jobs designed for male 'breadwinners'. The problem of discrimination against women workers would not be resolved by repealing the laws, any more than by retaining them. It was a case of Heads We Lose, Tails You Win: women would continue to be exploited while there was an unequal division of paid and unpaid labour, and while women were segregated in lower-paid jobs — with or without nightshifts and long hours of overtime.

Increasingly, women were taking work into their own homes. It was estimated in 1985 that there were at least 300,000 'homeworkers' or 'outworkers' in the UK, and their numbers tended to grow as in-company employment declined. Homeworking was an almost exclusively female activity — undertaken by women whose family commitments made it difficult or impossible for them to work elsewhere. The chronic shortage of child care facilities swelled the ranks of homeworkers. Many belonged to Asian communities where it was unacceptable for women to work outside the home. They sewed, knitted, packed, assembled and painted goods. There was also a new breed of homeworkers who operated computers — as programmers or systems analysts, or for certain kinds of clerical work. For a degree of control over their own time, most of them paid a heavy price. A report by the Department of Employment in 1984 warned:

Outworkers are treated as a secondary labour force, with pay and conditions inferior to those given to people doing similar work on the premises when they are given work, but vulnerable to short-term fluctuations in the quantity of work and even to being 'laid off' during the 'trough' months . . . Outwork plants were more likely than others to employ a typically-female work-force, and had relatively high proportions of ethnic minority and part-time workers . . .

Homeworkers were isolated and almost entirely unorganized. They might choose their own hours and pace of work, but they were otherwise powerless and could neither bargain for their pay nor secure a steady supply of employment. They had no legal protection

— against sacking, redundancy or the hazards of their work — unless they fought to be recognized as employees (rather than as self-employed workers) before an industrial tribunal. Some fought and won, but the great majority neither knew that the opportunity was open to them, nor dared risk their livelihood by taking action against their employer.

Women who worked relatively short hours were penalized in a similar way. Like homeworkers, they were not considered 'real' workers and did not get the same legal protection as full-timers. A person who worked less than sixteen hours a week had no legal protection from unfair dismissal or redundancy unless she had been in the same workplace for at least five years — and then only if she worked more than eight hours a week.[22]

Only certain kinds of work were available to people who could not work more than 30-odd hours a week. The labour market was designed in such a way that women whose time was taken up with domestic responsibilities had no choice but to do different jobs from men — jobs which carried lower status, fewer benefits and less pay. The very description 'part-time worker' carried a kind of stigma. Yet why should fewer than 30 hours (or 20 hours for that matter) be considered only 'part-time'? Only in a labour market regulated by men could such a definition be accepted.

So well established were these patterns that it made little difference whether or not individual women actually *had* family responsibilities, or whether they were suited to 'women's work'. They were edged into it by a combination of their own education, which prepared them for 'women's work'; the expectations of employers, who usually judged them according to their gender rather than their individual aptitudes; and by the reluctance of men in general to envisage any other way of arranging paid employment and domestic labour.

Pay and the patriarchal bonus

As we have seen, women and men were often segregated by employers in order that women could be paid less. Men monopolized work which was defined as 'skilled', commanding higher pay, and they appropriated the role of family breadwinner. Women were always more poorly organized than men. And where they were restricted by their domestic responsibilities to certain jobs (which men didn't do) employers were able to exploit them with greater ease. These were the main factors which determined the relative strengths of male and female pay.

Homeworkers were at the bottom of the pile. A survey by the Low Pay Unit in 1983 found that more than three-quarters of homeworkers earned less than £1 an hour, while one-third earned 50p an hour or less. (The LPU defines 'low pay' as less than two-thirds of median male earnings — in 1983, £2.25 an hour.)[23]

Part-time workers usually earned well below what was considered 'low pay' (£115 a week or £3 an hour in 1985) because of their restricted earning time. In addition, they earned less per hour than full-timers. In 1985, for example, 79.2 per cent of part-time women workers (i.e. 3.37 million) were earning less than £3 an hour, compared with 52.7 per cent of full-time women and 21.8 per cent of full-time men.[24]

Most women who worked full-time were excluded from higher-paid jobs because they could not spend as much time in paid employment as men, and because they were ill-prepared to compete on equal terms with men. As the tables on p. 81 show, in 1970, women's average gross earnings were £16.20 a week, which amounted to 54.5 per cent of the male average of £29.70 a week. By 1984, they had risen to £116 a week, but were still no more than 65.8 per cent of the male average £177. Their hourly earnings caught up a little faster, but not much — from 63 per cent of the male average in 1970 to 73.5 per cent in 1984.[25] (The reasons for this discrepancy between weekly and hourly earnings will soon become clear.)

Women remained concentrated in lower-paid jobs in all areas of employment. They also remained concentrated in the lower-paid industries, where unionization was weak, and where the only safe-guards against exploitation were Wages Councils. These were set up at the beginning of the century to mitigate the poverty of the 'sweated trades'. They included representatives of workers and employers and they established statutory minimum rates, below which they were supposed to ensure wages did not fall. These rates were very low.

For example, in 1986, the minimum was £68.60 for toy makers, £53.25 for employees in hairdressing and £75.10 for boot and shoe repairers. The Councils did nothing to cushion women from the effects of unequal pay. Women made up four of every five workers in industries covered by Wages Councils; a study by the Low Pay Unit in 1984 showed their average earnings to be just under 63 per cent of the male average within those industries. Employers who broke the law by under-paying did so with impunity — indeed, 9,842 were found to have broken the law in 1984, but there were only two prosecutions.

Weak and ineffectual though they were, Wages Councils came under heavy attack from the Thatcher government, in response to cries of pain from employers who resented any attempts to impose minimum pay. Legislation introduced in 1986 sought to exempt workers under 21 years of age from Wages Council rates and, for workers of all ages, to lift protection on holiday pay, weekend pay, shift premiums and skill differentials. The most vulnerable groups of workers were thus left exposed to even greater exploitation.

Not only were women located in lower-paid jobs and in lower-paid industries, but their pay was structured differently from men's. A range of extra payments had been organized by men to accompany the 'proper' jobs that 'real' workers did. A 1980 Department of Employment survey looked at the incomes of women and men who were doing the same work for the same employer. The researchers found that although both sexes were getting paid the same basic rates and were usually working the same basic hours, there was still a big difference in their take-home pay.

> Men work more overtime, do more shiftwork, have been employed for longer to qualify for length of service awards and hold a disproportionate number of merit or responsibility positions.[26]

This was confirmed by the results of the 1985 New Earnings Survey, which found that 39 per cent of male workers received overtime payments, compared with only 17 per cent of women; and that 16 per cent of men and only 12 per cent of women received shift premiums.

The fact that most women's working lives were divided into two phases had a devastating effect on their pay. It prevented them earning long-service increments and — even more damagingly — it closed off promotion to higher-paid jobs. As the NUT survey showed, this affected even women whose careers were not broken by family responsibilities.[27]

Productivity payments were another important source of extra money for men. The 1985 New Earnings Survey found that 39 per cent of men and only 17 per cent of women received additional 'payment by results'. Women were concentrated in service jobs which were often unsuited to productivity agreements. (How could you organize an incentive scheme for nurses, home helps or secretaries?) And women tended to have a different approach to their jobs — perhaps because they carried over into paid employment their attitudes to the work they did for their families. In November 1980 we visited a weekend women's school of the public employees' union, NUPE. The women were invited to consider a list of six bargaining issues (pay, child care, bonuses, and so on) and to list them in order of priority. Most of them put pay near the top of the list, but they all put bonuses right at the bottom. Later, when they discussed what they had done, there was great hilarity as they discovered their mutual hatred for the productivity bonus. They all felt it would taint their commitment to their work, and, moreover, in most of their jobs, productivity could not be measured.

The left in the labour movement has consistently opposed productivity deals on the grounds that they are divisive, give arbitrary privileges to some workers and penalize others, and threaten safety in some industries.

What all these factors add up to is that a significant proportion of men's earnings — something approaching a quarter of their pay packet — have accrued to them as a result of their special relationship *as men* to domestic life and to paid employment. This massive patriarchal bonus has proved to be immune both to the campaign for equal pay by the unions and the women's movement, and to the limp intervention of the Equal Pay Act.

During the 1970s, the character of the labour market began to change dramatically. One source of change was the spread of microtechnology; another was the economic recession and the government's commitment to public spending cuts and 'free market' economic policies.

A chip off the old block

The silicon chip was associated with the female sex as soon as it made its first major appearances in public. It was photographed on the tip of a model's nose, and as a tiny speck on a pretty woman's front tooth. What a little miracle! We were told it would improve the quality of our lives, give us more leisure, make our jobs more streamlined, cleaner and more pleasant, make Britain prosper again. By the time we began to foresee the extent of the problems it could bring, there it was already — the word processor on the desk top, the calculator in our pockets, the electronic gadgets in our homes, the robot on the factory floor.

In 1979, the TUC passed a composite motion which hailed the chip as a harbinger of a new utopia. It presented, said the motion, a

> unique and unparalleled opportunity for Britain to improve its economic performance and also its competitiveness in world markets whilst improving living standards, affording more

leisure to employees, eliminating dreary work and improving communications between people and nations.

In the years that followed, it became apparent that micro-technology alone would not improve our lives: what really mattered was the political and economic context in which it was developed.

One disturbing aspect of the new-tech revolution was its dependence on cheap, unorganized female labour, especially in developing countries. Rachael Grossman worked for ten weeks in the micro-electronics factories of Southeast Asia and published a report in the *Southeast Asia Chronicle* in 1979. The women in the factories mounted and tested chips under microscopes, for starvation wages, and in hazardous conditions, often resorting to prostitution when their usefulness on the assembly line had come to an end.

> After three or four years of peering through a microscope, a worker's vision begins to blur so she can no longer meet the production quota. Workers who must dip components in acids and rub them with solvents frequently experience burns, dizziness, nausea, sometimes even losing their fingers in accidents. It will be ten or fifteen years before the carcinogenic effects begin to show up in the women who work with them now.[28]

As the character of production changed, it became increasingly common for multi-national companies to spread work around the world, looking for labour wherever it was cheap and untroublesome. Exploitation of female labour in the new electronics industries ceased to be a problem exclusive to the Third World — as this 1984 report on Scotland's 'Silicon Glen' suggested:

> Between 55% and 60% of the Scottish electronics workforce are women, of whom half work as unskilled, or semi-skilled, operatives on an assembly line. Although in many ways the social position of Scottish women is vastly different from that of the Third World women workers, there are enough similarities to make them attractive to electronics employers. Sometimes the Third World seems very close — Nippon Electric company at Livingston initially (1982) recruited from among female school-leavers and the average age of its labour force is reputed to be below 25. Scottish women, like Third World women, are regarded as blessed with 'nimble fingers' and are segregated into low paying jobs with few prospects.[29]

Early optimism that micro-technology would improve job prospects in the UK soon disappeared. It was, of course, ideally suited to replace many of the unskilled and semi-skilled jobs that were normally done by women. And employers would find it much easier to introduce in areas where they did not have to reckon with strong trade unions. (In Fleet Street, trade unions resisted new printing technology for a decade and a half, until Rupert Murdoch's notorious stand against the National Graphical Association and Sogat '82 at 'fortress Wapping' in 1986, when 5,000 print workers lost their jobs.)

Among the most vulnerable areas of women's work were assembly-line jobs in manufacturing, stock control in retailing, telephone operating, banking and − above all − secretarial and clerical work. By 1980, the following changes had already taken place:

- Bradford Council reduced its staff in one section from 44 to 22 with the introduction of nine word processors, resulting in an increased productivity of 19 per cent and an estimated annual saving of £59,000.

- The British Standards Institute created a centralized specialist word processing department when it installed ten IBM word processors. The Institute handles a large quantity of long technical documents that go through several drafting and correction stages. The number of secretaries and typists employed fell by a third.

- The Provident Financial Group installed three IBM memory typewriters into a central typing pool. They reduced their full-time typing staff from 27 to 17, their part-time staff from 13 to 3, and increased the workload. (Jobs were cut through natural wastage.)

- The Halifax Building Society progressed from automatic type-writers which they had used for 10 years to a system of 16 IBM word processors. The workforce was not reduced, but the workload almost trebled. The typists are at the new machines all day apart from two 15-minute breaks and a lunch break.

- The Central Electricity Generating Board has reduced the number of 'girls' employed at its typing centre in Bristol from over 50 to 26. The advantage of the new machines, the supervisor reports, is that 'a less experienced typist is able to produce the same quality of work as a really skilled girl and almost as quickly'.[30]

It was predicted in 1980, in a report published by the Equal Opportunities Commission, that the installation of word processors in British offices would cut 21,000 secretarial and clerical jobs by 1985.[31] A study by the office workers' union APEX revealed in 1984 that for every one job created by new technology, 50 had been lost.[32] Another survey, based on 18 UK companies and published in 1985, showed that 7 of the 18 had reduced jobs by 60 per cent as a result of introducing word processors, while a further six had substantially increased their workload without hiring extra staff.[33]

New technology also transformed the nature of office work. As it became more sophisticated, it was able to fulfil an ever greater range of tasks previously done by hand and brain. Many women's hard-won skills became redundant, their work standardized and electronically monitored. The APEX study, which looked at office workers in the Midlands, found that 37 per cent had their working day monitored by computer. In the study, 15 per cent of firms had introduced shift systems to maximize use of new computers.[34]

In computerized offices, women lost control not only over their time, but also over their working routine and environment. Jane Barker and Hazel Downing described the 'culture of resistance' which was peculiar to the female office worker of the pre-computer age:

> She can sit on work and pretend to be too busy to have a chat, she can find any number of excuses for the lateness of a particular document ('I ran out of paper and had to go to stationery'; 'the ribbon got stuck'). Control also over her space and movements; going off to the loo for a chat and a cigarette, to touch up make-up or to read a book; going to visit someone on the next floor on the pretext of collecting a document. Those extra little jobs which women are expected to perform just because they are women, such as making the tea, watering the plants, organizing leaving present collections, going out to the shops to collect something for the boss, while on the one hand reinforcing ideologically their role as 'office wife', can be used to create *space* and time away from the routine of typing.[35]

In an automated office, they had no such options — as this account of a newly computerized local authority office suggests:

> The machines are in constant operation, and are programmed by the rate material comes in. The workers have one ten-minute break in the morning and afternoon, and otherwise have no contact with other workers during office time. All the new work comes in through a special anti-static glass box, and no non-section workers enter the room. The operator has almost no contact with the finished product . . . the existing tenuous relationship between a typist and her work is finally broken altogether. There is no sense any longer in which it is *her* work.[36]

It could be argued that the transformation of the 'office wife' into a semi-skilled manual labourer had its advantages. By breaking the (misconceived) bond of loyalty between the worker and her boss, it might encourage her to become involved in trade union activity, and so to replace one means of resistance with another — this time one that didn't depend on her sexual subordination. Both forms of employment were exploitative, for different reasons, and the crucial factor was how much control women could exercise over their work.

Mass unemployment and the new labour force

Between 1976 and 1986, unemployment rose from less than 1.5 million to nearly 4 million. During the 1970s, more women than men joined the dole queue in every year but two — as table 4 shows (p. 82). It was widely predicted that, as unemployment continued to rise, women would be eased out of the labour force and back into the home; men would have first claim on whatever paid work was available and women would simply do more unpaid work, caring for children, the sick and the elderly as welfare services were steadily cut back.

By the mid-1980s, the second part of that prediction had proved true, as we shall see in the next chapter. But the first part had not. Women had not been eased out of the labour force. Something else had happened.

Official figures showed that between 1979 and 1984, unemployment among women rose at a slightly higher rate than among men (see table 5, p. 82). This happened in spite of changes in the way the figures were collected, which, from 1982, removed 5 per cent of men and 14 per cent of women from the official statistics, by counting only those who claimed benefit at Unemployment Benefit Offices. So women were still losing jobs faster than men. But at the same time, the majority of new jobs were going not to men, but to women. In 1983, the Institute of Employment Research published projections to the year 1990: it estimated that there would be a net increase of 520,000 jobs over the period. Of these, 320,000 would be part-time — that is, women's jobs. In other words, at least two out of every three new jobs were expected to go to women.[37]

As table 6 shows (p. 82) this pattern was already well-established by 1984. The total number of people available for work had increased, but the size of the employed labour force had declined. In ten years, the number of men in employment had dropped by 1.8 million, and full-time women by 0.6 million. Meanwhile, two groups had increased their numbers: part-time women workers by 0.8 million, and self-employed men and women by 0.5 million. The self-employed included many of the growing army of homeworkers (an almost exclusively female preserve), whose numbers had more than doubled over the period.

As employers demanded ever cheaper and more malleable labour, the character of the workforce entered a period of dramatic transformation, to which women were the key. They held on to their place in the labour market — not in spite of their dual role as domestic workers and wage earners, but because of it. The more unpaid work they had to do at home, the less time and space they had to fight for better pay and conditions in the workplace, the more likely they were to do cheap, unprotected, part-time jobs . . . and the more attractive they became to the new employers of the 1980s and 1990s. Women could no longer be described as a 'reserve army of labour'; they had become the regular troops. They were not swept in and out of the workforce by fluctuations of the market. They stayed in, but paid a high price for the privilege, as their wages, hours and conditions ebbed and flowed, beyond their own control.

Against this trend, there were other, more positive developments. Since the early 1970s, there had been a change in women's consciousness; new ideas about what it was possible for women to do were becoming more familiar — even though they were seldom translated into action. These changes had emerged out of the women's liberation movement and had been reinforced by the 'equality laws' passed in the mid-1970s. The 'equal pay for work of equal value' amendment to the Equal Pay Act, introduced in 1984, provided the first serious legal challenge to discriminatory pay scales, as we shall see (p. 118).

Women's overall share of trade union membership had grown steadily, from 25 per cent in 1971 to 31 per cent in 1981 and (according to EOC estimates) 35 per cent in 1985 — although the continued increase in later years was mainly due to a relative decline in male employment. Women had marginally increased their share of union decision-making posts (see p. 182). A decade and a half of fighting for 'equal opportunity' had taught women some valuable lessons and led them to reassess their needs and demands.

We review women's experience of legal reforms and their efforts to establish a footing in the unions, in chapter 4 and 5. But first we look at relations within the family, and between the family and the state — for it was here, no less than in the workplace, that the struggle for women's liberation took place.

Table 1   Women workers in major occupation groups, 1911—1971

Female workers as a percentage of all workers in each of the major occupation groups identified by Bain and Price

Occupational groups	1911	1921	1931	1951	1961	1971
Employers and proprietors	18.8	20.5	19.8	20.0	20.4	24.9
White collar workers	29.8	37.6	35.8	42.3	44.5	47.9
(a) managers and administrators	19.8	17.0	13.0	15.2	15.5	21.6
(b) higher professionals	6.0	5.1	7.5	8.3	9.7	9.9
(c) lower professionals and technicians	62.9	59.4	58.8	53.5	50.8	52.1
(d) foremen and inspectors	4.2	6.5	8.7	13.4	10.3	13.1
(e) clerks	21.4	44.6	46.0	60.2	65.2	73.2
(f) salesmen and shop assistants	35.2	43.6	37.2	51.6	54.9	59.8
All manual workers	30.5	27.9	28.8	26.1	26.0	29.4
(a) skilled	24.0	21.0	21.3	15.7	13.8	13.5
(b) semi-skilled	40.4	40.3	42.9	38.1	39.3	46.5
(c) unskilled	15.5	16.8	15.0	20.3	22.4	37.2
Total occupied population	29.6	29.5	29.8	30.8	32.4	36.5

Source: Table 3 in G. S. Bain and R. Price, 'Union growth and employment trends in the United Kingdom 1964—1970', *British Journal of Industrial Relations*, 10, November 1972, pp. 366—381, quoted in Hakim, C. *Occupational Segregation*, Department of Employment, 1979. The authors' analysis of census data 1911—1961 was repeated with 1971 census data for Great Britain to update their time series, with the following modifications of their method:

(a) 1971 census separately identified/self-employed with or without employees. The self-employed with employees were classified in the 'Employers and proprietors' group and the self-employed without employees were added to their respective occupational group.

(b) Lists of occupational groups in each order as given in G. S. Bain, *The Growth of White Collar Unionism*, Clarendon Press, Oxford, 1970, pp. 189—190 were adhered to except when an overlap in definitions required 1971 figures to be split proportionately to the 1961 census distribution.

Table 2 Average gross weekly earnings (including the effects of overtime) for employees aged 18 and over, in £, 1970—1984

	1970	1975	1980	1981	1982	1983	1984
Men	29.7	60.8	121.5	137.0	150.5	163.3	177.0
Women	16.2	37.4	78.8	91.4	99.0	108.8	116.4
Differential	13.5	23.4	42.7	45.6	51.5	54.5	60.6
Women's earnings as a percentage of men's	54.5	61.5	64.8	66.7	65.8	66.6	65.8

Source: New Earnings Survey, 1970—84, Part A. Tables 10 and 11.

Table 3 Average gross hourly earnings (excluding the effects of overtime) for employees aged 18 and over, in £, 1970—1984

	1970	1975	1980	1981	1982	1983	1984
Men	67.4	136.3	280.7	322.5	354.8	387.6	417.3
Women	42.5	98.3	206.4	241.2	262.1	287.5	306.8
Differential	24.9	38.0	74.3	81.3	92.7	100.1	110.5
Women's earnings as a percentage of men's	63.1	72.1	73.5	74.8	73.9	74.2	73.5

Source: New Earnings Survey, 1970—84, Part A. Tables 10 and 11.

Table 4   Rate of increase each year of male and female unemployment, 1971−1980 (UK)

	Male		Female	
Year	*Increase in 000s*	*% increase*	*Increase in 000s*	*% increase*
1971−2	+ 11.3	+ 1.6	+ 12.1	+ 8.6
1972−3	−248.3	−35.0	− 57.9	− 37.9
1973−4	+ 70.3	+15.2	+ 23.2	+ 24.6
1974−5	+351.3	+66.0	+144.5	+122.8
1975−6	+176.5	+20.0	+133.7	+ 51.0
1976−7	+ 64.5	+ 6.1	+ 88.9	+ 22.5
1977−8	− 83.2	− 7.4	− 8.2	− 1.7
1978−9	−105.0	−10.1	− 18.2	− 3.8
1979−80	+442.7	+47.3	+202.3	+ 44.1

Source: Employment Gazette, 1971−80.

Table 5   Numbers registered unemployed 1979−1984, in thousands[1]

	1979	*1980*	*1981*	*1982*	*1983*	*1984*
Men	887.2	1129.1	1773.3	2055.9	2133.5	2109.6
Women	346.7	461.3	649.1	752.6	854.0	928.8

[1] All figures calculated on 'new count' basis.
Source: Employment Gazette 90(2), February 1984, March 1985.

Table 6   Employment trends 1974−1984, in millions

	1974	*1976*	*1978*	*1980*	*1982*	*1984*
Employed men	13.4	13.1	13.1	13.0	11.9	11.6
Employed women						
full-time	5.5	5.4	5.5	5.3	5.1	4.9
part-time	3.4	3.6	3.7	3.9	3.9	4.2
Self-employed	1.9	1.9	1.8	1.9	2.1	2.4
Employed labour force	24.6	24.3	24.4	24.7	23.3	23.4
Working population	25.1	25.5	25.7	26.2	26.1	26.5

Source: Employment Gazette 93(4), April 1985.

Notes to chapter 2

1   Hakim, C. *Occupational Segregation*, Department of Employment Research Paper no. 9, November 1979.
2   Ibid.; see also Coote, A. and Kellner, P. 'Women Workers and Union Power' in Coote and Kellner (eds) *Hear This, Brother, New Statesman*, 1980; and IFF Research Ltd, 'Inquiry into the Employment of Women', *Department of Employment Gazette*, November 1980.
3   Hakim, *Occupational Segregation*.
4   IFF Research Ltd, 'Inquiry into the Employment of Women'.
5   Lazonick, W. et al. 'Division of Labour in the Textile Industry', *Cambridge Journal of Economics*, no. 3, 1979.
6   Phillips, A. and Taylor, B. 'Sex and Skill: Notes towards a Feminist Economics', *Feminist Review*, no. 6, 1980.
7   Ibid.
8   See Chamberlain, M. *Old Wives' Tales*, Virago, 1981.
9   Gamarnikow, E. 'Sexual Division of Labour: The Case of Nursing', in Kuhn, A. and Wolpe, A. (eds) *Feminism and Materialism*, Routledge and Kegan Paul, 1978.
10 Cockburn, C. *The Machinery of Dominance*, Pluto Press, 1985.
11 Ibid.
12 Land, H. *The Family Wage*, Eleanor Rathbone Memorial Lecture, 1979.
13 Humphries, J. 'Class Struggle and the Working-Class Family', in Lamsden, A. H. (ed.) *The Economics of Women and Work*, Penguin, 1980.
14 NBPI Report no. 165, *Prices, Profits and Costs in Food Distribution*, Cmnd. 4645, HMSO, 1971.
15 NBPI Report no. 169, *General Problems of Low Pay*, Cmnd. 4648, HMSO, 1971.
16 *General Household Survey*, HMSO, 1978.
17 *OPCS Labour Force Survey*, HMSO, 1981.
18 *New Earnings Survey*, Department of Employment, HMSO, 1984.
19 *Woman's Own*, February 1979.
20 DES Statistics of Education, *Teachers in Service England and Wales*, HMSO, 1982.
21 *Promotion and the Woman Teacher*, Equal Opportunities Commission, 1980.
22 Sedley, A. *Part-Time Workers Need Full-Time Rights*, NCCL, 1980.
23 Bisset, L. and Huws, U. *Sweated Labour*, Low Pay Unit, 1984.
24 *Low Pay Review* 24, Low Pay Unit, 1985/6.
25 *Women and Men in Britain, A Statistical Survey*, Equal Opportunities Commission, 1985.
26 IFF Research Ltd, 'Inquiry into the Employment of Women.'
27 *Promotion and the Woman Teacher*, Equal Opportunities Commission.

28   Grossman, R. 'Changing Role of S.E. Asian Women', *Southeast Asian Chronicle*, Pacific Research, SRC no. 66/PSC, vol. 9(5).
29   *International Labour Reports*, July—August 1984.
30   Counter Information Service, *The New Technology*, CIS Anti-Report, no. 23.
31   Bird, E. *Information Technology in the Office: the Impact on Women's Jobs*, Equal Opportunities Commission, 1980.
32   'The Impact of Office Technology in the Midlands Area', APEX, 1984.
33   Faulkener, W. and Arnold, E. *Smothered by Invention: New Technology in Women's Lives*, Pluto Press, 1985.
34   'The Impact of Office Technology', APEX.
35   Barker, J. and Downing, H. *Office Automation, Word Processing and the Transformation of Patriarchal Relations*, January 1979.
36   Ibid.
37   *Review of the Economy and Employment*, Institute for Employment Research, 1983.

3 Family and state

The division of labour in the family home remained unchanged in the 1970s and 1980s. Women still did most of the work and — no less important — still carried the responsibility for getting it done. Women took care of planning meals, shopping, cooking, cleaning, washing, ironing, mending, equipping and running the household, clothing and caring for children . . . and much more besides. Women remembered to pay the milkman; they listened, soothed, praised and comforted their menfolk and their children; they anticipated needs, watched for signs of ill-health or distress, remembered where things were, kept spare light bulbs, telephoned relatives, and popped in to see the old lady round the corner . . . this is not a sentimental catalogue of How Wonderful Mum Is, but a job description.

This was the work women did while men put in a few more hours of overtime to increase their pay, or stayed late at the office to put themselves in line for promotion, or went to union meetings to improve their bargaining power, or went to the pub or a football match to maintain a sense of male solidarity, or kept pigeons or played snooker to amuse themselves, or tinkered with the car or pottered about in the garden (work of a kind, but not *essential* work), or read the newspaper or watched the television or rested after a hard day, or (perhaps a bit more than in the past) *helped* around the house. This was the way family work continued to be arranged in most British households, whether or not both partners were engaged in paid employment.

A major survey by the Department of Employment in 1980 asked how housework was divided between husbands and wives. Of women who were working full-time, 13 per cent said they did all of the housework and 41 per cent said they did most of it. Those who said they shared it equally with their husbands amounted to 44 per cent and only 2 per cent said their husbands did most of the housework. Not one said her husband did all of it. Among women working part-time, 77 per cent said they did all or most of the housework. (See table 7, p. 108.)

Child care seemed to be shared less unequally: 29 per cent of women working full-time and 44 per cent of women working part-time said they did most or all of it. (See table 8, p. 109.) However, the researchers commented:

Husbands and wives tended to be involved in rather different aspects of their children's care. Wives were more likely to be involved in the routine basic care such as feeding, dressing, washing and so on, while husbands spent time playing with the children or taking them out . . .

A Gallup Poll conducted for *Woman's Own* magazine in 1979 seemed to bear this out:

One in six husbands has never looked after his child on his own. One-quarter have never put their children to bed. One in three has never even read to their own children. Younger wives get slight help but, generally, wives are still left to shoulder the overwhelming majority of work involved in being a parent. Even in families where the mother works full-time, three-quarters of fathers never take time off work if their children are ill, and never collect them from school.[1]

Questions like these would probably not have been asked if it hadn't been for the women's liberation movement, which had begun to raise political questions about the division of paid and unpaid labour. In this chapter we look at some of the critical areas of conflict and change that emerged during the 1970s and 1980s, concerning women's role within the family and the relationship between the family and the state.

As we noted in chapter 1, much of the initial discussion and writing of new women's liberation groups focussed on the family. They drew on the analysis of Marx and Engels. They developed a detailed critique of the division of paid and unpaid labour between women and men, the economic dependence of women within the family, and the reproduction of polarized forms of femininity and masculinity, as children learned to copy their parents. They challenged the isolation of family life, which helped construct women's powerlessness, the 'myth of motherhood', which fetishized the role of women as sole and 'natural' child-rearers, and the contemporary ideology of marriage, which designated women as the sexual property of their husbands. They acknowledged that the liberation of women required fundamental changes in the structure of family life.

However, the women's liberation movement also had to discover for itself the limitations of the Marxist analysis. The family could not be understood in economistic terms. It had to be seen as a set of human relationships, where individuals had their first experiences of power and powerlessness, and where the roots of power went deeper than money or physical prowess. While the family could be a source of physical violence, economic oppression, psychic subordination and social control, it could — at the same time — be a source of care, affection, strength and security. For most feminists, then, calls for an end to the family, which came from sections of the left in the sixties and early seventies, made little sense. It was not a case of demolishing an institution, but of renegotiating relations.

This engaged the politics of the women's movement on three main fronts. One involved the efforts of feminists to change themselves and their relationship to men. Another took the form of challenging the way in which the woman's role within the family was regulated —

through the wages system which designated men as breadwinners, through matrimonial law, tax, benefits and services which institutionalized female dependency; this also meant waging a defensive action against Conservative politicians who wanted to promote the family as an alternative to the welfare state. The third involved carving out a new relationship between women and the state, a move which led to the emergence of 'municipal feminism' in the 1980s.

Changing lives

Many women tried — individually and collectively — to break out of the conventional mould of family life. In doing so they were continuing a pattern of change that had begun in the 1960s, before the women's liberation movement. Some 'reversed roles', leaving their husbands with the children while they went out to work. Some lived communally with men and women. Others set up networks of women's houses in towns and cities throughout the country.

At the same time, there were countless feminists who married — to please themselves or their parents, or to 'legitimize' their children. And there were countless more who set up home, nuclear-family style, complete in all details but for the marriage certificate. But even where the form was conventional, the content often was not, as women waged guerrilla warfare over the housework, 'nagged' and 'scolded' to get men to change their habits, and fought for their own space within the household.

Ironically, although women's liberation was founded on the principle that 'the personal is political', efforts to renegotiate family relations were not brought out into the open and asserted as political in the same way as other aspects of the struggle. The successes that women had in breaking with convention seemed like isolated incidents, and were not celebrated as part of a continuum, or placed within a political framework. The failures seemed purely — and painfully — personal. Yet the overall impact on popular attitudes was profound. The domestic roles of men and women had been publicly questioned. Variations on the conventional theme became more common. Even if individuals didn't change their habits, they were more likely to take on board the idea that the traditional division of labour was not 'natural' but socially constructed. The issues were on the agenda; change was at least a possibility. The long-term effect of all this, though impossible to measure, could not be underestimated. It was as much a part of the resistance of women as the more formal campaigns that were waged around the laws and provisions of the state.

Marriage on the rocks

The 1970s were rocky years for the institution of marriage, though this could hardly be attributed to the women's movement. The Divorce Reform Act of 1969 came into force in 1971 and the divorce rate soared — from 74,000 in 1971 to a peak of 148,000 in 1980, after which it levelled off. The number of single parents rose steadily, from 570,000 in 1971 to 930,000 in 1983 (nine out of ten were women). The number of first marriages — i.e. 'spinsters' or 'bachelors' marrying for the first time — declined sharply during the seventies, and people tended to get married later, often after a period of cohabitation. Meanwhile, remarriage became more common, especially among men, whose remarriage rate was three to four times higher than the rate for women. Redivorce became more common too. The broad picture seemed to be that people were using marriage in a more varied and flexible way. The crucial question, then, is how this new flexibility affected the conditions of women's lives.

The chief motivation behind divorce reform in the sixties had been to legitimize children of men who had set up second families outside wedlock. But of course it also gave women the option of choosing divorce — and choose they did, in greater numbers than men. And because women did not have sufficient earning power to keep themselves and their children, divorced men were expected to help support their former families. This could be financially crippling: it was not that ex-wives lived in the lap of luxury, but that men's wages, although higher than women's, were seldom enough to support one family, let alone two.

The courts ensured that divorced women got little enough if there was any matrimonial property to be shared out at the end of a marriage: one third was the most they could usually expect after a major test case in 1973. But there was often nothing to share out after divorce. Many men could not or would not pay anything at all. By 1982, nearly half of all families with dependent children on supplementary benefit were headed by a single parent; 50 per cent of all lone mothers were claiming supplementary benefit.

So divorce reform produced a crisis in family support, by enabling women to opt for legal independence within an economic system which was structured around their financial dependence on a male family breadwinner. In response to the crisis, men organized to reduce their financial obligations after divorce. The Matrimonial and Family

Proceedings Act, which came into force in 1984, not only made it possible to sue for divorce after one year's separation, but also sought to 'encourage ex-wives to become self-sufficient', by a series of measures which favoured short-term maintenance settlements or one-off lump-sum payments. During the parliamentary debate on the new law, Labour MP Jo Richardson described it as a 'powerful, well-organised and well-financed lobby of wealthy middle-class men'.

Shifting patterns of marriage, divorce and parenthood altered the character of family life in some respects. More women changed marriage partners, or lived alone with children. They had more choice, but if they chose independence, it usually meant poverty as well. Women might exchange economic dependence on men for economic dependence on the state. This shift from the private to the public sphere did not make them better off financially, but it did establish a different political relationship with the source of their support: it opened up the possibility of women organizing together to improve conditions — an option not open to them on the private, domestic front.

Financial independence

The call for financial independence, which was embodied in the fifth demand of the women's liberation movement, entailed an attack on the rules that governed state taxation and benefits. These rules were based on the 'family wage' proposition, that the man is the main breadwinner for his wife and children (see p. 63); the Beveridge Report of 1946, which formed the basis of social security legislation, enshrined this idea and set the pattern of different contributions and entitlements for men and women, which survived well into the 1980s.

One early target of feminist campaigning was a rule that prevented married women workers from claiming extra benefit for their children and non-employed husbands while they themselves were receiving unemployment or sickness benefit (men automatically had this right). Another was the unequal retirement age, which provided for men to retire five years later than women. Married women were also barred from claiming the Family Income Supplement or supplementary benefit. Under the rules governing the Housewives' Non-contributory Invalidity Pension (HNCIP), married women could not claim a special pension available to men and single women, unless they could show that their invalidity prevented their carrying out 'regular household duties'. In a similar vein, Invalid Care Allowance was designed for full-time, non-employed carers for disabled people, but was available only to single women and men, on the ground that caring was part of a married woman's regular duties, so she did not need compensation for loss of earnings. But perhaps the most notorious of all was the 'cohabitation rule': this reinforced the notion of female dependency by insisting that a women who was married to a man or thought to be living with him 'as husband and wife' had no right to claim supplementary benefit for herself or the household unit; the man had to provide for the family, or himself make the claim for supplementary benefit on their behalf. Women claimants were thus policed by DHSS officials who inspected their homes for evidence of cohabitation. (After 1978, under certain, limited conditions, women were allowed to 'swap roles' and claim benefit, instead of the husband/cohabitee, on behalf of the household unit; but the essence of the cohabitation rule did not change — the basic assumption was that female dependency was the norm and women were still not treated as independent individuals.)

Women's groups campaigned with claimants' unions and such organizations as the Child Poverty Action Group (CPAG), which became known collectively as the 'poverty lobby'. The influence of feminist ideas wasn't hard to trace — not least because many women with a background in women's liberation groups went to work in the organizations of the poverty lobby. While the CPAG began by stressing the needs of children and the interests of families, feminists made a point of insisting on the broader principle that women should be treated as independent individuals throughout the benefit and tax systems.

A breakthrough came in 1983 — not, however, because the government bowed to pressure from campaigners, but because the EEC directed member states that benefits should be awarded on an equal basis. Gradually, grudgingly, the UK brought its rules into line — often in ways which failed to bring positive advantages to women. Married women on unemployment and sickness benefit could at last claim additional allowances for dependants. However, male claimants could get extra for dependent children regardless of their wives' income; women could not do so unless their husbands' income fell below a certain level.

Married women won a limited right to claim Family Income Supplement. The Housewives' Non-contributory Invalidity Pension was replaced by a new Severe Disablement Allowance, equally available to men and women. But the new allowance had a much stricter test of eligibility. Of all the women who might have been able to claim the HNCIP if the 'household duties' requirement had been lifted, only one in twelve would be able to claim the Severe Disablement Allowance.

Even though women were gaining little in financial terms, the EEC was beginning to challenge the Beveridge model of female dependency within marriage — and campaigners could use EEC law to force change where the government refused to act. In 1986, retired dietician Helen Marshall secured a ruling from the European Court of Justice in Luxemburg that the UK's statutory retirement ages of 60 for women and 65 for men were in breach of EEC law. In another test case, Jacqueline Drake, a married woman caring full-time for her prematurely senile mother, claimed the right to receive Invalid Care Allowance. By 1986, her appeal had won the backing of the European Commission — and looked set for success in the final hearing at Luxemburg. Just how the UK government would amend its laws to comply with these judgements was not clear at the time of writing.

In one important respect, EEC law could not help achieve the objectives of the women's movement, and no progress was made. Women who were married or cohabiting with men continued to be judged on a different basis from women who were not. Their needs were 'aggregated' with those of their husbands or cohabitees; the family, not the individual, was the basic unit for assessment. The 'cohabitation rule' remained in force, as did a range of other regulations which discriminated between individuals and (hetero-sexual) couples.

Perhaps the greatest success of campaigners in the women's movement and the poverty lobby was the introduction of child benefit in 1977. This represented a real advance for women, as a tax-free, non-means-tested cash benefit paid directly to the mother. It guaranteed her some financial independence and recognized the inadequacy of the male breadwinner's 'family wage' as a means of child support. It was a popular innovation, but between 1977 and 1986 it declined in value, as the government failed to keep it in line with inflation. A campaign to raise child benefit ran parallel with a campaign to abolish the married man's tax allowance. This was, in effect, a large cash prize for male taxpayers who had been through a marriage ceremony more recently than divorce; it was founded on the same habit of discriminating between married and single people that bedevilled the benefit system (although it was not extended to cohabiting couples).

Women's groups and voluntary organizations in the poverty lobby argued that the married man's tax allowance should be abolished, and that the money saved by the Exchequer should be used to increase child benefit — as a way of redistributing wealth within the family, and directing resources towards larger families.

In 1986 the Conservative government launched proposals for overhauling the benefits system. There was no undertaking to maintain the value of child benefit. Supplementary benefit was to be replaced by 'Income Support', with a 'family premium' attached for claimants with dependent children. The universal £25 maternity grant was to be replaced by a £75 grant, restricted to women in families receiving certain benefits. Maternity allowance (based on National Insurance contributions) was to be taxed for the first time. And sweeping changes in pension provisions would make it much harder for women to keep out of poverty after retirement.

Parallel with these 'reforms', which were introduced in the 1986 Social Security Bill, the Tories proposed to abolish the married man's tax allowance and replace it with a system of 'transferable allowances': wife and husband would have equal tax allowances, but if one wasn't earning she or he could transfer it to the earning spouse.

The overall effect of these proposals to change the tax and benefits systems was to diminish incentives for wives to go out to work, reduce the means by which women had direct access to state benefits, and weaken child benefit as a source of family income available to women. They also represented a major step away from universal family support towards the means-tested safety-net, or — put another way — away from the collective principle and back to the workhouse mentality.

During the 1980s, women's groups became involved in campaigns to encourage unemployed women to 'sign on' — because this gave them certain entitlements (even if they weren't eligible for the dole) and made sure they were counted in government statistics, which tended to underplay the numbers of women who were unemployed. Meanwhile a major national campaign to defend child benefit drew support from more than 60 organizations. A formidable alliance, which bore witness to the success of an essentially feminist argument, it ranged from the National Federation of Women's Institutes, the Mothers' Union and Church of England Children's Society, to the Women's Aid Federation, the Fawcett Society and the National Childcare Campaign. Just how much it would achieve remained to be seen at the time of writing.

One tangible new benefit which women won from the state, and which looked like surviving the 1980s in some form, was maternity leave (as distinct from maternity allowance). The 1975 Employment Protection Act introduced six weeks' paid leave for women who had two years' service with their employers, plus the right to return to work up to 29 weeks after the birth. Research published in 1980 showed that 45 per cent of women who were employed during their pregnancy received the statutory pay. However, the provision for reinstatement was found to have very little impact, with only five per cent of women who returned to their jobs doing so according to the statutory formula.[2] The Act laid down a string of conditions for women to fulfil in order to claim their right to reinstatement, and these were intensified by the Employment Act of 1980. The legal obstacle-course no doubt deterred many women, but there were two further problems. There was no statutory provision for men to take parental leave; and the great majority of women who qualified for reinstatement could not take advantage of it even if they managed to jump all the hurdles — because they could not combine their old job with their new child care responsibilities.

Where women were disposed to return to work but did not go back, the chief reasons were the lack of anyone to look after the baby or the lack of accessible local jobs with convenient hours . . . women's suggestions for change concentrated on the needs primarily for improved child-care facilities.[3]

Farewell to welfare

Provision by the state of high-quality, flexible child care was, as we've seen, the subject of one of the main campaigns of the women's liberation movement. Feminists looked to the state to provide services which would improve the quality of women's lives and help change their role within the family: day-care centres for the elderly, home helps, meals on wheels, good public housing and transport, a well-resourced education system and health service . . . these features of the state were of critical importance to women, as an expression of collective — rather than private and individual — responsibility for the care and welfare of the community.

In the early 1970s, it seemed possible that there would be a trend towards more, not fewer, social services to relieve the burden of women's domestic labour. But by the end of the decade, the trend had been reversed — discreetly at first by a Labour government under James Callaghan, and then, in the full cry of an ideological offensive, by a Conservative government under Britain's first woman prime minister.

Labour had begun to cut public spending in the mid-1970s, to meet the conditions of a loan from the International Monetary Fund. Public opinion was shifting. There was a growing sense that Britain was a nation in decline and no longer deserved its welfare state. Services frequently came under attack, and not without justification. Schools were said to be too large and unruly . . . hospital waiting lists were too long . . . social workers left children to be battered to death . . . there were too many bureaucrats . . . too much red tape . . . too many 'scroungers' . . . all such shortcomings were diligently noted in the Tory press. Feminists, too, criticized the machinery of the welfare state for its methods of policing women within the family and its assumption that women should be financially dependent on the men with whom they slept.

So the ground was well prepared when the Conservatives launched their attack on the welfare state in the run-up to the 1979 general election. They were not interested simply in cutting expenditure on state services to make the books balance; they were strongly committed to 'rolling back' certain features of the state, replacing public with private enterprise, and collective with individual responsibility. They began by reconstructing the family in popular ideology.

The family takes a bow

On 12 October 1977, Conservative social services spokesman Patrick Jenkin reminded the Conservative annual conference that the family was 'an enduring institution':

> It had been the foundation for virtually every free society known to history. It possesses strength and resilience, not least in adversity. Loyalty to the family ranks highest of all, higher even than loyalty to the state. It is no accident . . . that dictatorships whether of the Left or the Right seek first to devalue and then to destroy the family . . .

This 'enduring institution' was under pressure, Mr Jenkin went on. What were the signs?

> The rising tide of juvenile crime, the growth of truancy, the break-up of marriages, family violence, the loneliness of the aged, the growing dependence on the social services, the steadily mounting numbers of children in care — these are the toll exacted by the strains on family life.

And what were the causes? A 'profound change', he said, had been 'occasioned by the number of married women who now take a job outside the home':

> I am told there is now a word for 'latchkey kid' in every European language . . . in more and more families mothers are combining earning with home-making . . . There is now an elaborate

machinery to ensure her equal opportunity, equal pay and equal rights; but I think we ought to stop and ask: where does this leave the family?

More to the point, where did this leave women? The Conservative spokesman was in no doubt: 'The pressure on young wives to go out to work devalues motherhood itself . . . Parenthood is a very skilled task indeed and it must be our aim to restore it to the place of honour it deserves.' Once women were restored to their 'place of honour' in the home, they could, he implied, take a lot of expensive work out of the hands of the social services:

> We hear today a great deal about social work . . . perhaps the most important social work of all is motherhood . . .

And the second most important social work, it seemed, was caring for the elderly at home: 'The family must be the front-line defence when Gran needs help.'

This was to be the theme of all Conservative electioneering around the welfare state. On 17 June 1978, at a National Children's Centre conference, Patrick Jenkin (who continued as chief propagandist) attacked the new TUC *Charter for the Under-Fives*. The Charter called for care and education to be made available to all children under five whose parents wanted it. Mr Jenkin was 'dismayed'; he could not 'conceive of any change which would do more to turn a highly personal individual service into yet another arm of the bureaucracy'. Instead, he wanted more pre-school playgroups. Young mothers, he said, were 'often isolated and depressed' (though why they should be when they were in the bosom of such a splendid institution as the family he did not explain); and when 'the only alternative may be increasing isolation and a course of Valium', what could be better than a voluntary stint at the local playgroup?

This new campaign by the Conservatives, who claimed to be 'the party of the family', soon had the Labour leadership engaging in the sincerest form of flattery. At the National Conference of Labour Women in May 1978, Prime Minister Callaghan made the same connection as the Tory spokesman between 'the impact on the family . . . [of] more mothers going out to work', the 'growth of vandalism and hooliganism' and the need to preserve 'the beneficial influence of the family as a whole . . . in this changing situation'. And he too linked the idea of strengthening the family with caring for the old and the sick:

The nature and strength of the family and our attitude towards it will include our attitude to care for the old and weaker members of our society.

But this put Labour in a bit of dilemma. Think of all the wonderful things the party had done to help women *go out* to work! Equal pay and opportunity laws ... statutory maternity leave ... protection from unfair dismissal during pregnancy ... a special new pension scheme ... If they all went off to be plumbers and computer analysts who'd be left to 'preserve the beneficial influence of the family'? For, as Callaghan noted in the same speech, 'the woman usually is the centre of the family'. Well, she would just have to do both — and that would evidently require shorter and more flexible hours, and more peripheral jobs. As Callaghan put it:

> We have to pay much more attention than we have done in the past as to how industry organizes woman's *role* at work, so that her influence as the centre of the family ... is not weakened. [Our italics]

A month later, on the same day as Jenkin's Valium speech, Callaghan took another tack, announcing in the Market Hall, Brecon, that 'change' must be harnessed 'to our principles and to our values'. Among these he named not only 'care and compassion for those in need' and 'the unique bonds of family life', but also 'the qualities found in the home', which included 'service before self'. Labour, said Callaghan, had done a lot 'to open up new opportunities for women who go out to work' and that was all very well.

> But equally — and here I want to make a very important point, one which I think is not made often enough — those women who choose their families as their lifework, devote their energies to their homes, their husbands and their children are equally valuable members of society and fulfil themselves.

This new focus on the family represented a greater ideological leap for Labour than for the Conservatives; it expressed confusion at the level of policy and a degree of conflict within the Labour Party. Public spending on the caring services had increased massively under the Wilson governments of the late 1960s and early 1970s. This directly affected women's workload — both by providing paid employment, and by taking into the social sphere responsibilities which had previously been left to mothers, daughters and neighbours. However, this particular effect of the expanding welfare state was never celebrated as a benefit for women. It did not seem to be a conscious part of Labour's thinking, and it was never a priority.

After the publication of the Seebohm Report and the 1974 reorganization of health and social services, there was a new emphasis upon reducing institutional care and speedily returning the sick, the geriatric and the disabled to the 'community'. The idea was popular not only with professionals in the field, but also with the public, because the alternative — large, impersonal institutions into which the sick and needy were dispatched and forgotten — seemed indefensible. The trouble was that a clear distinction had not been made between care *in* the community and care *by* the community. The former could mean well-resourced local services and facilities, accessible and accountable to the community and staffed by trained public servants. The latter could mean shifting responsibility to the family (which was, of course, the basic unit of the community) and converting paid employment into more unpaid work for women. The Labour Party had not thought this through; it retained a traditional view of the role of women in the family.

The Conservatives had a much clearer idea of what they were trying to achieve. In July 1980, Patrick Jenkin — by then a senior member of the new Tory government — addressed the Church of England Children's Society on the problem of handicapped children. 'Every child deserves a proper family life,' the Secretary of State for Social Services declared. The aim must be to keep the family together, with the child at home; that might be difficult and the family would need support, advice and encouragement; but *professional* help could 'actually undermine the confidence and competence of ordinary parents'. In its place should come support 'from people operating on a self-help basis and making use of resources within the community'. And in case anyone doubted who these 'people' were, Mr Jenkin was already on record with the following statement, delivered during a BBC *Man Alive* programme the previous year:

> If the good Lord had intended us all having equal rights to go out to work and to behave equally, you know he really wouldn't have created man and woman.

Cuts take their toll

There was far less talk about the family at the next general election in 1983. It was hard to find evidence that the Thatcher government had done anything positive to help the family — and so perhaps the less said about it, the better. In any case, the Conservatives were now fairly confident that they'd captured the ideological ground they needed to proceed with dismantling the welfare state. The shift in consensus was towards the anti-social and the individualistic, as public spending cuts took their toll on services and jobs.

Margaret Thatcher and her team managed to deflect opposition to the cuts away from themselves by making local authorities do the cutting. Local authorities had become the big spenders of the state sector. Between 1951 and 1975, their share of the gross national product almost doubled, from 9.8 per cent to 18.6 per cent; and their share of all government spending rose from a quarter to a third. Yet only ten per cent of their revenue came from rates. As the scale of their operations increased, so did their political significance and their power, but at the same time their financial dependence on central government grew. The Conservatives broke their political autonomy by insisting on strict cash limits.

The Thatcher government ordered local authorities to cut spending by 3 per cent in 1979 and by a further 5.6 per cent in 1980. Some Labour-controlled councils were unwilling to cut services, but found they were damned if they did and damned if they didn't. If they did, they incurred the wrath of their Labour supporters, who accused them of reneging on election promises; and if they didn't, they had to raise the rates, which incurred the wrath of ratepayers, many of whom were also Labour voters. They had no hope of being bailed out if they failed to stick to the limits. On the contrary, the government resolved to 'fine' recalcitrant authorities by taking an extra cut out of their next grant.

Many councils tackled the problem by deciding on an order of priorities and making deeper cuts in some areas, so that others would suffer less. Nursery care and education were often the first to go. East Sussex, for example, planned in 1980 to close all nursery schools and classes by 1982, shedding forty-five jobs and saving £233,600; at the same time its social services department named the day nursery services among its 'lowest priority items'. In Nottingham, more than two hundred nursery nurses were sacked. Oxfordshire announced it would close all its nursery schools rather than pare down the service all round. These patterns were repeated throughout the country. Nursery nurses and nursery teachers — almost all women — lost their livelihood. Working mothers who had previously relied on the services now had to choose between leaving their jobs and allowing their children to become (in Patrick Jenkin's favourite phrase) 'latchkey kids'.

School meals were another early target. Some authorities hiked up prices, greatly reducing the numbers of children who ate the meals. Others cut the quality. Bromley Council in Kent replaced hot dinners with cold snacks and issued redundancy notices to four hundred staff; two local independent nutrition experts were able to show that on every score (protein, energy, fibre, Vitamin C content) the new snacks would have a detrimental effect on the children's health. Dorset County Council rid itself of 950 school meals staff and in September 1980 abolished all school meals for children under twelve. A survey carried out by the National Union of Public Employees in November 1980 found that throughout the country some twenty thousand school meals staff (almost all female) had lost their jobs. And where jobs were not cut altogether, hours were cut — reducing women's earning power as well as the quality of their work, as meals suddenly had to be prepared in two hours rather than three. Mothers were left with the responsibility of providing alternative midday meals, or extra nutrition in the evenings, or of coping with the adverse effects on their children's health.

Homes for children, old people and the disabled were closed down. Some councils seized upon Mr Jenkin's familiar theme. Tory-controlled East Sussex, for one, declared proudly that its aim was 'to provide the help and support that families and the community need to look after these frail members of society', and stressed that 'voluntary organizations are vital in strengthening community life.' Kent came up with the idea of paying 'neighbours' a nominal fee to look after old people in need of residential care. Nicholas Stacey, director of social services in the Tory-controlled council, explained: 'By paying neighbours fairly little we get quite excellent, loyal and devoted service. You pay a neighbour £15 a week and get £50 service.' Not one of these neighbours was a man and that was quite appropriate in Stacey's view:

> When you've got male unemployment, how much better that women, who more naturally incline to a community-based life, do this sort of thing.[4]

The Thatcher government went on to produce a series of new laws and administrative measures designed to increase central control over local authorities and enforce further spending cuts. Councils which refused to stick to spending targets imposed by the government were heavily penalized. They were 'fined' through reductions in the rate support grants they received from central government; they were forbidden by law to raise local rates beyond strict limits; if they flouted the law, councillors could be taken to court, fined and banned from holding public office. Some authorities had much harsher limits imposed than others. In 1985—6, for example, Leicester was ordered to decrease its rates by 56.61 per cent and Southwark by 24.74 per cent, while Merseyside was allowed to increase its rates by 27.48 per cent and Basildon by 17.59 per cent.

Between 1979 and 1986, the real value of Exchequer grants to local authorities was cut by 12.3 per cent — an accumulated loss of nearly £8.5 billion. By 1986, local government's share of all public spending had fallen back from a third to a quarter.

Councils had to lop millions off their budgets to comply with government spending limits. The London borough of Southwark estimated that it would have to cut spending by £22.6 million in 1986; if cuts were spread evenly through all services, it would mean a reduction of £5.4 million in social services, leading to:

- the closure of seven residential homes for children;
- the closure of five old people's homes;
- the closure of all day centres for the mentally ill;
- a 21 per cent cut in the number of social workers;
- the ending of all grants to voluntary organizations working with the vulnerable and needy.[5]

The Inner London Education Authority estimated that for the same year, keeping within the government's target could mean:

- the loss of over 5,000 teaching and non-teaching jobs;
- a 30 per cent cut in cash allowances to schools for books, equipment and stationery;
- a 43 per cent increase in school meals prices;
- major cuts in adult education classes and soaring fees for what remained.[6]

Housing became a major victim of spending cuts, as council house building programmes were slashed and private enterprise failed to make up the difference. Fewer than 40,000 council houses were started in 1984: about 65 per cent down on 1978. Taking public and private house building together, the number of homes started under the Tories was 40 per cent below the numbers started under Labour. The Association of Metropolitan Authorities estimated in 1985 that there was a shortage of 517,000 dwellings. Standards declined, while rents went up. In 1985, one million dwellings in England and Wales lacked one or more basic amenities; 2.5 million homes in the UK were seriously affected by damp and three million required repairs costing £2,300 or more. Between 1979 and 1984, council rents in England and

Wales increased on average by 40 per cent, discounting the effects of inflation.[7] Inevitably, those most severely affected by deteriorating conditions were women, since they were largely responsible for managing the domestic environment and making it work for their families; and their lives were more likely than men's to centre on the family home.

Child care suffered too — though in ways that were harder to measure, because provision was already so patchy. Local authorities had no statutory obligation to provide services. For some, child care was the first to be cut back to meet government spending targets. Others improved their services, only to be forced into retreat by a funding crisis precipitated by rate-capping. The Greater London Council and other metropolitan authorities had funded a wide range of child care facilities, before their abolition in 1986. Overall, the most serious effect of spending cuts was to make any improvements impossible (beyond a few privately funded or voluntary experiments). The needs of women and children could not be met. Plans for improving the quality of care could not be put into practice. The rich hired nannies; the poor were left with nothing. Only handicapped children, or those deemed 'at risk' from 'inadequate' homes, had any right to claim access to local authority services, which were themselves inadequate:

> The concentration of unhappy and disturbed children in many day nurseries is so high that often care can be no more than custodial . . . As Professor Jack Tizard commented, 'a service to the poor is a poor service'.[8]

Meanwhile, the National Health Service was being whittled down to its bare bones. The process had been set in train by Labour, during the Callaghan administration. Capital spending on NHS hospitals and community health services declined from £586 million to £359 million between 1971 and 1977 (at 1977 prices). Between January 1976 and June 1978, 143 hospitals in England and Wales were closed down or otherwise 'rationalized'. In an attempt to redistribute resources more fairly between the regions, some districts lost out badly. For instance, between 1977 and 1979, London's health budget rose by only 2 per cent, compared with 5.8 per cent in the North-West. A report published by NUPE estimated that London would lose 31 per cent of its hospital beds between 1975 and 1986, with a total loss of 24,548 health service jobs.[9]

As young people moved out of central London, so the average age of the population increased, putting ever greater strains on services for the elderly. NUPE reported in 1978:

> Many geriatrics are already occupying beds in acute wards; and demand will also increase for these facilities due to lack of earlier treatment. Patients are being transferred to inadequate local authority social services, or *returned to friends or relatives.* [Our italics][10]

Many health districts tried to cut costs by sending hospital patients home earlier than before. In the London health district of Brent, hospital beds were reduced by 25 per cent in four years, without any increase in waiting lists. According to an official report from the Area Health Authority:

> This has been done by discharging patients earlier (five days earlier, for example, in General Medicine) and by drastically cutting the time between one patient going out of hospital and another one coming into the bed. This has all happened *without any extra community staffing.* [Our italics][11]

The Conservatives came to power intent on boosting the private health sector — which was geared far more to the needs of middle-class men in work than to the needs of any women (except where abortion was concerned). They claimed not to be cutting funds to the National Health Service, but by failing to increase resources in line with increased costs and demands, they drove it into decline. Screening for cervical cancer was badly hit after the government closed the national recall system in 1980, leaving millions of women without access to systematic checks. The British Medical Association found in 1983 that waiting times for hospital appointments had increased by an average of 20 per cent over the previous year. The Royal College of Nurses reported the same year: 'Nurses want the public to know that standards of care are already threatened, that staffing levels on wards hover just above danger level and that out in the community increased numbers of patients are over-burdening community care and making good nursing practice practically impossible.'[12] In 1983−4, health authorities had to cut 11,400 jobs.

Health, housing, education, welfare . . . as cuts in public spending went deeper, they did not simply diminish these services, but changed their meaning. What had been intended as an expression of collectivity, in which everyone benefited from pooled resources, was becoming a tawdry safety net to catch the nation's have-nots. Anyone who could afford to buy something better was encouraged to do so. The idea that there might be public solutions to private problems, shared across society, went right out of style. Responsibility was returned to the private sphere, which meant the family, where needs were met, if at all, by the unpaid work of women.

It's worth remembering how swiftly this change took place. When the feminist writer Zoë Fairbairns published her novel *Benefits* in 1979, her image of the future still sounded fantastic and fictional. By the mid-1980s, it sounded almost unremarkable, so closely did it resemble the rhetoric of the time.

> The dying welfare state brought its own Newspeak as well: government's failure to link child benefit, unemployment pay and so on to the cost of living was *the fight against inflation*; putting children on halftime schooling was referred to as *giving parents a free hand*; closing hospitals and dumping dying relatives on the doorsteps of unwarned and distant relatives was *community care*; and a new political movement that saw remedies to the whole predicament, if only the nation's women would buckle down to their traditional role and biological destiny, was known quite simply as FAMILY.[13]

Challenging the state

The character of the campaign against spending cuts, which was led by the public service unions, was largely reactive, focussing on saving jobs and reinstating services. But as the 1980s progressed, another dimension emerged which bore the hallmark of feminist influence. This involved a critique of the welfare state and proposals for changing it. It recognized that the state could contribute to the subordination of women and could perpetuate oppressive hierarchies, as well as sexist and racist practices. It called for women and men in the community to be involved in planning, so that services responded more effectively to real needs and could be held accountable, through democratic, local control. It sought a more creative use of resources and a reordering of priorities.

If school meals were to be defended, for example, the point was not simply to save the jobs of the women who provided them, but to improve the meals themselves. Likewise, it was not enough to fight for a new public housing programme if it perpetuated the traditional pattern of privatized, 'nuclear' family life. Homes and communities needed to be designed and equipped to create more flexibility, with services and facilities that could create conditions for change. Child care needed to be reorganized, to integrate care and education and to combat racism and sexism. The health service was desperately in need of a shake-up, which would change its priorities to favour preventive measures and free it from the high-tech wizardry of a male-dominated medical profession. Ideas like these had little practical impact while the Conservatives remained in power, but they began to change the climate of opinion among defenders of the welfare state, in ways which could prove important in years to come.

As an autonomous, locally based movement of heterogeneous elements, the women's movement developed no single party-political affiliation, nor any specific orientation towards constitutional politics. Yet some of its major practical innovations were self-help endeavours at a community level, which supplemented the functions of the welfare state, or challenged traditional state practice. Women's Aid refuges, for example, filled a gap in municipal provision: by mobilizing some state resources for women, on the side of women, they endorsed a critique of what had been regarded as 'normal' masculine behaviour. The success of these and other projects (children's community centres were another example) was a result of engagement *in and against* the local state by the women's movement. It was easier for the movement to operate at this level, because local government corresponded more closely to its non-centralized form than did the strictures and protocols of national politics.

The process which began with feminist groups entering a dialogue with local authorities, to gain access to funds and premises, fed back into the wider campaign to defend jobs and services. It also produced a new feature on the face of local government — official committees and support groups run by and for women, within the machinery of state.

'Municipal feminism'

The first of these Women's Committees was formally established by the Greater London Council in May 1982. It came into being partly because the new Labour administration at the GLC had as one of its basic objectives the channelling of 'power, resources and opportunities to the deprived, marginalized and disadvantaged sectors of London's population', but primarily because the GLC came under pressure from feminists working in and around the Council to translate policy into practice. It was a full committee of the GLC, with wide terms of reference:

- The promotion of the welfare and interests of women in Greater London.

- The implementation of policies to promote equal opportunity for women and to increase the range and level of opportunities open to women within the Council's employment in conjunction with the Staff Committee. The promotion of adoption by London Borough Councils and other employers in Greater London of equal opportunity policies for women.

- Advocacy of the abolition of policies which discriminate against women on grounds of sex.[14]

By the time the GLC was abolished in 1986, women's committees or working parties had been set up in 33 local authorities, including 10 London boroughs. They varied in nature, and in the emphasis and scope of their work, depending on the degree of local political support and the size of their budgets, but all shared similar objectives. The GLC Women's Committee had a shorter life than most of them, but was more influential — not only because it was the first, but because it was by far the largest and most powerful. It pioneered an approach to politics which was to affect the work of other women's committees after its own demise.

The Committee had its own budget, which ran to some £90 million by its fourth (and final) year, and its own Support Unit, which in January 1986 consisted of 96 posts. It set up an elaborate consultative framework, beginning with open meetings in the Council chamber: scenes like these had not been seen at County Hall before, as up to 500 women from all over London met in open sessions to discuss the needs of women and how the Committee should go about its business. Extra members were co-opted to represent Black and ethnic minority women, lesbians, women with disabilities and trade union women, and special areas of interest such as peace, planning and child care. Strategies were planned with working groups drawn from different sections of the community. Child care costs were met for women attending meetings, and crèches were set up wherever possible. In these and other ways, the GLC Women's Committee helped to create a distinctive new style in local government, based on accessibility, wide consultation, positive action to redress discrimination, and re-distribution of power and resources. It was part of a general pattern of change brought about by the Labour administration at County Hall (and by certain other Labour-controlled authorities), and it was large and powerful enough to play an important role in shaping that initiative.

In its first four years, the Committee gave out £30 million on nearly

1,000 grants to women's voluntary sector groups. Nearly 14 million went to child care projects: by 1986 the Committee was funding 12 per cent of all full-time provision for under-fives in London. In addition, it made 151 grants to social and resource centres for women, 69 to health projects, 60 to information and advice projects, 55 to counselling and support services, and 37 to women's refuges. Grant-aided projects were encouraged to reflect the values of the Committee — by being accessible to all women, pursuing anti-racist, anti-sexist policies and providing high quality services and conditions of employment.

As well as funding independent groups of women, the Women's Committee tried to ensure that other GLC committees took women fully into account — not just in rhetoric, but by following detailed plans to consult women in the community, to promote equal opportunities and to meet women's needs. Special efforts were made to involve women in planning; a survey of women's transport needs was conducted, a range of publications was produced to spread information about services and campaigns for women, and a large building in central London was set up as a resource centre . . . it would be impossible to do justice here to all the Committee's activities. What counted most, in a sense, was the very presence of the Women's Committee, and the scale on which it was operating. For a short time, women had a taste of what real power might be like, and what could be achieved if women could command extensive resources in women's interests, over a longer period.

Women's committees and working parties in other local authorities had to cater for different kinds of constituencies under different conditions, and their priorities varied accordingly. A Standing Conference of Local Government Women's Committees was set up in January 1985, as a forum for discussion and a network for women councillors and officers. Through it, the committees could learn from each others' experience, develop common policies and co-ordinate strategies. After the abolition of the GLC, the Association of London Authorities set up a women's unit, financed by London boroughs, to carry on some of the functions of the GLC Women's Committee.

The politics of the new women's committees reflected — and to a certain extent shaped — a new phase of the women's movement. There was a determined shift of emphasis towards Black and ethnic minority women, working class women, women with disabilities, lesbians, older women. This was based not so much on a new theoretical analysis of where the roots of oppression lay, as on a critique of the white, middle-class character of the women's movement of the 1970s, and on the simple observation that groups which had been deprived and disregarded in the past should now be recognized and empowered.

The women's committees represented a move from the private into the public sphere, from autonomy to a new relationship with established state power. They gave expression to a developing feminist critique of the state, as well as suggesting a route by which women could begin to put their own policies into practice. It was not just a question of going for local authority funds (some women's committees had little to offer in the way of resources), but of carving out a new place for women in the local state. So elusive was the power that women wanted that they had to build their own bases first, and start transforming the conditions under which power could be achieved, and the ends for which it was exercised.

Table 7   Wives' and husbands' views about how the housework is shared between them (percentages)

	Wife does it all	Wife does most of it	Shared half and half	Husband does most of it	Husband does it all
Families where wife works full-time					
wife's view	13	41	44	2	0
husband's view	9	46	43	2	—
Families where wife works part-time					
wife's view	26	51	23	0	—
husband's view	15	61	24	0	—
Families where wife is not working					
wife's view	32	49	17	1	1
husband's view	22	58	19	0	1
All married women					
wife's view	25	48	26	1	0
husband's view	16	56	27	1	0

Source: Department of Employment, OPCS, *Women and Employment*, 1984.

Table 8 Wives' and husbands' views about how the child care
is shared between them (percentages)

	Wife does it all	Wife does most of it	Shared half and half	Husband does most of it	Husband does it all
Families where wife works full-time					
wife's view	5	24	67	4	0
husband's view	2	24	72	2	—
Families where wife works part-time					
wife's view	8	36	55	1	—
husband's view	5	44	51	—	—
Families where wife is not working					
wife's view	11	48	41	0	—
husband's view	6	64	30	0	—
All married women with children under 16					
wife's view	9	40	50	1	0
husband's view	5	51	44	0	—

Source: Department of Employment, OPCS, *Women and Employment*, 1984.

110 *Family and state*

Notes to chapter 3

1 *Woman's Own*, 17 February 1979.
2 Daniel, W. W. *Maternity Rights: the experience of women*, Policy Studies Institute Report no. 588, June 1980.
3 Ibid.
4 Campbell, B. 'In a Family Way', *Time Out*, September 1979.
5 Labour Party Research Department, *Breaking the Nation*, Pluto Press and *New Socialist*, 1985.
6 Ibid.
7 Ibid.
8 *Under Fives and Under Funded*, Equality for Children, 1984.
9 *Under the Axe: London's Health Service Crisis*, NUPE, 1978.
10 Ibid.
11 *Cuts and the NHS*, The Politics of Health Group Pamphlet no. 2.
12 Labour Party Research Department, *Breaking the Nation*.
13 Fairbairns, Z. *Benefits*, Virago, 1979.
14 Hunt, L. *The GLC Women's Committee 1982−6*, GLC, 1986.

4 Law and politics

> The Women's Liberation Movement protests against the term
> 'Sex Discrimination Bill' being used for what is only a limited
> equal opportunities Bill. The movement severely condemns
> obvious fundamental omissions of discrimination such as
> pensions, taxation, social security etc. We demand of the
> Government a comprehensive sex discrimination Bill so that
> women are no longer defined as dependants; and a Bill that
> provides for no less than genuine equality of treatment under
> the law for both sexes.

This resolution, passed by the National Women's Liberation Conference
in Manchester on 6 April 1975, only hinted at the range of views held
by feminists in that period.

There was a strong current of opinion which held that the
parliamentary battle was a side-issue, which would do little or nothing
to help end female oppression: these women weren't opposed to it, but
they were preoccupied with other matters. Some groups were eager
for Parliament to legislate, believing with varying degrees of optimism
in the efficacy of law. Some saw themselves carrying on the work of
feminists who had campaigned for women's suffrage — taking their
victory a step further by using Parliament to enshrine the principle of
equality in a Sex Discrimination Act.

Few were in doubt that the Labour government's Bill, which was
cruising through Parliament at the time, had serious weaknesses. Yet
even fewer believed that (as the resolution suggested) any law could
work the miracle of providing 'genuine equality of treatment'. The
motion was proposed by a women's group in Watford, Hertfordshire,
which in 1973 had launched the Women's Liberation Campaign for an
anti-discrimination law. One of its members, Pat Howe, chained herself
to the railings outside the House of Commons on 19 April 1975, as
part of a National Day of Action, organized by her group, against
Labour's Bill. But the demonstration attracted little support. Most
women welcomed the Bill, warts and all.

Such differences as there were among feminists did not reflect the
radical/socialist divide. The campaign for law reform had supporters
on both sides. It was a popular cause, well publicized, which drew
countless newcomers into the women's liberation movement. More-

over, it was a crucial stage in the development of feminist politics. It was an opportunity to remove some of the outer wrappings from the system which sustained inequality. Once that had been done, it was found that — like a parcel on April Fool's Day — there were layers upon layers beneath. Something of the kind was suspected by most women, but now they could get a clearer idea of how the monstrous item was constructed.

In this chapter we look at the campaign for 'equality' legislation, at how far the new laws changed women's lives, and at the reasons why they have had such a feeble effect. Some of these reasons can be found in the laws themselves, others in the methods of law enforcement. We describe the emergence of a new campaign for 'positive action', which grew out of women's experience of ineffective legislation. And finally we examine the changing relationship between the women's liberation movement and the machinery of party politics and parliamentary government.

Equality — good in parts

Labour's new Bill was a great deal better than women had been led to expect, after all the ups and downs of the seven-year fight for an anti-discrimination law. Joyce Butler, Labour MP for Wood Green, had introduced the first Private Member's Bill to outlaw discrimination against women in 1967. It failed to get a second reading. Bills along the same line were submitted every year after that, but it was not until 1972, when Edward Heath was Prime Minister, that a Bill introduced into the House of Lords by the Liberal peer Nancy Seear got over the crucial second hurdle. It might have gone on to become law had it not been referred (rather unusually) to a Select Committee of the Lords. This Committee heard an impressive range of evidence between June and December 1972, and eventually reported in the spring of the following year. Meanwhile, on 29 November 1972, Willie Hamilton, Labour MP for West Fife, submitted another, similar Bill to the Commons.

The two Bills now became the focus of a large and energetic campaign, uniting for the first time the new women's liberation groups and some trade unions with such long-established feminist organizations as the Fawcett Society (set up to continue the work of the suffragist Millicent Fawcett) and the Six Point Group (which belonged to the more militant tradition of the suffragettes). Both Bills were far less detailed and more narrowly focussed than the one which eventually became law.

At its second reading on 2 February 1973, Willie Hamilton's Bill narrowly missed a sudden death. As the feminist newsletter *Women's Report* explained at the time, 'Only the uproar on the crowded opposition benches and the massive support of British women (as manifested by the unabashed claps and jeers in the packed gallery) kept Speaker Selwyn Lloyd from killing the Bill for lack of time.'[1] A mass meeting followed at the old suffragette venue, Caxton Hall, where between three and four hundred women listened to speeches from MPs, women's liberation campaigners, trade unionists and others, under pre-1914 banners urging 'Dare to be free'. Then, at the call of May Hobbs of the Night Cleaners Campaign, they 'erupted into the night to march in torchlight procession to the House and 10 Downing Street'. It was a stirring occasion, with a scent of victory in the air. On 14 February, Hamilton's Bill completed its second reading, unopposed; but to the surprise and disappointment of many, it was referred to yet another Select Committee.

Neither Bill could succeed without some measure of support from the government. The strength of the campaign and the degree of enthusiasm inside Parliament made this seem a possibility. It therefore came as a bitter blow when on 14 May 1973, as Baroness Seear's Bill returned to the Lords, amended and strengthened from committee stage, Home Office minister Lord Colville announced that the government would not support it (nor Hamilton's, by implication), but planned instead to introduce proposals of its own.

The Tories' Green Paper was published in September 1973 and — as MP Renée Short declared at that year's Labour Party Conference — it was altogether 'flabby and toothless'. Education and training were omitted entirely, thanks to the intervention of Education Secretary Margaret Thatcher. There were wide exemptions in the provisions relating to employment: for example, it would remain lawful to discriminate 'where it could be shown that for performance of personal services strong preferences among customers or clients make the employment of a man (or a woman) essential to the business'. There was nothing to stop discrimination by trade unions; the proposed Equal Opportunities Commission had no enforcement powers at all; and no mention was made of penalties for offending employers, or arrangements for compensation. The Bill died an unlamented death when the Heath government fell in February 1974. Labour returned to power and introduced its own legislation, drawing on the findings of the two Select Committees, and going further than either Seear's or Hamilton's proposals. The Labour Bill embraced not only education, training and employment, but also housing and the provision to the public of goods, facilities and services, and, more important still, the concept of 'indirect discrimination', imported from the United States, which extended its influence in all these fields. Debate now homed in comfortably on the details: should there be an exemption for midwives? Should private clubs be included? Should new 'equal opportunities tribunals' be set up to enforce the law, instead of industrial tribunals? By this stage, many women wanted to give the Bill — which was finally enacted on 29 December 1975 — the benefit of the doubt. In any case, there was a strong feeling in 1975 that progress was being made, at least towards eliminating the more blatant forms of female disadvantage.

Along with the new Sex Discrimination Act, the Equal Pay Act, passed in 1970, came into force and an Equal Opportunities Commission was set up with a statutory duty to enforce these new laws. The 1975 Social Security (Pensions) Act introduced a new state pension scheme which made special provision for people who spent some time out of waged work because of their 'home responsibilities' and gave women a new chance to earn a full pension of their own. And the Employment Protection Act, passed that same year, gave women a statutory right to paid maternity leave, protection from unfair dismissal during pregnancy and the right to their jobs back up to twenty-nine weeks after the baby's birth. So the year designated 'International Women's Year' by the United Nations brought a shower of benefits — or so it seemed. It was not altogether unreasonable for women to assume they were making headway and that things would go on getting better.

The principle of equal rights now bore the official seal of approval and it ceased to be respectable to treat women less favourably than men — at least without making some effort to disguise what one was doing. The effect of having the principle of equality formally endorsed is hard to measure, but it must have helped to develop new expectations and a new sense of confidence among women, and it must have begun (however sluggishly) to change public opinion about what was 'natural' and immutable about the differences between women and men. The focus of argument shifted: open disputes about whether or not women were men's inferiors, worthy of unequal treatment, gave way to disagreements over what exactly constituted the equal rights that women were acknowledged to deserve, and how these could now be achieved.

On the other hand, the material circumstances of most women's lives remained almost entirely unchanged by the new legislation.

Equal pay — some more equal than others

The Equal Pay Act said that a woman should be paid the same as a man if she was doing work that was 'the same or broadly similar' to his; at the very least, she should get no less than the lowest male rate in the lowest grade. The five-year gap between its enactment in 1970 and its coming into force in 1975 was officially the period in which equal pay was to be 'phased in'. It was never expected to cost employers much: a 1970 Department of Employment report estimated that it would add only 3.5 per cent (on average) to employers' wage bills if they enforced the law by 1975.[2] In fact, those years were a gift for employers who needed time to work out ways of avoiding their obligations under the Act. The first government report on the implementation of the Equal Pay Act is worth quoting at some length because it lists many of the typical measures adopted to keep down women's pay.[3] One company, where 80 per cent of employees were women engaged on semi-skilled work similar to men's, set about separating women and men into distinct categories:

> For example, the machine shop has had a female day shift and a male night shift; men are now being recruited for day work and women are being transferred to other departments. The more technical inspection jobs are being allotted to men and the women are being transferred to simple inspection tasks; central packing is becoming a male area, line packing is reserved for women; work in the finishing and paint shops and in the Stores, is to be a male preserve; this also applies to sign-writing, even though many women are considered to be more skilful at this.
>
> White collar jobs are to be graded into three grades: the lower one predominantly women, the middle one mixed and the upper one predominantly for men. As a result of this reorganization it is expected that by the end of 1972 very little of the work undertaken by women will be even broadly similar to that of men.

All this was done 'with the acceptance of trade union representatives who are concerned about male unemployment'. In many areas, the Equal Pay Act was actually doing women more harm than good — and they were to suffer well beyond the end of the decade from this rigid segregation of male and female jobs, which depressed their pay and limited their opportunities. The company referred to above was by no means an isolated exception. A memorandum from the British Paper Box Federation, representing an industry of 26,000 employees, 70 per cent of them women, was quoted in the *Sunday Times* on 25 February 1973. It recommended to the Federation's member firms that if they had not made 'proper provision for an acceptable differential between the take-home pay for men and women, the following discriminatory factors [were] available: Long Service; Merit; Attendance Bonus; Willingness to work overtime to a given number of hours . . .' And, the memorandum went on, 'Jobs should be changed now where areas of conflict are likely to arise: i.e. the Lavatory Cleaner.'

When a research team from the London School of Economics embarked on a three-year project to study the effects of the new legislation, they found that sixteen out of nineteen organizations they were monitoring went on paying all female manual workers less than the lowest rate paid to men, until the Equal Pay Act came fully into force.[4]

So much for the five-year 'phasing-in' period. Once the Act was in force, a great many women were unable to benefit from it, there being no men with whom they could compare their pay. The most they could expect was that they should now be brought up to the lowest male rate, which was the minimum stipulation of the new law.

The Act was supposed to give women the right to claim equal pay not only if their work was 'the same or broadly similar' to a man's, but also if their work had been 'rated as equivalent' to a man's in a job evaluation scheme. These schemes had become quite common by the mid-1970s. They involved assessing each job for its value, according to particular criteria: how much skill did the job require, for instance, and how much responsibility did it carry? The job would then be placed in what was thought to be the appropriate grade, and paid at the agreed rate for that grade. It was (and remained) common practice for employers and unions to cooperate over job evaluation, jointly agreeing the criteria and negotiating the value of each job.

The problem for women arose over which criteria were chosen and how they were applied. As we explained in chapter 2, the notion of skill was by no means neutral or fixed, but part of a political process in which certain workers fought for better pay over more than 150 years. As a result, greater value was routinely attached to heavy or dirty jobs normally done by men than to jobs requiring manual dexterity or non-stop concentration (such as assembly-line work), normally done by women. Where women were not in a strong bargaining position, which they seldom were, opinions of this kind prevailed, leaving them on their own in the lowest-paid grades, still unable to claim equal pay. There was a provision in the Equal Pay Act for discriminatory wage structures to be referred for amendment to the Central Arbitration Committee, a statutory body set up in 1970. But this net could only catch the more blatantly unequal arrangements.

On 10 February 1975, a directive was issued by the EEC defining the principle of equal pay set out in the Treaty of Rome (of which Britain was a signatory). It clearly stated that equal pay should be given to women and men doing the same work or *work of equal value*. This 'equal value' principle was not enshrined in Britain's Equal Pay Act and it was not until 1984 that the necessary amendment was made.

In the nine intervening years, women could not get equal pay for work of equal value. The kind of absurdity that could arise was illustrated by the case of Leicester community worker Sue Waddington. Ms Waddington made a claim in 1976 for equal pay with a male playleader whom she had employed to run an adventure playground which she herself had set up. His pay, determined by the national scale for youth leaders and community centre wardens, amounted to 14 per cent more than hers, which was fixed under a separate national pay scale for social workers. She lost — on the ground that her job carried more responsibility than his and was therefore not 'broadly similar'![5]

Unamended, the Equal Pay Act had only limited use. Most employers found it easy to avoid litigation by segregating the workforce. After a couple of years, relatively few could be caught in breach of the law. The number of applications under the Act fell dramatically — from 1,724 in 1976 to 35 in 1983. Meanwhile, the gap between male and female pay actually grew wider: in 1977 women's gross hourly earnings were 75.5 per cent of men's; by 1984, they were down to 73.5 per cent.

On 1 January 1984, the government finally bowed to its obligations under the Treaty of Rome and amended the Equal Pay Act to allow women to claim equal pay for work of equal value. In the following two years, more than 600 applications were made, involving around 100 employers. Industrial tribunals could now appoint an independent expert from a panel drawn up by ACAS (the Advisory, Conciliation and Arbitration Service), to analyse the jobs of the applicant and those with whom she was claiming equal pay, to assess whether they were of equal value.

The first woman to win an equal value case was Julie Hayward, a cook at Cammel Laird Shipyard on Merseyside. She based her application on the fact that she had obtained a City and Guilds Certificate in cookery by going to day-release classes over four years, yet was paid considerably less than three young men who had qualified in a similar way — as painter, joiner and thermal insulation engineer. She was also expected to work at a higher level, standing in for the canteen chef for substantial periods of time. Her job, she claimed, was of equal value to those of the three men in terms of effort, skill and decision-making. The independent expert assessed the jobs by breaking them down into five main factors and scoring them 'low', 'moderate' and 'high': physical demands, environmental demands, planning and decision-making, skill and knowledge required, and responsibility. After five months, he reported in Julie Hayward's favour. The tribunal upheld his decision.

Early victories under the amended Act were also scored by 14 fish-packers who claimed parity with a labourer; a data processing clerk who did work of equal value to that of a machine operator; and a college housemother who won equal pay with a housefather. All these cases were decided by different methods of assessment, there being no standard system. By 1986 it was still not clear how the law would be interpreted in future cases, but it looked as though it had considerable potential — since it struck at the heart of the job evaluation process on which pay scales and collective agreements were based.

Sex discrimination — early promise not fulfilled

As we explained earlier, the Sex Discrimination Act was born with something of a silver spoon in its mouth. People looked kindly upon it and expected it to do well. It was left to a small band of sceptics in the women's liberation movement to reject it for the chinless wonder that it really was.

In theory, the Act made it unlawful to treat a woman less favourably than a man would be treated in the same circumstances, just because she was a woman. (It applied, conversely, to men.) It covered the fields of education, training, employment, housing and the provision to the public of goods, facilities and services. It made it unlawful, too, to treat a married person less favourably than a single person (though not vice versa) in the fields of training and employment.

The Act embraced not only straightforward, 'direct' discrimination, but also 'indirect' discrimination — defined as imposing a condition which could be met by more people of one sex than the other, and which was not 'justifiable'. An obvious example would be an employer's requirement that applicants for a job should have 'O' level Physics, even though the job could be done perfectly well without it. Since far more boys than girls take 'O' level Physics, the requirement would amount to an unjustifiable condition which could be met by more members of one sex than the other.

The Act may have seemed far-reaching at first glance; but it was also exceedingly complicated. It was ringed around with 'ifs' and 'buts' and shot through with loopholes. It was often very difficult for an individual to discover whether she was a victim of unlawful discrimination. If she had applied for a job and failed to get it, how would she know if she had been turned down because of her sex? If she asked for a mortgage and was turned away, how could she find out whether the mortgage company had rejected her simply because she was female? And it was up to *her* to prove the point.

In 1978, Mrs Nasse, who worked as a clerical officer for the Science Research Council, applied for promotion, but was passed over in favour of two people whom she considered less well qualified than herself. She suspected discrimination on grounds of her marital status — having heard that the SRC considered married women to be lacking in mobility and therefore unsuitable for promotion. In order to prove her case, she applied to an industrial tribunal for disclosure of confidential documents relating to the other candidates. Disclosure was ordered, but the SRC fought it all the way to the House of Lords, where it was finally ruled that she would not be allowed to see the documents, but that the industrial tribunal should look at the relevant ones first, and then order discussion of any that it considered necessary for a fair hearing.[6] This was not altogether unhelpful, but the right of women to see documents which may help to prove discrimination against them remained indistinct. (And, of course, discrimination was not always documented.) The position might have been improved if the Act were worded differently, so that the individual applicant simply had to show that she had been treated differently and to her disadvantage, with the burden of proof on the respondent (the employer, for example, or the mortgage company) to show that the treatment *did not* amount to unlawful discrimination. While the burden of proof remained on the individual complainant, it was relatively easy for employers and others who were practising sex discrimination to cover their tracks.

Even where a woman had successfully brought a case under the Sex Discrimination Act, her victory rarely improved conditions for other women. Employers could just go on behaving as before, until the next individual brought another complaint — and her victory, in turn, affected her situation alone. This was true of most cases of direct discrimination. However, a successful complaint against *indirect* discrimination could have a wider impact, as the case of Belinda Price showed.

Belinda Price, a single mother of two, wanted to return to full-time employment at the age of thirty-five, having spent several years at home while her children were young. She applied for an executive officer's job in the Civil Service, and although she had suitable qualifications she found that entry to executive officer grade was restricted to people aged 28 or under. She brought a complaint of indirect discrimination, claiming that the age bar amounted to a condition which could more easily be met by men, since so many women take a break from paid employment in their twenties and early thirties, to look after young children. There was ample statistical evidence to support her claim. The Civil Service argued that all women could go out to work in their twenties if they wanted to, it was a matter of 'choice'; but the Employment Appeals Tribunal ruled that

> it should not be said that a person 'can' do something merely because it is theoretically possible for him [sic] to do so; it is necessary to see whether he can do so in practice.[7]

As a result, the Civil Service has raised its age bar to forty-five, opening the rank of executive officer to many more women than before. So the benefits in this case spread far beyond the individual litigant.

Relatively few formal complaints of indirect discrimination were made in the first ten years of the Sex Discrimination Act (less than 15 per cent of the total). Not that such breaches of the law were rare. When the London School of Economics' Equal Pay and Opportunities Project monitored nineteen employing organizations, 16 cases of possible indirect discrimination were identified. These included age bars; restriction of certain jobs to people who had served a formal apprenticeship, where this was not necessary for the job; and requirements that employees be geographically mobile or undertake lengthy periods of residential training in order to qualify for promotion. None had become the subject of a formal complaint. Reporting the results of the LSE Project in 1979, Mandy Snell, one of the researchers, commented:

> Indirect discrimination is a complex concept and there was little awareness and even less understanding of its implications among women, unions and employers. This situation is not confined to the workplace; unions at a national level, the media and many women activists have failed to recognize the potential importance of this provision of the Act.[8]

In the early 1980s, the proportion of indirect discrimination cases increased significantly (from 28 applications in 1982 to 98 in 1984) — and some useful precedents were set. The case of *Hurley* v. *Mustoe* involved Ms Hurley, a mother of four, who had been refused a job as a waitress on the ground that the employer, Mr Mustoe, considered women with children to be unreliable. Mrs Hurley won her case at the Employment Appeal Tribunal, which established that her treatment amounted to direct sex discrimination (since men with children were not assumed to be unreliable) and indirect marriage discrimination (since it was not justifiable for an employer to exclude all women with children on the ground that some would be unreliable).

The case of Brenda Clarke and Sandra Powell, part-time workers at a company called Eley Kynoch, had far-reaching implications. The company had a policy of making full-time workers redundant on a last-in-first-out basis, but making part-time workers redundant before full-timers, regardless of their length of service. Ms Clarke and Ms Powell, who were made redundant with 58 other part-timers, complained of indirect sex discrimination. Far fewer women than men, they argued, could meet the company's condition for being selected for redundancy on a last-in-first-out basis, because of the predominance of women working part-time. The Employment Appeals Tribunal upheld their complaint — an important step towards establishing the principle that part-time workers should not be treated less favourably than full-timers.

Problems of enforcement

From 1976 to 1983, a total of 4,296 applications were made under the Equal Pay Act and 1,792 under the employment section of the Sex Discrimination Act. Less than half of all these applications proceeded to industrial tribunal hearings, and just over one in ten produced a favourable tribunal decision. Thirty-five per cent of all applications were withdrawn; 15 per cent of equal pay claims and 25 per cent of sex discrimination complaints were settled 'out of court'.

Were women simply getting it wrong? Or was there a problem with the way the laws were enforced? A study published in 1981 cast doubts on the role of ACAS, which had been given the job of helping 'the parties in an independent and impartial way to try to reach a settlement . . . acceptable to them.'[9] Jeanne Gregory surveyed women who had withdrawn their applications and concluded that many had been unnecessarily deterred by ACAS officers. The officers were predominantly male. Gregory reported this woman's experience as typical of many:

> He [the ACAS officer] said that if you take a case to the tribunal the onus is on you to produce evidence and prove your case. If you lose the case you have to pay the costs and you can't ask for a reference from your employer if you leave. He said the number of cases which go through successfully is virtually nil. All this information succeeded in putting me off. He also asked me who

had told me I could make a complaint about sex discrimination and I told him the Job Centre had. He said they shouldn't do that.

As Gregory pointed out, the officer was wrong on several counts. A woman who took a complaint to an industrial tribunal would incur no costs of her own unless she chose to employ a lawyer; only in exceptional cases where the tribunal took the view that a complaint was 'frivolous' or 'vexatious' would the applicant be ordered to pay the costs of the other side. The number of successful cases could not be described as 'virtually nil'. And it was the duty of Job Centres to provide complaint forms to women who wanted to take action under the Sex Discrimination or Equal Pay Act.

More detailed research published in 1985 confirmed that many applicants were dissatisfied by the intervention of ACAS.[10] The authors, Cosmo Graham and Norman Lewis, found that applicants needed help of a different order:

> It is the entire set of circumstances in which they find themselves which is the fundamental cause of their difficulties, and which can be expressed as being unbefriended in a hostile environment. They need to be courageous enough to object to things which many others regard as normal currency, in circumstances where they are told, as they often are by ACAS officers, that the respondents are represented by clever and experienced solicitors, and that cases such as theirs are notoriously difficult to prove. They are intimidated by terms such as 'preliminary hearings', and even more so by the prospect of appearing before a tribunal where, they are told, vexatious claims might be penalised by the award of costs. They frequently have no trade union or one which is indifferent to them or simply outclassed when it comes to invoking the legislation. They are informed by a supposedly 'neutral' party of [the] respondent's side of the story, which they often regard as being a tissue of lies. And they believe that standing up for themselves could jeopardise their jobs or cause them to be blacklisted . . .

No wonder so many abandoned their complaints. Graham and Lewis concluded that the search for compromise, with which ACAS had been entrusted, was inappropriate in many cases. They reported that settlements were usually produced on the basis of the lowest common denominator between the parties, even if the strict requirements of the law were being flouted. 'Equal pay means equal pay and not a bargained reduction in the current differential between men and women.'

By 1986 the first exhaustive analyses were published of applications to industrial tribunals under the Equal Pay and Sex Discrimination Acts.[11] It emerged that tribunals often misinterpreted or misapplied the law, and accepted with only superficial questioning employers' explanations of their actions: 'tribunals generally, and with striking frequency, accepted vague and generalised explanations from respondents, ignored noted inconsistencies in evidence, and even accepted in proof of non-discrimination, evidence that was irrelevant to the issues presented.' Standards of decision-making varied enormously from one tribunal to another. Cases were allocated in such a way that tribunals had little or no chance to build up expertise in this area. Applicants were more likely to succeed if there was at least one woman on the panel, and a full-time chair (full-timers were more experienced). Yet too often cases were heard by all-male panels, headed by a part-time chair — and the situation appeared to be getting worse:

> Complainants lacked either a full-time chairman or a woman on the panel, or had neither, at 33% of the hearings in 1980, 40% of the hearings in 1981 and 45% of the hearings in 1982. Only 5% of the hearings from England and Wales were heard by a woman chairman [sic] . . . During the period of this study, chairmen received no specific formal training of any kind about sex discrimination or equal pay issues. Panel members were given two half-day training sessions each year, though a few regions did more. These sessions sometimes dealt with equal rights legislation and issues . . .

Applicants were often poorly advised and lacked sufficient help in presenting their case to the tribunal. Those represented by a lawyer were much more likely to win than those who were not, especially if they called witnesses. Employers, on the whole, had a far higher standard of representation. 'Only one-fourth of the complainants took witnesses to their hearings, and less than one in twelve took more than one witness; but over half of the respondents took more than one person to testify, with over half of these presenting two, three or more witnesses in addition to their primary witness.'

Trade unions were more help in representing applicants in equal pay cases than in sex discrimination cases. In the latter, applicants represented by unions had a 19 per cent success rate, compared with

21 per cent of those who represented themselves and 39 per cent of those represented by lawyers. There was sometimes a conflict of interest between the applicant and her union:

> Of 215 cases, five decisions indicated there was entrenched and active workforce and/or union opposition to the complainant's position; and in about 10, the complainant's claim for equal pay or unfair selection for redundancy was counter to a union-agreed or supported wage structure or redundancy procedure. And there were several in which particular actions of union stewards or other officials either before or at the hearing were directly contrary to the complainant's interest. In several cases, the conflict between the complainant's claim and the union position meant the complainant was unrepresented; in others, simply that the representative was in the very awkward position of propounding a position that was counter to union policy.

What should be done to improve women's chances of getting a fair deal? The author of this research, Alice Leonard, recommended that tribunal members should be properly trained and issued with detailed guidelines; a small number should specialize in equality cases. The Equal Opportunities Commission should 'encourage and assist the development of expert representatives on a far more widespread level than currently exists'; in cases where it was not directly involved, it should be allowed to submit *amicus curiae* briefs, explaining the law to the tribunal. There should be more joint claims by groups of women (known as 'class actions' and widely practised in the United States).

Leonard went on to propose some more basic changes. Once an applicant had shown that she had been treated less favourably than a man would have been treated in the same circumstances, the burden of proof should be shifted to the employer, to show that his action was justifiable. Tribunals should play a different role, moving from the 'adversarial' to the 'inquisitorial' model of operation: in other words, instead of either side preparing its case for the tribunal to judge between them (as was the present case), there should be a specialist officer, acting as an independent investigator on behalf of the tribunal, who would step in at an early stage to establish the relevant facts.

Whether any such changes would be made remained to be seen. Meanwhile, the overall picture produced by the studies of Leonard and others was of a system that was not designed to meet women's needs or bring them justice. It is worth recalling that the Equal Pay and Sex Discrimination Acts were drafted by politicians and civil servants (mainly men) who were lodged very near to the heart of the

established order, and who had been forced to respond to outside
pressure (mainly from women). Well-meaning liberals, they had taken
care to study the example of US equal opportunity law, and to turn
out a product which was, if anything, an improvement on the US
model. But their guiding principle was not 'How can we make sure
those bastards don't get away with it any more?' (which might have
been the feminist approach); but 'How far can we go without causing
too much trouble?' It wasn't a priority for them to close loopholes,
minimize exemptions or install the strongest possible means of
enforcement, but to avoid anything approaching a showdown with the
entrenched powers of the CBI and the TUC. Their product was then
fed into a system of courts and tribunals controlled, in the main, by
men with similar attitudes (or worse). It turned out enough decisions
in favour of women to prevent a national scandal, but not enough to
disturb the time-honoured practice of treating women less favourably
than men, or to upset the traditional balance of power between the
sexes.

Goods, facilities and services

We have dwelt so far upon the application of the new laws to pay and
opportunity in employment. Cases under the non-employment
sections of the Sex Discrimination Act had to be taken to the county
court and occurred far less frequently. In the first ten years of the Act
a handful of cases was won, but not enough to build up an influential
body of law.

In a test case which went to the Court of Appeal in November 1980,
June Quinn of Leicester obtained a ruling that Williams furniture
store had discriminated unlawfully when it asked her husband to act
as guarantor for a hire purchase agreement. Ms Quinn asked the store
whether they would have required a similar guarantee for her husband
if his material circumstances had been the same as hers; they admitted
that they would not.[12] By the end of the 1970s this type of overt
discrimination in the granting of credit, mortgages and tenancies had
become quite rare — which was progress of a kind. Nevertheless,
stores and credit companies retained the privilege of refusing credit
to anyone, on their own undisclosed terms. If they wished to
discriminate against women on the quiet, they could usually do so
without fear of reprisal. The same was true of mortgage companies,
for whom it remained common practice to lend *less* money on the basis
of a wife's earnings than on a husband's.

In 1986, the Equal Opportunities Commission published the results
of a survey about a new method of assessing credit-worthiness called

'credit scoring.' People applying for credit would fill in a questionnaire and points were awarded for different factors — length of service in a job, or home ownership, for example. The final score determined whether they got credit. Women were more likely to have interrupted their careers, to have low-paid jobs, and to be working part-time — factors which attracted lower scores. The EOC concluded that unless there were significant changes in credit scoring methods, women would not get a fair deal.

In the first case dealing with accommodation, a Ms Taylor complained that she had been refused the opportunity to take over a caravan in Hilltree Park Ltd, because she was a woman. The county court found in her favour and awarded £100 compensation for injury to feelings. Pubs which refused to serve women with pint mugs of beer were taken to court and found guilty of unlawful sex discrimination. Sheffield's Wellington Inn was ordered to pay £10 damages for refusing to allow a young woman called Gay Rice to play snooker. But progress on this front could be remarkably heavy-going, as the case of El Vino illustrated.

El Vino was a little wine bar in Fleet Street, whose clients were mainly lawyers and journalists and which cherished the tradition of forcing 'ladies' to drink only while sitting down. Because of its strategic position in the heart of the male establishment, its habit of discriminating against women took on a symbolic significance — as the last stand of the Old School Tie against the Monstrous Regiment. Photographer Sheila Gray was the first to take El Vino to court alleging sex discrimination; but in 1978 Judge Ruttle ruled against her at Westminster County Court. El Vino, he said, treated women differently from men, but not less favourably: 'It would be very wrong to my mind if this statute were thought to obliterate the differences between men and women or to do away with the courtesies and chivalry we expect mankind to give womankind.'[13]

Sheila Gray did not appeal, and seven years after the Sex Discrimination Act had come into force El Vino was still allowing men to choose whether they stood up or sat down, while giving women no choice in the matter. Another case brought by lawyer Tess Gill and journalist Anna Coote went before the Court of Appeal in November 1982, where the judges finally ruled that El Vino had been breaking the law. Shortly afterwards, the management issued a new rule that women would not be served (sitting or standing) if they were wearing trousers: this was hard to fault legally because El Vino had traditionally refused to serve men not wearing ties, and so it could be argued that it simply operated parallel and appropriate dress rules. At least the Court of Appeal had set a legal precedent, upholding the principle that deprivation of choice for one sex amounted to unlawful sex discrimination. Licensed premises would have to take note, or risk court action that was almost bound to go against them.

Unlike pubs and wine bars, private clubs were exempted from the Act, which meant that a vast range of 'facilities and services' continued to be out of bounds for women. London's gentlemen's clubs, the working men's clubs of the North, and countless political, sporting and recreational clubs were free to exclude women altogether, or to allow them in sometimes, on special conditions. When Wakefield City Working Men's Club banned Sheila Capstick, a long-standing member, from playing snooker, the Equal Rights in Clubs Campaign was launched (with its slogan, 'A Woman's Right to Cues'). ERICCA challenged the restriction on women's membership and participation in the four thousand clubs affiliated to the Club and Institute Union. Some individual clubs relaxed their rules, but the CIU remained staunchly opposed to ERICCA's demands.

Only a change in the law would force the CIU to treat women as equals, for instance by prohibiting unequal treatment by clubs of their members. But to lift the Sex Discrimination Act's exemption for private clubs, to treat them on the same basis as public services and facilities, could cause a new set of problems. In certain circumstances, women wanted to meet and organize without men and the law had already created some difficulties for them: a women-only taxi service set up in London to help women get home safely at night had fallen foul of the Sex Discrimination Act. Other services could suffer a similar fate, unless organized as private clubs. If the exemption were lifted, women would find they were breaking the law not only by running women-only services, but by holding meetings and conferences of women-only organizations. A possible solution lay in scheduling for exemption certain kinds of organization, services and facilities which were expressly designed to combat particular disadvantages suffered by one sex.

Sport presented a similar problem. Twelve-year-old Theresa Bennett wanted to join Muskham United, her local football club. The Nottingham Football Association and the Football Association Ltd barred her because she was a girl — and she sued them. In the Appeal Court, Lord Denning ruled that it made no difference whether she was as good as any boy of her age. The Sex Discrimination Act exempted 'any sport . . . where the physical strength, stamina or physique of the average woman puts her at a disadvantage to the average man'.[14] So Ms Bennett was to be judged not on her own ability, as any boy would have been, but on the average ability of all women of all ages. Lifting the exemption for all sport would mean that men could compete against women, whether women liked it or not — yet in some sporting events, women were able to compete on an equal footing and wanted to have the choice of doing so. A more selective exemption, which did not include children up to a certain age, might have improved matters. At the time of writing, there was no sign of any such amendment — for sport or clubs and services — being made.

So what did we have to show from our experience of a law prohibiting sex discrimination in the provision of housing, goods, facilities and services? A handful of colourful cases, which may have helped to publicize the intention of the Act, but which were not all successful. A little more circumspection on the part of those who wished to continue treating women as second-class citizens. In a few areas real changes which extended opportunities for women . . . but on the whole, life went on much as ever.

As in employment cases, many women may have felt they were being unfairly treated, but they were seldom aware that they were victims of unlawful discrimination. It was even more difficult to take a case to a county court than to an industrial tribunal: an alienating and expensive procedure, for which legal aid was seldom granted. Most judges continued to take a traditional view of male and female roles and so interpreted the law narrowly. And — perhaps most important — there was no base from which women could organize to enforce these sections of the Act. The trade unions may have had only a limited effect in helping to enforce the employment provisions of the law, but at least they held out an opportunity for women to overcome resistance and use their combined strength to claim their rights.

Discrimination in education

In the field of education, the Sex Discrimination Act had even less impact. Schools continued, in various ways, to educate girls and boys differently, narrowing their horizons and restricting their job opportunities. (We shall look more closely at this in Chapter 6.) In the first ten years of the Act, only two notable cases went to the county court. Helen Whitfield, a pupil of Woodcote High School, Croydon, Surrey, wanted to participate in a 'craft' course which covered woodwork, metal work and design technology. The school refused: the course was for boys and a separate course in 'home economics' was provided for girls. Helen's mother threatened legal action. Later, when a boy dropped out of the craft course, Helen was offered a place, as a special concession. But she didn't want to be the only girl in a class of boys and turned the offer down. She and her mother pursued their legal action, alleging that if the school admitted boys automatically to the course but did not admit girls unless they made a special application, that amounted to 'less favourable treatment' under the terms of the Sex Discrimination Act. When the case came to court in December 1979, Helen's lawyers called expert witnesses to testify (among other things) that a craft course provided better prospects than a home economics course because it was more likely to lead on to skilled employment. Judge Perks, in Croydon County Court, disagreed. He decided that Helen had suffered no damage, and that she never genuinely wanted to take the craft course 'but acted throughout under her mother's influence and was used as a weapon, or perhaps an ally, in her mother's campaign for women's rights'.[15]

Schools went on providing 'vocational' courses for girls and boys on an effectively segregated basis — without much fear of legal reprisals. Occasionally one or two rather unconventional girls would ask to be let into a 'boys-only' course and, to avoid trouble, the school would usually admit them. But classes in woodwork, metal work and other technological subjects retained a strong 'boys-only' image, which was enough to deter the majority of girls.

In its guidance to schools, the Equal Opportunities Commission pointed out that opportunities for pupils to study non-traditional subjects 'should be real opportunities and not token gestures . . . While many schools operate an apparent choice, the grouping of the subjects and the timetabling arrangements can discourage pupils from selecting a subject which is non-traditional.'[16] In 1984, the EOC reported that, although it interpreted the practice of allocating home economics to girls and craft, design and technology to boys as unlawful and educationally undesirable, 'individual schools persisted with these arrangements'.[17] It seemed able to change — through persuasion — the practice in some schools when it received specific complaints, but remained incapable of overturning the general pattern that prevailed in schools throughout the country.

One other case that went to court under the education section of the Act concerned three ten-year-old girls at St George's Church of England Primary School in the London borough of Bromley. In September 1982, Michelle Debell, Selmin Sevket and Michelle Teh returned to school after the summer holiday to find that, instead of being moved up to Class 10 as they expected, they were to be kept down in Class 9 for another year. This was done not on a basis of age or merit, but because the school wanted to maintain a balance of boys and girls in class 10, and had decided it could not accommodate any more girls. The parents took the local education authority and the headteacher of the school to the county court in August 1983. A settlement was reached in November 1984, when the defendants

admitted breaking the law and agreed to pay a (small) sum in damages as well as the plaintiffs' costs. This could not undo the harm done to the three girls, who by then had moved on to secondary schools.

A major problem with this section of the Act was that it could be extremely difficult and risky to take a case to court. Since minors could not take legal action on their own, a girl who wanted to pursue a complaint needed the full cooperation of her parent or guardian. Few children would be keen to stand out from the crowd by challenging their school in court, and probably even fewer parents (having been brought up in awe of educational authorities) would want to 'make trouble' in a daughter's school. They might worry that it would damage her chances of achieving good results, or earn her a poor reference which could count against her later on (teachers' references were usually kept secret). Or they might feel thoroughly daunted at the prospect of going to court. A special 'cooling off' period was required, in which parents had to write to the Secretary of State for Education and wait two months to see if anything changed before going ahead with a court action. This could serve as a further deterrent. And, as the Bromley case demonstrated, legal action took so long it could rarely bring practical help to the individuals involved.

While this section of the Act remained largely untested in court, it was impossible to predict how judges would interpret it, in anything but the most clear-cut of cases. Most schools ceased to display blatant sex discrimination: the practices that still needed to be challenged were of a subtler nature, harder to prove. So parents would need expert help to pursue a complaint. They could apply for assistance from the Equal Opportunities Commission, but this could well be refused — the EOC being far from bold in such matters. They could apply for legal aid but their chances of getting it were slim. In view of what Judge Perks had to say in the Whitfield case, it is ironic that if Helen's mother had not been a campaigner for women's rights, she would not have taken up the case at all.

As the 1980s progressed, it became clear that individual cases brought by parents would not be a catalyst for change. The hope lay with radical education authorities instituting anti-sexist programmes, and enforcing them. This approach was pioneered by the Inner London Education Authority and we look at it in more detail in chapter 6.

The EOC — 'a passionate caution'

Set up in a great rush so that its launch could coincide with the new laws coming into force, the EOC opened the doors of its Manchester headquarters on 29 December 1975 — amid cries of 'Personchester!'

and other hilarious jokes from the nation's media people. The powers and duties conferred upon it by the Sex Discrimination Act sounded rather impressive.

In general, it had a duty to monitor the working of the Sex Discrimination and Equal Pay Acts, to combat discrimination and to promote equal opportunity. In particular, it had the power to conduct formal investigations where it suspected that sex discrimination was being practised. The scope of these enquiries could be broad, covering a whole region or industry, or narrow, looking into the conduct of a particular organization — such as a factory, school or credit company. In the course of a formal investigation it could compel people to supply relevant information; it could order a course of action to prevent further breach of the law; it could issue a 'non-discrimination notice' requiring the offender to stop breaking the law; and if that didn't do the trick it could apply to court for an injunction, which carried the threat of fine or imprisonment if not obeyed.

The EOC had power, too, to give financial and legal assistance to individuals who were pursuing complaints under the two Acts — especially if the case involved a key principle and would serve the purpose of testing the law. It had a duty to see that the law was properly enforced; to conduct research into relevant areas; and to recommend to the government necessary changes — including amendments to the Equal Pay and Sex Discrimination Acts, and reforms to end discrimination in other fields not covered by those laws (such as tax, immigration and provisions for retirement).

In addition, it was responsible for chasing up certain kinds of discriminatory behaviour, such as advertisements which conveyed an intention to discriminate unlawfully; cases where a person had been instructed or encouraged to discriminate unlawfully; and cases of persistent discrimination, where patterns of inequality were so firmly entrenched that no woman was likely to get as far as raising a complaint.

An innocent onlooker might have been tempted to imagine that with powers such as those, with an annual budget of more than £3 million and more than 170 employees (1984 figures), and with a dozen commissioners meeting regularly, the EOC would be blazing a fair trail — striking fear into the hearts of powerful men. ('My God, Basil, they're on to us — we'll have to let the women through! . . . Take down that Pirelli calendar and get Miss Jones a cup of coffee at once!') It has not been quite like that.

Back in 1975 a considerable amount of hope and optimism was invested in the EOC. Many women believed it would champion their cause and fight hard to enforce the laws. By 1980, few were left who

expected much action. By the mid-1980s, that early hope and optimism had been consigned to the realm of fantasy. This was partly due to a dramatic change in the political climate; it was also due to the nature of the organization itself.

The EOC was set up according to the same unwritten rules by which most commissions and 'quangos' have been established. These rules are designed first and foremost to satisfy the interest groups which carry most weight with the government, and only secondly to enable the organization to perform its statutory duties. Since Labour was in power when the EOC came into being, the Labour Party's Women's Officer, Betty — later Baroness — Lockwood, was given the chair. Lady Elspeth Howe, a prominent and rather well-connected Tory, became her deputy. It kept the two parties happy, but was not the best recipe for a strong, determined leadership to launch the enterprise.

The TUC and CBI had to be given equal representation on the Commission, with three seats each. The educational establishment had to be satisfied next, then Scotland, Wales and the Home Office itself (which of course made all the appointments). The idea that the Commission might be filled by individuals most noted for their enthusiasm and ability to work for equality was not entertained. It was intended to be (and remained) a disunited group of the 'Great and the Good', who had prior and sometimes conflicting allegiances, who were busy with other commitments and saw their work on the Commission as peripheral to the rest of their lives, and who approached their statutory task with a passionate caution. As time went by, the cast list changed. A Tory peer, Baroness Platt, replaced Baroness Lockwood in the chair and the Commission gradually took on a bluer complexion. But the political mix made little difference — so thoroughly had radicalism, inventiveness and campaigning courage been programmed out of the original design.

When advertisements went out for staff to fill the Manchester office, they appeared to present ideal opportunities for energetic young women with impressive qualifications and a high level of commitment to the work in hand. Clashes were inevitable. One commissioner complained in 1978: 'There are too many people (on the staff) who are committed to the women's cause, so they can't think straight. They just go barging through.' There were massive defections in those early years: in 1978 staff turnover was 38 per cent — more than three times that of an average office. One senior officer explained in her resignation letter that she was leaving because of a 'total disillusion-ment with the lack of direction and commitment to decisive action by EOC Commissioners in all areas of the EOC's work'. The fact that it had four Chief Executives in the first five years of its life suggested an organization severely at odds with itself, unable to reconcile the grand scale of its mission with the disabling knots of its constitution.

Inevitably, it was in areas which were least politically sensitive that the Commission made most progress. There were no major disagreements between political parties, or between the TUC and CBI, or between feminists and non-feminists, as to whether job advertisements should have a non-discriminatory form, or whether credit companies should treat women as favourably as men. Consequently, in these and other areas outside employment and education, the EOC built up a fairly uncontroversial record of diligence. It developed a good line in commissioning academic research, which illuminated important issues (notably on women's caring roles) without treading on too many toes. But with the TUC and CBI commissioners guarding their traditional spheres of influence, the EOC was less likely to stick its neck out in the employment field and confined itself mainly to individual casework. When it went so far as to issue guidelines for employers, these could not be published until 17 different drafts had passed back and forth between staff and commissioners.

Its work in education grew a little bolder as time went by. It sponsored some useful research as well as some (rather inconclusive) formal investigations, and a major project designed to find ways of encouraging girls to study science and technology (see p. 199). Overall, however, it did little to disturb the status quo.

Its record was least impressive when it came to formal investigations. These were not easy to carry out: the EOC had to jump through a long row of legal hoops, allowing for a series of delays and appeals before getting an investigation under way. It needed political will and experience to make the most of a complex but potentially valuable weapon. The Commission for Racial Equality, which had similar powers, made some considerable headway, but the EOC never had the political will and so never built up the necessary experience. In its first eight years it launched only nine investigations, completed four and issued one non-discrimination notice. The CRE (which came into being a year and a half later) launched 47, completed 24 and issued 10 non-discrimination notices during the same period.

A report analysing the EOC's record in formal investigations was published in 1984.[18] It concluded that the EOC revealed 'no coherent policy as to what might be regarded as key targets in dismantling strongholds of sex discrimination'; it was inattentive to essential legal detail, sometimes with 'disastrous' results; and it was 'noticeably reluctant to use its enforcement powers'. It had deliberately chosen to act by persuasion wherever possible: 'although an excellent way of short-circuiting the legal difficulties, this policy has the disadvantage of being heavily reliant on the co-operativeness of the subject and also of involving limited publicity.' The EOC's timidity on this front was attributed 'to a lack of direction within the Commission itself', with members at odds with each other about how to use its enforcement powers. It was also alleged that the commissioners from the TUC and CBI tended to combine forces to prevent the EOC meddling in industrial affairs:

> The six commissioners representative of management and work-force in practice vote together and have obstructed the launching of investigations with significant industrial relations repercussions. In one case, an investigation was proposed into an engineering firm in the North-West which had segregated male and female workforces, but the investigation was effectively blocked by this means. The primary allegiance of these commissioners has been said to be to the T.U.C. and C.B.I. rather than to the principle of sex equality.

The report concluded that the EOC's record in this area was 'so unsatisfactory that the time may well have come for an investigation into the Commission itself'. A more general investigation of the EOC, published in 1986, was also highly critical and concluded that if it were to be effective in future, it would have to 'go public' and lay siege to the political citadel:

> The Commission could, by stimulating debate and by organising a parliamentary lobby, planting parliamentary questions and providing answers to them, place on the political agenda those equality issues which the parties must address . . . the way forward now — 10 years on — is for the Commission to come in out of the cold and remind the political world that 'equality for women requires the active support and intervention of Government itself.'[19]

Within the women's movement, some efforts were made to compensate for the shortcomings of the Equal Opportunities Commission. The Women's Rights unit of the National Council for Civil Liberties, the Equal Pay and Opportunities Campaign and Rights of Women (ROW) worked hard in their various ways — helping individual women, producing guides to the law, proposing amendments, lobbying Parliament and holding seminars and workshops to teach people how to enforce the legislation. They were also responsible for putting new issues on the agenda, such as positive action and the issue of sexual harassment. They operated on a tiny fraction of the Commission's budget. Between them they seldom had more than two salaried workers and two dozen volunteers. Compared with the EOC, their achievements far outstripped their resources. The *Sunday Times* commented in 1977 that the NCCL women's rights officer seemed to be doing more to enforce the legislation than the whole of the EOC![20]

Later, the Women's Committee of the GLC emerged as a new champion. Though not primarily concerned with enforcing the law, it had money and power, and a brief to fight sexism and promote equal opportunity. It started by asking local women what they wanted. It dispensed funds to voluntary groups and enabled a wide range of projects, facilities and activities to come into being. It made mistakes, it was confined to London and it didn't last. But it showed what could be done with a magnanimous budget, a strong political will and no institutional fear.

The EOC was neither representative of women, nor accountable to them. MPs would find it easier to keep an eye on the work of the Home Office — and that was hard enough — than on the EOC. Neither MPs nor members of the public could sit in on Commission meetings, or get sight of its unpublished documents. There was never any question of its being answerable to a constituency of women. Its quasi-independence from government was supposed to make it more effective. Yet it was entirely dependent on government funds and at the mercy of the Home Office's powers of patronage. The relationship made it behave like a poor cousin on the annual visit to the Big House: dull, over-dignified, obsequious and desperately anxious about the next handout.[21]

The need for 'positive action'

Women who fought for the vote in the early 1900s saw it as a means of improving their position in society generally, but until they won it they could only guess at how little or how much it would help to change their circumstances. In the same way, women who have fought for equal pay and sex discrimination laws, and then experienced them in practice for a few years, have been able to appreciate more fully the extent of their oppression and to work out further strategies. By the early 1980s it was clear that laws *against* unequal pay and sex discrimination would do nothing to tackle the entrenched patterns of inequality that had built up over centuries. In some quarters — notably, at first, the NCCL and the TUC — people began to insist that *positive* measures were needed in order to compensate for past discrimination.

In the United States, this principle had been accepted at an official level since 1970. Many US employers were obliged by law to implement what became known as 'affirmative action programmes', aimed at increasing the numbers of women in jobs done mainly or exclusively by men. Those who held government contracts had to show that they already employed women at all levels in equal proportions with men, or that they were making a 'good faith' effort to do so. If they failed they risked losing their contract. In order to prove they were making a 'good faith' effort, they usually had to introduce an 'affirmative action programme'. The same principle was applied to ethnic minorities, whom employers were expected to hire in proportion to what percentage of the local working population they constituted.

The basic idea behind 'positive' or 'affirmative' action was that women were constrained by more than just overt discrimination ('We don't hire women in this job'). A woman might be deterred from coming forward because she felt the job was not for her. She might lack confidence in her ability, or have the impression that a particular job was intended for a man. She might not have had the opportunity in the past to develop the necessary qualifications, or the job might be organized in such a way that she could not easily make it fit in with the rest of her life. None of these factors amounted to personal failure, but were products of an unequal system, in which strong habits had been developed about the way women and men were perceived and treated. They could be overcome if certain measures were adopted which helped women change themselves and encouraged them to think they could do the job. The kind of measures that were appropriate would depend on the nature and circumstances of each job.

A 'positive action programme' was a package of measures which were considered appropriate to the organization in question. It would ideally include a set of goals and timetables, with the intention of achieving certain levels of female employment by certain dates in the future (for example, that 25 per cent of trainee drivers in a company would be female in five years' time, and 50 per cent in ten years' time). It was not expected that changes would occur overnight, but if goals were not met within the required time, the programme would need to be reviewed and strengthened.

The programme would be written out in detail and usually monitored by a team representing management and employees. It might include such measures as aiming job advertisements specifically at women and publishing them in women's magazines; reassessing the skills and qualifications required of applicants, to weed out any which favoured males and were not strictly necessary for the job; scrutinizing selection procedures; and providing special training to enable women to qualify for promotion. (As we shall see, more sophisticated policies were developed later in the UK.)

In some US organizations, women made substantial early gains as a result of positive action. For example, a programme set up in 1972 by the Bank of America aimed to fill 40 per cent of jobs at officer grade with women by 1978; in fact, the goal was exceeded by 3 per cent. General Motors introduced a programme which increased the proportion of female students at its engineering college from 0.6 per cent in 1970 to 32 per cent in 1977.

Positive action usually proved more effective where there were groups of articulate, middle-class women who were prepared to fight to ensure that programmes were properly implemented. It had no apparent effect on the gap between male and female average pay (which was even greater in the United States than in the UK). It did little to change patterns of employment among lower-paid, blue-collar workers. Nevertheless, in some areas it helped to change attitudes and provide new opportunities for women. As a strategy it was important for feminist politics, because it shifted the focus of the campaign for equality towards recognition of the system which sustained male supremacy, and suggested that men themselves should actively participate in the process of change.

Gradually, the idea began to attract attention in Britain. In the early 1970s, it was widely believed, even among some feminists, that if women were to be equal they should be treated the same as men; anything else would demean them, or inhibit their progress, or be unfair to men. However, when the Sex Discrimination Act was drafted, an allowance was made for women to be treated differently in some circumstances. The Act said that certain training organizations could provide women-only courses for jobs which were monopolized by men, and special training for women returning to work after raising their families. Employers could encourage women to apply for jobs traditionally done by men, and provide single-sex training for them. Trade unions, employers' organizations and professional associations could take steps to increase the levels of female participation. These provisions were largely ignored for some years. But by the end of the 1970s, it was becoming increasingly clear that unless they were utilized, women would make no progress at all.

In September 1980, a resolution was passed by the Trades Union Congress which called for 'positive action in favour of women' to help break down job segregation and raise the level of women's pay. The dismal record of the Equal Pay and Sex Discrimination Acts helped to win the assent of Congress. It was necessary to reassure delegates that positive action in favour of women need not entail discrimination *against men* — for example, it would not mean that a woman could be hired for a job who was less well qualified than a male applicant. Two months later, the TUC held a special conference to discuss draft guidelines for positive action programmes which might be negotiated by unions.[22] (It is interesting to note how vigorously — and with what comparative success — men have resisted any threat of discrimination against themselves, as though this were an even greater evil than continuing discrimination against women. Some of the most celebrated cases brought under the Sex Discrimination Act have been fought and won by men.)

With funding from the EOC, the National Council for Civil Liberties launched Britain's first positive action project in 1979. Its purpose was to introduce pilot schemes in two or three different workplaces, in collaboration with unions and management, so that the idea could be tested in practice. Thames Television responded to the idea, and barrister Sadie Robarts was employed by the NCCL to investigate patterns of employment at Thames and help the company to devise a plan for extending opportunities for women. An important early consequence of her intervention was that women at Thames formed a group and began to meet regularly to discuss their employment conditions and to find ways of improving them. This provided a strong impetus for a positive action programme.

In 1981, Ms Robarts made her recommendations to the Thames Board of Directors. A programme of action was begun later the same year, well-publicized inside and outside the company. It did not only involve setting goals and timetables for the employment of women in areas where they were under-represented. It stressed the importance of equal opportunities as 'an aspect of good personnel practice, which benefited all employees and not just particular groups'. In 1984, the programme was extended to ethnic minorities.

The company invested its Director of Personnel and Company Secretary with overall responsibility for the programme, and publicized its policy widely. It appointed a full-time equal opportunity adviser whose job it was to evolve training schemes, provide counselling and advice, and implement the programme on a day-to-day basis. It set up an Equal Opportunities Committee, representing different groups of employees. It provided nursery places or financial assistance with other child care arrangements, as well as paid maternity leave well above the national minimum. It introduced a range of training schemes — in television programme-making, basic science and technology and 'personal effectiveness', to assist career development for women; and awareness training for managers. Women's progress was monitored after they'd taken the courses. By 1985, 61 per cent of those who had been on the courses remained in the same job; 30 per cent had been upgraded, taken on wider responsibilities or a new job within the company; and 9 per cent had left.

London Weekend Television, the capital's other main independent station, followed suit, with a programme of action which involved removing age limits for entry; promotion and training; assistance with child care; women-only training courses; a job attachment scheme which gave employees an opportunity to gain new skills and experience; and a monitoring exercise of the race and gender profile of the workforce.

Other private sector companies which developed high-profile equal opportunities policies included the Midland Bank, Marks and Spencer, Boots the Chemist, Littlewoods and Smiths Industries. The amount of real 'positive action' which accompanied these policies varied from company to company. Boots seemed to confine itself to improving the terms on which it provided maternity leave, re-entry after prolonged absence for family responsibilities, and paid time off to cover domestic problems. Littlewoods went further. It set up an Equal Opportunities Committee, chaired by John Moores, the company chairman, which met four or five times a year and scrutinized quarterly returns showing where women and ethnic minorities were employed. It took on an equality officer, monitored job applicants and introduced 'equality awareness' training programmes for recruitment staff and managers. It dropped a requirement that all management trainees should be completely mobile within the UK. The Midland Bank set up a Group Equal Opportunities Unit responsible for collecting and analysing data on recruitment and promotion of women and men, putting on sex equality awareness workshops and mounting development programmes for women managers. It also introduced a retainer scheme which allowed potential high-flyers (male and female) to take up to five years off, for pre-school child care.[23]

Most of these schemes, like the 'affirmative action programmes' in the United States, were bound to favour articulate white-collar workers. By the mid-1980s, however, a more sophisticated approach to 'positive action' was being developed. This took on a broader perspective, aiming not only to promote equality for white-collar women and 'high-flyers' from ethnic minorities, but also to combat sexism and racism suffered by working-class people, to fight discrimination against lesbians and gay men, and to ensure that people with disabilities got a fair share of all opportunities. As a policy it was easy to declare, as a kind of blanket condemnation of injustice, but it was much harder to put into practice. It needed strong political commitment and generous resources. Private companies, however much they wanted to be seen as progressive and benevolent, usually stopped short of pursuing policies that could not easily be justified as cost-effective. (It was one thing to safeguard investment in trained 'career women'; it was another thing to take a stand against 'heterosexism', or to spend money on child care and training for working-class Black women.) Pioneering this approach was left to a small group of Labour-controlled public-sector authorities — of which one of the most influential was the Greater London Council.

Any visitor to London's County Hall in the last year or so before the Council's abolition in 1986 could not help noticing that there were far more women and Blacks moving around its corridors than would normally be found in a government bureaucracy. An ambitious equal opportunities policy was fully supported at the highest level of authority and implemented by a special unit of senior officers within the personnel department. It began with regular, detailed monitoring of employment in all grades. The head of each department within the vast organization was charged with setting and monitoring targets for ethnic minorities, women and people with disabilities — their efforts co-ordinated centrally by the GLC's Equal Opportunities Group. A range of training schemes was linked with changes in job advertising and selection procedures, as well as with a new form of 'career appraisal', which replaced secret judgement of candidates' promotion prospects with an open and agreed system which assessed an employee's current skills, but combined this with a plan for future training and career development. Child care facilities were provided for GLC employees.

There were 'basic skills' courses for part-time manual workers, to build confidence in dealing with written material and prepare for further study. Day-release courses were specially designed for keyboard operators, almost all of whom were women, with a high proportion of Black and disabled; these covered topics such as health and safety, women in trade unions and self-assertion. There were courses to introduce manual workers to new areas of work, including office work; and Open University courses in effective management for ethnic minority employees. There were special courses to train women for non-traditional jobs, career development workshops for lesbians and people with disabilities, and courses for Asian and Afro-Caribbean women. Other short courses for women covered 'first steps to management', assertiveness training, and a project for women returning after maternity leave. The GLC made a point of publicizing its training opportunities well beyond County Hall, especially among Black and Asian women.

Overall, between 1981 and 1985, the proportion of ethnic minority employees at County Hall rose from 7 to 11 per cent; the proportion of women from about 17 to 21 per cent.[24] In assessing its progress, the Equal Opportunities Group analysed varying trends in different grades, to identify where specific blocks occurred, and to take steps to deal with them. While the practical emphasis of the programme was on opening opportunities at all levels, the philosophy behind it was to achieve 'a substantial shift in the balance of power from white, able-bodied men towards groups of workers and groups in society who have previously been excluded . . .' and the purpose was to achieve a workforce 'better suited to meet the needs of the community'.

The impact of the GLC experiment outweighed its immediate effectiveness. Though short-lived, it was well documented and widely publicized. It established useful guiding principles and suggested what might be achieved with time (which the GLC didn't have) as well as money and commitment (which it did). A small but significant group of Labour-controlled councils continued to pursue positive action policies.

Contract compliance

The same was true of the GLC's initiative in 'contract compliance'. A special unit was set up, serving the GLC and the Inner London Education Authority. Its purpose was to use the considerable purchasing power of these two large organizations to encourage equal opportunities in the private sector. The idea was imported from the USA, where it had been in operation since the early 1970s and had proved highly effective in some areas.

Companies who wanted to do business with the GLC and ILEA had to be on an approved list of contractors and suppliers. A condition for getting on to the list was that they answered a questionnaire about the composition of their workforce and their equal opportunities policy. If they failed to fill in the questionnaire, they were recommended for exclusion from the list. If they filled it in, their answers were assessed to see whether they were meeting required standards, and in particular whether they were complying with codes of practice produced by the Equal Opportunities Commission and the Commission for Racial Equality. The Contract Compliance Unit would meet with the companies, to discuss ways of implementing these requirements — which could entail a programme of action to promote equal opportunities, to be monitored for its effect on women, ethnic minorities and people with disabilities. Companies who failed to cooperate could be recommended for exclusion from the approved list. However, that implied failure on both sides, and the emphasis of the project was on persuading the companies to change their ways. The Unit began its work with a review of building companies on the approved lists held in the Architect's Department. By December 1985, 106 companies had been selected for detailed investigation, of which 77 agreed to undertake specified programmes of action to bring them into line with the GLC's requirements. A further 17 were still negotiating and 12 had been taken off the approved list. After the GLC was abolished, the Unit continued to work for the ILEA.

Contract compliance was a complex and controversial business, especially while it had no backing from the government and carried almost no legal force. Section 71 of the Race Relations Act said that local authorities had to carry out all their functions with regard to promoting good race relations and eliminating discrimination, but there was no parallel clause in the Sex Discrimination Act. Equal opportunities programmes cost money and could push up the price of contracts; public sector authorities had to tread very carefully while they were under heavy political and legal pressure to control spending. Companies who relied heavily on contracts from the GLC and ILEA, and who feared losing out to competitors, might be more easily persuaded than others. But those who held a near-monopoly over whatever goods or services they provided could cause serious problems by refusing to cooperate.

In 1985, the Conservative government issued a Green Paper which proposed to stop local authorities making any requirements of contractors which were not directly related to the quality, timing and cost of the work to be done. This was intended to 'promote the extension of free competition in the provision of local authority services' — and the clear implication was that contract compliance policies interfered with free competition. At the time of writing, no law had yet been passed, but the chips were down. Meanwhile, other authorities were beginning to investigate the potential of contract compliance and pressure was building to persuade the Labour Party to give it full backing as a national policy. The GLC/ILEA experiment was starting to show positive results, demonstrating how much could be achieved if the policy were ever to be adopted by central as well as local government.

Isolation at the centre

We have seen that the women's liberation movement had little influence over the way the 'equality' laws were drafted and even less over the design of the Equal Opportunities Commission. It might have been different if there had been a strong force of women within

Parliament. Law-makers were not generally inclined to undermine their own interests, and the British Parliament had always been packed with men.

In May 1979, when Margaret Thatcher became the first female Prime Minister of the UK, 19 women were returned to Parliament, the lowest proportion in 20 years. In the 1983 general election, 23 women were returned as MPs and by 1986, by-elections had increased the total to 25. If there was any cause for optimism, it was that more women were standing: in 1983, there were 276 female candidates out of a total of 2,579 — 10 per cent up on the previous general election.[25]

It was, of course, no accident that men continued to outnumber women in Parliament by more than 25 to 1. In her book *Women in the House*, Elizabeth Vallance identified a wide range of social and political constraints on women.[26] They were not encouraged from an early age (as men were) to be bold with their opinions, to articulate them in public, or to seek out power. Parliament's hours of business had been arranged for the convenience of male barristers, not women with young children. Selection committees in the constituencies still tended to assume that women could not deal with certain 'heavy' political issues. It was possible, too, that 'the ritual and ceremonial of the House, its slow, ponderous processes, its interminable committees and talk rather than action, did not appeal to women whose experience is largely practical, pragmatic and here and now.'

Moreover, it seemed that women who had 'made it' in Parliament were not paving the way for others as they were doing in many walks of life: 'A few outstanding individuals may make their own way and achieve great personal success,' said Vallance, 'but this does not accrue to women in general. Each time, it appears, the ground has to be ploughed anew.' Margaret Thatcher's arrival as Prime Minister was 'most unlikely to pave the way for women any more directly than Margaret Bondfield's achievement did over forty-eight years ago. In 1930 there was one woman in the Cabinet, and in 1978 there was also one.' In 1986 there was none.

If the feminist tradition was weak in Parliament, it was partly because the women who were in the House had always been so isolated. When feminists organized around parliamentary politics they usually did so as lobbyists only. Until the 1980s, there were few concerted attempts to increase the numbers of women in Parliament, and few efforts to combine lobbying with organization of feminist support for elected female MPs.

Getting women into Parliament did not figure among the aims of the women's liberation movement in the 1970s. Abhorring leaders, hierarchies and all man-made power structures, feminists saw little merit in fighting such a battle. Some took the view that all MPs were elitist time-servers, out of touch with the needs of ordinary people, and that women who joined their ranks were bound to be corrupted — so there was no point encouraging them. Those who put themselves forward were commonly dismissed as 'opportunists'. There was also the awkward question of whether one favoured a woman on account of her sex before one rated her in conventional political terms. Few women in the movement felt they had a common cause with Tory women; but there remained the problem of whether a woman with feminist views at the centre or centre-left of the political spectrum was preferable to a man with traditional left-wing credentials and a wife at home looking after the kids.

More important was the general alienation of the women's movement from parliamentary politics. It was one thing to write letters to MPs, sign petitions and carry torches down Whitehall — to beat on the front door from the outside. It was quite another to go round the back and fight one's way inside — past forbidding doormen, through long corridors of protocol and compromise, up grubby, hypocritical stairs, into uncomfortable ante-rooms of self-advertisement — to seek out the place where power was meant to lie but seldom could be found. So women continued to lobby a male-dominated legislature, which had little understanding of their needs and less intention of making them a priority.

By the 1980s, there were at last some signs that this was changing. Elizabeth Vallance pointed out that a new sense of unity had already begun to develop among Labour women MPs — and the spur for this was the challenge they faced from a series of anti-abortion Bills between 1975 and 1979.

> This unity was, according to many of the women involved, at least in part the product of male apathy. Even the men who were willing to support them saw the issue as not important enough to devote a great deal of time to. And it did take a great deal of time simply not to allow the stages of these Bills to go through almost by default.

When the abortion debate was in full swing in 1976, the women gathered in the Chamber one evening, waiting to intervene:

> At one stage there were twelve of them sitting, as they do not typically do, together, on the back benches awaiting the Speaker's sign. This apparently was too much for some of the men who came into the Chamber from elsewhere in the Palace . . . to view

this unholy alliance, [the men were] laughing and making suggestive remarks, perhaps more than anything to cover their own trepidation.[27]

Vallance suggested that women MPs were becoming less apologetic about concentrating on 'women's issues' instead of proving themselves in the big, strong, masculine arenas of economics, industry and foreign affairs. Why should women have to steer clear of feminist contention, or risk being stigmatized as emotional and tendentious?

Isn't political debate always tendentious, they ask, doesn't it always involve talking about what you know, and isn't it often extremely emotional? No one castigates a union-sponsored MP for putting his members' case. No one suggests he is not being objective or only talking about what he knows. This response seems largely to be reserved for women, talking about women.

Mary Kaldor, the disarmament campaigner, published an astute critique of the 'parliamentary career' in the *Guardian* (22 June 1981) which illustrated why so many women — however talented and politically active they might be — were reluctant to stand for Parliament. When she was a prospective parliamentary candidate, she says people were always saying to her, 'I hear you're going into politics':

What a funny phrase, I thought, since I have been 'in politics' all my life. What they meant, of course, was going into a well-paid job, with a career structure, a job which is called 'politics'. And the fact that this 'politics' is a career separates Westminster from the rest of politics — constituency parties, community activities, single-issue campaigns. The chasm . . . is entrenched by the sexual divisions in society. So long as we think men ought to have careers, it will be difficult to end the isolation of Parliament.

She maintained, nevertheless, that women *should* stand, and she remarked that when she was standing for selection in the London constituency of Dulwich, she got to know two of the other female candidates rather well:

Perhaps because we were women, we became friends. Kate Hooey, who was eventually selected, and I thought we should turn the job into a collective enterprise so we could all do it together, helping each other with the difficult questions and spreading the issues around. Nevertheless, the situation was competitive. We were competing for a job which we might have for life. We were getting trapped into a male situation . . . As long as being an MP is a career, and that means the combination of good pay, tenure, and patronage, Parliament gradually gets sealed off from other activities: a separate male institution . . .

Labour MP Harriet Harman took up a similar theme when she wrote in the *New Statesman* a feminist critique of the 'good Labour MP' who 'works 24 hours a day, seven days a week, 52 weeks a year. He travels the length and breadth of the country, making stirring speeches to serried ranks of (mostly male) activists . . .' It was wrong, she said, to equate socialism with absenteeism from home. People could not be properly defended against Tory attacks by 'a cadre of burnt out workaholics who either never see their family or don't have one':

The movement would be much better represented by people whose minds are focussed on shopping and the school holidays — as well as pit closures and overseas investment . . . We should be encouraging the sort of socialist who hates exploitation in the home as well as exploitation in the workplace.

If the influence of the women's movement — so evident in the comments of Mary Kaldor and Harriet Harman — were to continue to spread and to bring more women into the House of Commons, parliamentary politics might start to be transformed. If women accounted not for *3* per cent of MPs (as at present) but for 20, 30 or 50 per cent, we might even see the beginnings of a useful legislative programme.

Organizing for change

In the autumn of 1980, a Woman's Action Committee was launched by feminists in the Labour Party, as a 'major campaign to give women political equality'. Its aims included getting the women's section of Labour's National Executive Committee elected by the party's annual women's conference; selected resolutions to be carried forward from the women's conference on to the agenda of the party's national conference; at least one woman on every shortlist for parliamentary candidates; and a reformed parliamentary working day.

Over the next five years, the Women's Action Committee grew in strength and influence, winning support from Labour's national women's conference, though it periodically antagonized female activists in trade unions, thanks to the uncompromising views and acerbic style of some of its protagonists. It had little success with Labour's National Executive Committee, which stood out against most of the constitutional changes it proposed. But WAC's real achievement was to stimulate a higher level of participation among women, and a higher awareness — among men as well as women — of the issues it had put on the agenda. It fought for, and won, the right to set up women's sections in constituency parties without prior permission from General Committees (which were usually dominated by men). The provision of crèche facilities at Labour's conference became the norm rather than the exception. A number of Labour's Regional Committees introduced direct election of their women's sections by regional women's conferences.

More women were encouraged to stand for selection as parliamentary candidates. The NEC went as far as to recommend that there should be at least one woman on each shortlist (though this did not become a rule), and constituency parties were increasingly aware of the need to consider female candidates. Men still managed to monopolize the safe seats, at a ratio of more than ten to one, but the proportion of women selected for marginal constituencies in 1985/6 was higher than ever before. Parallel with these developments was an increased level of activity among Blacks and Asians in the Labour Party, and the controversial campaign for Black Sections, which WAC supported. Diane Abbott, a member of WAC as well as the National Black Sections Steering Committee of the Labour Party, became the first Black woman to be selected as a parliamentary candidate in a safe Labour seat. The work of WAC, the legacy of the GLC Women's Committee, the growth of the Black women's movement and Labour's Black Sections, combined to change the atmosphere within the Labour Party. There was a new focus of radical activism which did not belong to the traditional base of white, male trade unionism, and which entailed a critique of that base. It helped break down some of the barriers that had stood between the women's movement and parliamentary politics in the 1970s.

Outside the Labour Party there were other positive developments. The 300 Group, formed in 1980, aimed at uniting women from all parties to fill half the seats in Parliament with female MPs. It organized conferences and workshops to give women training and encouragement, and aimed at building support networks for women standing for selection or running as candidates in local, national and European elections. It monitored election results and campaigned through the media, consciously identifying itself with the feminist tradition of the constitutional suffragists. Although it did gain some support from left-

and right-wing women, its cross-party approach inevitably made it more attractive to women at the centre, where the idea of eschewing conflict between left and right was the very stuff of politics. Like Labour's WAC, the 300 Group stimulated a higher level of female participation in parliamentary politics; it played an important role in raising awareness about the obstacles that stood in their way, and helping to break them down.

In March 1981, the Social Democratic Party was founded, claiming to 'break the mould' of British politics. Women had quite a high profile in the SDP. From the start, it required every shortlist of parliamentary candidates to contain at least two women, and the party developed a range of policies which reflected a feminist influence. Later the same year, it joined with the Liberal Party to form the SDP/Liberal Alliance. The Alliance built up a presence in Parliament, winning 23 seats in the 1983 election (though with no female MPs). By the mid-1980s it looked capable of becoming a significant third force. In March 1986 it had 24 MPs and 2,732 District and County Councillors. Later that year, Liberal Elizabeth Shields won a by-election, to become the first female Alliance MP. In public opinion polls, the Alliance often came second and occasionally first, as Labour and Conservative fortunes waxed and waned. One of its main objectives was to reform the electoral process, introducing proportional representation which would strengthen its own position in Parliament and break the hegemony of the two-party system.

By the mid-1980s, both the SDP and the Liberals had drawn up detailed policies on women's issues, supporting equal pay for work of equal value, strengthening the Sex Discrimination Act, abolition of the married man's tax allowance, positive action to improve women's position in the labour market, setting up a network of 'Well Woman Clinics', improving child care provision and caring services, and equalizing pensions and social security benefits. A discussion document entitled *Policy for Women*, published by the SDP, went into more detail — for example, proposing Family Centres in every locality, tax relief for workplace nurseries and crèches, extended parental leave, improved shopping facilities, new family courts, a special charter for carers, equal rights for part-time workers, equal opportunity in training and education, and an end to sex discrimination in immigration and nationality laws.

During the same period, the Labour Party published the *Charter for Women and Work*. This committed the Party (on paper, at least) to equal education and training opportunities, expanded nursery education and child care provision, improved services for the elderly and disabled, shorter, more flexible working hours, better parental leave, equal rights for full-time and part-time workers, measures to protect homeworkers, to combat health hazards at work and sexual harassment, positive action policies at work and a system of contract compliance, a statutory minimum wage, equal pay for work of equal value, abolition of the married man's tax allowance, increased child benefit and equal pension rights.

There was considerable overlap between Labour and the Alliance on women's issues. In terms of official party policy, Labour was committed earlier to a wider range of measures. Where the Alliance stressed the need to boost the voluntary sector to ease the burden of women's unpaid work, Labour stressed the need to expand state services. Labour looked first to the unions as a source of strength for women while the Alliance looked to 'the community'. Labour's starting point was the rights and needs of women in paid employment; the Alliance placed more emphasis on women's unpaid work as carers. These distinctions were significant, but would remain academic — as would the policies themselves — while the Tories were in power.

What counted was how far a new government would put a genuine effort into redistributing wealth and power between women and men. As a party that claimed to be socialist, Labour stood for redistribution. But would it give priority to its policies for women, or would it be hampered by its traditional allegiance to a trade union movement dominated by white men? In 1985, it published a proposal for a Ministry for Women's Rights: a department placed within the Cabinet Office, with a minister in the Cabinet. The plan included a network of Regional Equal Opportunity Units to monitor progress in education, training and employment, and to liaise with local women's organizations. The new Ministry would take over from the Home Office supervision of the Equal Opportunities Commission and make sure that other government departments carried out the Party's policies regarding women. Though far from perfect, the plan for a Women's Ministry represented a serious approach to the problem of putting policy into practice. But would Labour get elected and then act on such a proposal? Change would only come if women themselves wielded power in government. How to break the deadlock of women's powerlessness? We return to this question in chapter 9.

Table 9 Applications to industrial tribunals in percentages, 1976 – 1983[1]

	Settled	Withdrawn	Heard	Success rate at IT
Sex Discrimination Act				
All applicants	25	35	40	27
Represented by:[2]				
self	30	42	28	21
trade union	17	30	53	19
lawyer	28	22	50	39
other	21	39	40	34
Equal Pay Act				
All applicants	15	35	50	20
Represented by:[3]				
self	25	45	30	25
trade union	15	40	45	30
lawyer	16	18	65	25
other	22	36	42	38

[1] Figures based on analysis of Department of Employment statistics. Some analyses for 1980 not available. Data refer to individual applicants rather than cases.

[2] Representation of 2% of SDA applicants unknown; these figures omitted.

[3] Representation of 18% EPA applicants unknown; these figures omitted.

Source: Leonard, Alice M. *The First Eight Years: A Profile of Applicants to the Industrial Tribunals under the Sex Discrimination Act 1975 and the Equal Pay Act 1970.* Equal Opportunities Commission, 1986.

Notes to chapter 4

1   *Women's Report*, vol. 1(2), January—March 1973.
2   'Cost of Equal Pay', *Employment and Productivity Gazette*, January 1970.
3   *First report on the implementation of the Equal Pay Act*, from the Office of Manpower Economics, HMSO, 1972.
4   Glicklich, P., Povall, M., Snell, M. W. and Zell, A. 'Equal Pay and Opportunity', *Department of Employment Gazette*, July 1978.
5   *Waddington* v. *Leicester Council for Voluntary Service*, Employment Appeals Tribunal (EAT), 1976.
6   *Nasse* v. *Science Research Council*, House of Lords, November 1979.
7   *Price* v. *Civil Service Commission*, EAT, July 1976.
8   Snell, M. 'The Equal Pay and Sex Discrimination Acts: their impact in the workplace', *Feminist Review*, vol. 1(1), 1979.
9   Gregory, F. 'The Great Conciliation Fraud', *New Statesman*, 3 July 1981.
10 Graham, C. and Lewis, N. *The Role of ACAS Conciliation in Equal Pay and Sex Discrimination Cases* EOC, June 1985.
11 Leonard, A. *The First Eight Years: A Profile of Applicants to the Industrial Tribunals under the Sex Discrimination Act 1975 and the Equal Pay Act 1970*, EOC 1986.
12 *Quinn* v. *Williams Furniture Ltd*, Court of Appeal, November 1980.
13 *Gray* v. *El Vino*, Westminster County Court, May 1978.
14 *Bennett* v. *the Football Association and the Nottinghamshire Football Association*, Court of Appeal, July 1978.
15 *Whitfield* v. *the London Borough of Croydon and Woodcote High School*, Croydon County Court, December 1979.
16 *Do You Provide Equal Educational Opportunities?*, EOC.
17 *Ninth Annual Report*, EOC, 1984.
18 Appleby, G. and Ellis, E. 'Formal Investigations: The Commission for Racial Equality and the Equal Opportunities Commission as Law Enforcement Agencies', *Public Law*, summer 1984.
19 Sack, V. 'The Equal Opportunities Commission Ten Years On', *Modern Law Review*, 1986.
20 Ashdowne-Sharpe, P. 'Women's Rights — the missed opportunity', *Sunday Times*, 20 February 1977.
21 See also Coote, A. 'Equality and the Curse of the Quango', *New Statesman*, 1 December 1978.
22 The TUC published a discussion document, *Equal Opportunities: 'Positive' Action in Women's Employment*, in May 1980.
23 Income Data Services Study 340, June 1985.
24 *Equality Moves Forward*, GLC Equal Opportunities Second Annual Monitoring Report, April 1984—March 1985.
25 'Plenty of Room at the Top', Polly Toynbee, *Guardian*, 16 September 1985.
26 Vallance, E. *Women in the House*, Athlone Press, 1979.
27 Ibid.

5 Unions

From the early stages of the women's liberation movement, efforts were made to forge links with the trade unions. Indeed, this was a key strategy of the socialist—feminist element of the movement. The unions were seen as a central site of struggle — around employment, pay and conditions. It was a way of reaching women who were not yet acquainted with feminist politics, as an organizational base for feminist campaigns, and as a means of anchoring women's liberation in working-class politics — which was essential to those who regarded feminism as an integral part of the struggle for socialism.

There was also a general trend, beginning in the 1960s and continuing through the 1970s, alongside the development of the women's movement, of massive numbers of women (especially white collar workers) joining unions for the first time. For many women, then, the start of trade union activity coincided with, or prompted, an introduction to feminist ideas.

In 1961 there were four male trade unionists for every female union member. By 1980, the ratio dropped to barely two-to-one. Female membership increased during that period by 110 per cent — more than twice the rate at which women joined the labour force (an increase of 48.5 per cent). Within the same years, the number of men in the workforce remained fairly stable, while they increased their union membership by only 17.6 per cent.

The unions held out considerable promise to women, especially during the 1970s. They had power in the workplace. They had a hot-line to government (under Labour, at least). Their business was to represent women and help them to win better pay, benefits and conditions. The British trade union movement was perhaps the most experienced and influential in the Western capitalist world. Through the unions, women had a chance to enlist male support in order to fight with them, rather than fighting alone.

Many radical feminists — and others too — considered the trade union movement a bastion of male power which was inimical to women's liberation. Socialist feminists were not under any great illusion about the extent of male dominance in the unions: it was plain to see that men were in control of almost all the top positions, both in individual unions and in decision-making posts throughout the trade union structure; and the special needs of women workers were low

down on the list of union bargaining priorities. The fact that socialist feminists were determined nevertheless to engage in trade unionism was an expression of their approach to politics generally. They saw it as necessary to organize within the unions, to campaign through them and to struggle to change them — all at the same time.

In the course of the 1970s, women began to discover what a slow, difficult business it was going to be to change the unions. They made some inroads and they achieved some material gains. However, just as they had to discover, through campaigning for equality at work, that inequality was deeply built into the structure of the labour market, so they learned, through their involvement in the unions, that female powerlessness was not a superficial problem, but a profound and intractable one.

In this chapter we look at the record of the trade union movement in fighting to improve the position of women since the early 1970s. We examine the reasons for women's continuing powerlessness, and we assess attempts by the TUC and individual unions to increase the participation of their female members.

The impact of feminism

During the 1970s the unions notched up some notable gains for women. Each one had its own favourite examples — and it is worth recounting a few to indicate the range of their activities. APEX, the office workers' union, made a string of successful applications to the Central Arbitration Committee, which led to the scrapping of low-paid 'women's grades' in several large companies, including the tobacco giants, Imperial and Gallaghers. TASS, the white-collar engineers' union, conducted a campaign under the slogan 'Men's pay for women', which went beyond the scope of the Equal Pay Act and demanded that women should be paid the rate that a man would be paid for doing the same job; according to the TASS salary census, between 1975 and 1980, the pay of female clerical workers increased on average from 74.4 to 81.3 per cent of the male average — which was considerably better than the national figures. The National Union of Public Employees negotiated maternity pay agreements for two large groups of public sector workers, which went well beyond the statutory awards. The General and Municipal Workers' Union won several important victories at industrial tribunals and at the Employment Appeals Tribunal in equal pay and sex discrimination cases (including two that were abandoned as no-hopers by the EOC). ACTT, the film and television workers' union, commissioned an exhaustive study of female employment in those industries, published in 1975, which became a classic reference point for feminists and trade unionists, as well as a valuable bargaining counter for women in the ACTT.[1]

The first positive action agreement to be signed between unions and management was negotiated by the national and local government officers' union, Nalgo, and the same union produced a series of negotiating guides for its members, *Negotiating for Equality*, *Workplace Nurseries* and *Rights for Working Parents*[2] — all with a distinctly feminist tone.

The influence of the women's liberation movement could easily be traced. Feminists had taken jobs in unions' expending research departments and played a part, as lay activists, in the development of policy. Small but conspicuous incursions of women into manual trades, directly inspired by the women's movement, brought tiny contingents of feminists into such solidly male enclaves as the building workers' union, UCATT, and the electricians' union, the EETPU. At the TUC's annual conference of women workers, the feminist presence grew visibly stronger year by year. There were growing numbers of younger delegates with prior experience in women's groups and, at the same time, older delegates and those in traditional blue-collar jobs were voicing their demands in increasingly feminist terms. From the mid-1970s, the cultural and political gap between the women's liberation movement and women in the trade union movement narrowed considerably. The impact on TUC policy was unmistakable.

When the feminist campaign around the Working Women's Charter reached its height in 1974, the TUC set about revamping its own charter, *Aims for Women at Work*. Its motives were not entirely admirable: it wanted to head off the initiative of the charter campaign, which had an unofficial base, a grass-roots orientation and an ambitious list of demands, including a national minimum wage. Nevertheless, the TUC was obliged to include many of the same points in its own charter, which was published in 1975 and updated in 1978 to include a pro-abortion statement. The feminist campaign for child care, which began in the early seventies, eventually found expression in the TUC's *Charter for the Under-Fives*,[3] published in 1978, which called for a 'comprehensive and universal service' of care and education for children from birth to five years, with 'flexible hours to meet the needs of working parents'.

A resolution carried at the 1979 TUC Women's Conference brought the feminist debate on domestic labour into the trade union debate on the unemployment crisis. It called on the General Council

> to campaign for a shorter working week for all waged workers to offset the effects of unemployment and to campaign among male trade unionists to use the extra time available to spread the burdens of housework and child care.

At the 1981 TUC Women's Conference, a resolution was passed which recognized 'that the unequal division of work in the home is one of the main obstacles to equal pay and employment opportunities, and to the full participation of women in the trade union movement.' The conference called 'upon the General Council and the Women's

Advisory Committee to launch a campaign to raise consciousness amongst male trade unionists about the importance of taking an equal part in housework and child care.' And later that year, the TUC Congress passed a resolution which recognized that the 'outdated concept of the family wage' was a basic cause of rising unemployment among women.

The idea of positive action had been imported from the United States via the British women's movement and, as we noted in the previous chapter, it marked something of a watershed for feminist politics. It expressed an understanding that simply ending discrimination against women was not going to achieve equality and that special measures had to be taken to tackle the underlying causes of oppression. The TUC held a special conference on positive action and drew up a useful set of guidelines for introducing positive action in employment. Nalgo, the finance union BIFU, and ACTT began to work towards setting up positive action programmes in a handful of workplaces. This was not followed by any widespread practical demonstration of the unions' commitment to positive action. Nevertheless, their official approval of applying positive action to their own organizations provided a real chance for feminists to make headway in their efforts to transform the character of trade unionism. (We return to this subject on p. 169.)

One dramatic manifestation of union support for women's demands came in 1979 with the TUC's official demonstration against the restrictive abortion Bill introduced into Parliament by John Corrie, Conservative MP for Bute and Ayrshire North. When some 80,000 women and men marched from Marble Arch to Trafalgar Square on 31 October that year, it was the largest union demonstration that had yet been held for a cause which lay beyond the traditional scope of collective bargaining; it was also the biggest-ever pro-choice march.

It came as the culmination of four years' hard labour by the feminist National Abortion Campaign, which had been launched in 1975 to defend the 1967 Abortion Act. As the 1970s wore on, attacks on the 1967 Act became more concerted and in response, individual unions began to pass pro-abortion resolutions at their national conferences. This was often at the instigation of feminist members already active in NAC or other pro-abortion groups. At the 1976 TUC Women's Conference, when an earlier anti-abortion Bill, introduced by Labour MP James White, was before Parliament, the medical practitioners' union (a section of ASTMS) put forward a resolution which pledged support for abortion 'on request'. It was moved by a young doctor who was a founder-member of NAC, and it was carried by a large majority.

Later that year, Terry Marsland, deputy general secretary of the tobacco workers' union, took a similar motion to the TUC Congress — and that, too, was passed.

James White's Bill fell for lack of time, as did its successor, introduced the following year by William Benyon. But further trouble was anticipated. At the 1978 TUC Women's Conference, a delegate from the National Union of Journalists, who was a member of NAC's steering committee, moved a resolution from her union which called upon the TUC to organize a national demonstration in defence of the 1967 Act, in the event of another restrictive Bill. It was passed overwhelmingly. Once again, Terry Marsland carried a similar resolution through Congress. So when John Corrie brought his Bill into the new Parliament, under a Tory government which had no inclination to defend the 1967 Act, it was time for the TUC to fulfil its pledge.

When the big day came, the TUC had arranged for general secretary Len Murray and a group of General Council members to head the procession as it moved off down Park Lane, and inevitably this meant it would be led almost exclusively by men. A contingent of young radical feminists staged an angry protest. Women, they insisted, without a shade of respect for the official grandeur of the occasion, should lead the march. Len Murray, by all accounts, was beside himself with rage. So was Marie Patterson, chairperson of the TUC Women's Advisory Committee and one of the two women on the General Council, who had the place of honour at his side. Many other senior trade unionists railed against the folly of the protest. ('After all we've done for you . . . don't expect to be so lucky next time!') If feminists wanted TUC support, they were going to get it on the TUC's own terms. Such an open challenge was considered an intolerable breach of protocol and there was no question of giving way. For the women in NAC who had worked so hard for this moment it was an excruciating ordeal to be caught between elements of mutual distrust and intolerance in the two movements they wanted to bring together. Only the impressive size of the demonstration, which took more than four hours to file into Trafalgar Square, could sweeten the atmosphere.

It was indeed a big success and it clearly confirmed that public opinion was leaning towards a woman's right to choose. (There remained, however, some strong support for making it more difficult to obtain abortions late in pregnancy.) Corrie's Bill ran out of time in Parliament; the government did not give it any more, and it fell. Male trade unionists would cite the event for some time to come as evidence of their commitment to the women's cause.

The defeat of Corrie's Bill was remarkable because it was, thus far, one of the trade unions' few major, tangible achievements for women. They passed many excellent resolutions and they won some impressive piecemeal gains for their female members. But there was little evidence that they had the political will to mount an effective challenge to the traditional distribution of jobs and pay between women and men.

No action on low pay

In 1979 the TUC endorsed a ten-point charter, *Equality for Women within Trade Unions*. Point Two of this charter demanded 'complete equality of job opportunity for women with men'. Point Four called for 'an end to all pay discrimination against women workers'. For some groups of women, unions negotiated a real improvement in their basic wages, relative to men's. But, as we have seen, the overall gap between female and male take-home pay scarcely diminished at all. The extent to which women's jobs were segregated from men's increased during the 1970s. And in some instances, trade unions deterred women from pursuing claims under the new equality legislation.

The laws were intended to compensate for past failures of collective bargaining: had the unions succeeded in negotiating adequate pay and conditions for their female members, there might have been less need for Parliament to step in. The unions backed the campaign for legislation, but at the time many trade unions argued that the laws were an unnecessary intrusion into their own territory: wages and conditions were a matter for collective bargaining; they did not want the autonomy of the unions undermined by courts or tribunals or quangos — and anyway, they argued, the laws wouldn't work.

A resolution carried by the 1975 TUC Congress declared that the Equal Pay Act could not close the gap between the average earnings of men and women:

> The aim of this Congress is that a woman should be paid the wage a man would be paid if he were doing the job. This will only be achieved by intensive industrial campaigns for higher wages for women.

Those intensive campaigns did not take place.

At the same 1975 Congress, TUC general secretary Len Murray tried, successfully, to head off left-wing opposition to the new 'social contract' between the unions and the Labour government, and to the £6 pay limit which was part of its first phase. He argued that this was neither a wage freeze nor an anti-working-class policy.

Our voluntary policy of a £6 a week increase will help, and it will work, because it can be operated without disunity. It is fair and socially just, in that the greatest benefit goes to the lowest-paid . . . the policy before you is an attack on low pay.

The trouble with this approach to low pay was that there were no means of ensuring that the low-paid actually got the £6. Many poorly organized workers (including women and in particular part-timers and homeworkers) did not have the bargaining strength to win more than a fraction of it. Many got nothing at all. It was a strategy for holding down wages at the top of the ladder, not for increasing those at the bottom. It was a bonus for employers, an empty promise for many of the lowest-paid and weakly organized workers, and it was bound to build up trouble for the future, since it was seen as no more than a temporary interruption of the traditional function of trade union bargaining — which was to safeguard differentials between weaker and stronger groups of workers, between the 'skilled' and the 'unskilled', between women and men.

The statistics show that women's pay did improve in relation to men's between 1975 and 1977 (see p. 81). This was partly because there were still some blatant cases of unequal pay which could be swept up under the new Equal Pay Act, and these settlements were exempted from the limits of the 'social contract'. It was also partly because certain groups of lower-paid women did not get pay rises which increased the overall female average, while there was a temporary brake on stronger groups of (male) workers who might otherwise have got more than £6. It was a brief respite.

In June 1976, when the TUC held a special congress to ratify Phase Two of the 'social contract' (this time a 5 per cent pay limit), the problem of low pay seemed almost forgotten. Lord Allen of the shop workers' union, USDAW, who chaired the congress, declared:

We all know that differentials have been squeezed . . . what we are saying is that in a freer situation ability must be rewarded, skill must be rewarded, effort must be rewarded.

The TUC came out in favour of a 'planned return to free collective bargaining' in which priority would be given to the 'satisfactory restoration of differentials'. Kevin Halpin, one of the leaders of the rank-and-file Liaison Committee for the Defence of Trade Unions, later summed up the disdain for 'soft' struggles which were all that remained on the bargaining table when demands for pay were fettered. The social contract had inhibited negotiations, he told *Morning Star* readers on 4 February 1977; shop stewards were 'reduced to arguing about such things as soap and towels and redundancy'. By the end of that year, the gap between female and male pay had begun to widen — a trend which continued for the rest of the decade. 'Free collective bargaining' was unlikely to help low-paid women while their bargaining power remained weaker than the traditionally higher-paid and predominantly male sectors of the workforce. An incomes policy would be no help to women while it was based on restoring or maintaining differentials, and it would be no help to anyone except employers while its effect was simply to hold down the wages of the higher-paid.

The issue of low pay returned to the headlines during the 'winter of discontent' of 1978/9. NUPE had tabled a demand for a minimum basic rate equivalent to two-thirds of the average male wage, plus a 35-hour week — which suggested that it was at least trying to grasp the nettle of female disadvantage. On 22 January 1979, 80,000 came out in support of a National Day of Action for the Low Paid, and shortly afterwards the unions organizing public service workers launched a programme of industrial action, to protest both at low pay and at Labour's cuts in public spending, which threatened jobs and the quality of the services. The Tory press made a meal out of it, ensuring the defeat of the Callaghan/Healey government in May 1979. It did nothing much for the low-paid. At Downing Street in the small hours of 10 February, a deal was struck between James Callaghan, Len Murray and the general secretaries of the four unions whose members were involved in the action. The demands for a 35-hour week and a minimum earnings guarantee were abandoned; the public service workers were given £1 'on account' and it was agreed to instigate a comparability study with a view to increasing their pay in line with the private sector. Terms of reference were drawn up which left plenty of scope for the new Standing Commission on Pay Comparability, set up under the chairmanship of Professor Hugh Clegg. NUPE suggested that the Commission should compare women's pay with men's pay rather than with that of workers doing similar jobs in the private sector (where, if anything, they were less well organized and lower paid). This fell on deaf ears.

Clegg reported in August 1979. He recommended pay increases for cleaners, kitchen assistants and domestic assistants (who were all female and already the lowest paid) of between 2.9 and 4.9 per cent. For ambulancemen, storekeepers, caretakers, refuse collectors, heavy plant operators and other male workers in higher grades, he recommended increases ranging from 9.7 to more than 20 per cent. It amounted to a massive betrayal of the low-paid women who had been involved in industrial action during the 'winter of discontent'. By the time the seeds of that betrayal bore their bitter fruit (in the form of actual pay awards) Margaret Thatcher was in Downing Street, the unions were demoralized and there was no effective protest.

The problem of powerlessness

As the economic crisis deepened in the late 1970s and early 1980s, the unions became increasingly preoccupied with saving their members' jobs and defending the purchasing power of wages. The fight against female disadvantage was not a top priority. It seemed that women's economic equality had to be a no-cost benefit, which could only be sanctioned in a period of economic growth, because redistribution of wealth between women and men was not seriously considered.

The most obvious cause of the failure to improve the lot of women was that women themselves still had no real power in their unions. They had little or no control over the making or implementation of policy. They were severely under-represented on their unions' executive committees, among full-time officials and on delegations to the TUC, as table 10 shows. In 1985, nearly half a million women who belonged to Britain's two largest unions (the Transport and General Workers' Union, TGWU, and the General, Municipal, Boilermakers' and Allied Trades' Union, GMBATU) had only two female executive members between them; and if the two major public sector unions (Nalgo and NUPE) wished to achieve the same proportion of female full-time officials as female members, they would need to hire 185 more women. In spite of the massive increase in female membership since the 1960s, this pattern of male dominance remained entrenched at almost every level of the union structure — from regional councils to the shop-floor, from industry-wide negotiating teams to specialist committees (except those concerned with equality).

It wasn't just that women failed to fill key posts in the unions; they remained absent from a whole range of union activities. Polls conducted by MORI in 1976 and 1979 showed that although female union activity increased in that period, more than one in four women still had no record of union activism by the end of the decade. (This meant they had never been involved in industrial action, nor held union office, nor attended union meetings.)[4]

'What can women expect if they don't get involved? . . . They've got no-one to blame but themselves . . . women are their own worst enemies . . .' These were familiar refrains, but were they accurate? What were the real reasons for women's continuing powerlessness?

Men, too, often found themselves powerless in their unions, cut off from the centres of activity and authority. Evidently, there were difficulties about the way trade unions were organized which affected both sexes. For example, there were increased bargaining advantages to the unions if they grew in size; but the larger they became, the harder it got for them to meet the needs of all their members. At the same time, the scope and complexity of their business grew steadily, with the changing structure of industry and the worsening economic climate constantly demanding new strategies. If solutions to general problems such as these were found, they would no doubt help women improve their position. But that would not be the end of the matter. For it was still men, not women, whose voice was heard, whose strength was felt, whose investment in the organization yielded greater dividends.

There were no formal bars to female participation, and there were few overt acts of discrimination against women. So we need to look deeper — at the history of trade unionism, at the structure of paid and unpaid labour, and at the way these shaped the different traditions and attitudes of female and male workers.

As we saw in chapter 2, the character of British trade unionism had its roots in the early craft unions, developed during the nineteenth century by skilled male workers to protect their own interests. Women were at that time excluded both from skilled work and from the means of organization. Then (and ever since) they mainly did work that was designated as unskilled or semi-skilled, at much lower rates of pay than men.

In the latter half of the century, new trade unions were developed for workers outside the traditional crafts; but for these, women were at best a problem, to be accommodated in some special way, and at worst a menace, to be driven out of the labour force. As Henry Broadhurst put it to the 1875 TUC, one of the aims of a union was to

> bring about a condition . . . where [men's] wives and daughters would be in their proper sphere at home, instead of being dragged into competition for livelihood against the great and strong men of the world.[5]

Cheap female labour (a consequence of women's exclusion from organization) was regarded by men as a threat to their jobs. However, rather than ensure that women were paid more, men tried to control their access to the labour market by keeping them out of the unions.

Women began to set up their own organizations to fight for better pay and conditions, and in 1906 the National Federation of Women Workers was established, with some 2,000 members and Mary

McArthur as its first president. Effective and militant, it built up its membership to 80,000 by the end of the First World War. But by that stage there had developed a strong feeling that the separatist 'experiment' should come to an end. Mary McArthur argued at the Federation's national conference in 1920 that it should merge with the National Union of General Workers, to become 'a great industrial organization of men and women, in which women are not submerged but in which they take as active part as the men'.[6]

At first, the Federation kept its own executive council and became a 'district' of the NUGW, with special officers to cater for women. In the next three years, however, the separate women's district and the National Women's Committee were abolished. All signs of separate identity swiftly disappeared and the number of women's officers fell from sixteen to one. By 1930 the voice of women was so thoroughly silenced that the NUGW did not send a single female delegate to the TUC Congress. (Almost half a century was to pass before the union — which became the General, Municipal, Boiler Makers' and Allied Trades' Union — stirred itself to make good the damage and actively encourage women to participate in its affairs.)

In other unions women were silent too. Whether they would have been more effective if they had remained separate is difficult to judge. They were not deliberately suppressed. They believed their future lay in fighting alongside men on equal terms and they did not foresee how hard that would be.

Just as the silence of women in the unions stretched into the last quarter of the twentieth century, so the principle which justified and encouraged it remained firmly embedded in trade union philosophy. This was the idea that men had the right to earn a 'family wage', which we have already described (p. 63). Although it never bore much relation to working-class life — since women continued to do paid work to support their families — it helped to perpetuate the unequal division of labour between women and men, with men retaining economic control within the family and women bearing the full burden of unpaid domestic work.[7]

As long as the myth of the family wage persisted, there was bound to be a conflict of interest between women and men in the trade union movement. For if men saw themselves as breadwinners-in-chief, how were they to view the prospect of women gaining equal opportunity and equal access to all jobs, with equal pay and job security? Especially at a time of recession, when jobs and money were in short supply, they would probably conclude that there would be less to go around for themselves. (Some would argue that employers' profits were the rightful source of extra pay and benefits due to women. But that amounted to an excuse for delay in putting the unions' own house in order and women would not 'wait until the revolution'.)

Thus, for men to champion the women's cause wholeheartedly required a degree of altruism that had no part in the tradition of British trade unionism. The unions' chief purpose had always been to look after their members' interests, and self-protection was their business. Pure altruism, requiring self-denial without hope of future gain, was not. Of course, there were brave acts of comradeship, but that was another matter. The thousands who turned out to support the Grunwick strike in 1977—8 (for example) felt that the struggle of those workers (for the right to organize) was their struggle too — it was, after all, a defence of the general right to organize. Men did not identify with the struggle of women in the same way. Instead, seeing it as a threat, they dug in their heels and with the passing of time they developed increasingly diplomatic ways of doing so.

This conflict of interest lay beneath the surface of the trade unions' fight for equality like a wrecked tanker — polluting the waters and impeding all passage. Nobody wanted to admit that it was there. Men often recognized it only subconsciously, acting upon it instinctively more than deliberately. Women were perhaps reluctant to look too closely at the reasons men did not support them. It wasn't easy to confront a conflict of interest with men at work while trying to build a domestic life which was based on an assumption of common interest. Women themselves were often affected by the 'family wage' propaganda, even though it diminished their status as workers, undermined their claim to equality and contributed to a feeling that the trade unions were not primarily for them.

So what of men's support for women's abortion rights? Unlike the fight for equality at work, the defence of the 1967 Abortion Act entailed no threat — present or future — to men's material circumstances. Indeed, a great many men were spared financial hardship and social embarrassment by the 1967 Act. And there was no danger of women gaining real control over their fertility while they still had to obtain the consent of two doctors before terminating a pregnancy. This is not to say that self-interest was the only motive behind men's support of abortion rights, but that there was not necessarily a serious conflict of interest between women and men over the issue.

As we showed in chapter 2, women's experience of paid employment was radically different from men's. They did different jobs and earned a lot less money. Their employment was less likely to be continuous. They worked shorter hours and they often had part-time jobs. When they went home from their work they began another job, whose hours were unlimited and for which they received no pay. If they had children, the job of parenthood carried with it full-time cares and responsibilities which often intruded into their paid employment. None of these factors was inevitable or immutable; they were a result of the unequal division of labour between women and men; and they all had a bearing on women's relationship with the trade unions.

In his analysis of a 1980 MORI survey, Peter Kellner demonstrated the impact of child-bearing and -rearing on working patterns and union membership. A smaller proportion of women aged between 25 and 34 did paid work than among any other age group between 18 and 55; a smaller proportion of 25- to 34-year-old women who had jobs worked full-time than in any other age group; and a smaller proportion of women in this age group who worked full-time belonged to a union than in any other age group. The cumulative result of these biases meant that one man in two aged between 25 and 34 had a full-time job and belonged to a union — compared with one woman in 20 in the same age range. Kellner concluded:

> As a result, the typical male union member in his late thirties or forties has had work and union experience over twenty years; whereas for the typical female union member, work and union experience will be nothing like as continuous. It follows that wherever buggins' turn applies, buggins is seldom a woman.[8]

Here women were caught in a vicious circle. There was strong evidence that they would work if they could in their late twenties and early thirties, but they were largely deterred by the lack of adequate child care facilities. Child care could have been a priority in trade union bargaining. However, it was not — and according to another MORI poll, only 19 per cent of female (and 15 per cent of male) trade unionists thought their union 'should do more to meet the needs of workers with young children'. Women who could not work because of child care difficulties didn't join unions until these difficulties no longer affected them, so when they were in membership, they were less likely to demand policy changes which could radically improve their freedom to go out to work and participate fully in union activities.

Collective bargaining traditionally reflected male, not female, experience. Men saw themselves as wage earners, playing only a minimal part in the day-to-day lives of their families; they seldom saw fit to use their power in the unions to win improvements which did not relate directly to the workplace. Their bargaining strategy didn't express any responsibility as active parents, because they had none.[9]

The male view remained the dominant view of what mattered most in a trade union context, since women had insufficient power to assert other priorities.

The consciousness-raising effect

The reasons for women's low pay and powerlessness ranged well beyond the economic relationship between workers and employers. The day-to-day concerns of working women — different from men's because of their different role in the home — were not part of traditional trade union discourse; there were no established channels for talking about them. There was no bank of experience within the unions which could be drawn upon in order to tackle the particular problems that confronted women.

For us, these points were vividly illustrated when, in the autumn of 1980, we interviewed two groups of women factory workers in the north-west of England. In both factories, the women saw each other every day at work, but had never before met together as a group. Therefore, although they experienced low pay and powerlessness, they had had little opportunity to articulate them as grievances, less still to work out what to do about them. As they began to discuss the link between their jobs and their pay, and their participation in their union (the GMWU), their attitudes swiftly changed.[10]

Early in one of the discussions, which took place in a glass factory on the outskirts of Liverpool, one woman expressed strongly her view that it would make no difference if there were more female shop stewards at the plant. 'Why should it?' she demanded; 'the union treats you the same whether you're a man or a woman. I mean, I'm paying my 35p the same as any man. They've *got* to treat you equal!'

Jobs in her factory were divided into nine grades; the women were concentrated in the lower four. She said she thought her job — which involved stamping the glasses as they came off the assembly line — was graded too low. 'We're in grade three, but we ought to be in grade seven. Machine operators are in grade six and it's an easier job. In our room, when the machines are running smoothly, the operators can sit there all morning and read a paper, while I put in four and a half hours continuously, like a robot.' She didn't know who had devised the grading system, but guessed that management alone had been responsible. She was surprised to hear that it had been negotiated with the unions. Could her union get her on to a higher grade? At first she shook her head: 'They've tried.' But then she decided they hadn't tried hard enough: 'Well they can't have, can they, because we're still on grade three!'

One of her colleagues said at first that she thought men should be paid more than women, but later after discussing the problem of redundancy (two of the women were afraid their husbands would lose their jobs), she changed her mind, explaining: 'Nowadays you get a lot of women on their own, and women left working when their husbands are put out of work. I never really gave that thought before.'

In the second factory, which made pharmaceuticals, the women outnumbered the men by more than four to one, yet the men ran the union. The women were paid no more than the lowest male grade, although they worked more intensively than most of the men. One of them explained that they barely had time to get to the canteen and back for their ten-minute tea break:

> You run the length of the factory, up four flights of stairs, run right down to the canteen, get a drink, sit down, scald your tonsils and you've got to be back on the line before the buzzer goes again. But the men, they saunter in and saunter out. If *we're* late back, it's marked down on the lost time paper, but they're not as hard on the men. The management bend over backwards towards the men.

Asked why, she said the men 'stuck together' in a way that the women didn't. The men themselves, who joined the discussion later, agreed that they were strong in the union because they got together more often. 'The women are tied on the line and they can't stop,' said one. 'There's plenty of time during the day when we can meet up. Quite often all the men are in the same cloakroom.' Couldn't the women get together at lunch time? Apart from practical difficulties — they were on different shifts and (as one said) the married women had to go out shopping — it hadn't occurred to them to congregate in that fashion. The men had got into the habit of meeting in the cloakroom during the day just as they gathered in the pubs at night. The women were not in the least downtrodden or disinclined to unity; they had simply lacked the opportunity to meet and exchange views.

Not only did they miss out on informal gatherings, but they also had problems getting to official union meetings. One of the female stewards at the pharmaceutical factory explained: 'A lot of women have to go home and cook tea for their husbands. Or they can't get out because they've got to do their washing or their ironing.' Some said their husbands would disapprove if they knew they were going to a pub for a union meeting; and who would look after the children? (Who indeed?)

Most striking of all was the link between the prospect of 'responsibility', which deterred so many women from union office, and the role they played at home. It was not simply that the women had less time: they were reluctant to add to the mental and emotional burden — of looking after other people, having to remember to do things, always being on call — which they already carried with their domestic responsibilities.

Many of our impressions were confirmed by Jane Stageman's study of women trade unionists in the Hull area.[11] With a grant from the Equal Opportunities Commission, Stageman set out to discover why women did not participate more fully in trade union affairs, and what might encourage them; 108 women from five union branches (spanning the public and private sectors, servicing and manufacturing) answered questions about what they thought would increase the level of women's union activity. As table 11 on p. 183 shows, one vital practical measure came top of the list: 'holding meetings in work time'. This was followed closely by measures to increase women's sense of involvement ('making union matters easier to understand' and 'making more information available about how unions work'). More than half said they would participate more if they had 'more interest in union affairs' and if they had 'fewer home responsibilities'. Next, they thought participation would be encouraged if opportunities were created for women to 'get together and discuss matters of interest to them'; if they felt 'more confident'; and if they knew that women could be 'as competent as men in union affairs'.

First steps towards positive action

Throughout the 1970s, there were fierce arguments in the trade union movement about whether or not special steps should be taken to increase women's activity. Should there be special conferences for women, special courses, special committees, special seats? Or would these amount to tokenism, would they ghettoize women's issues? Would it be an insult to women to treat them as something other than the exact equals of men?

Some white-collar unions made vigorous efforts to disband the TUC Women's Conference (inaugurated in 1925) on the ground that it was a ghetto and an anachronism. The last serious attack came in March 1977, when the Civil and Public Services Association and the National Union of Journalists moved a resolution that the conference be discontinued, chiefly because of 'the fact that women can now claim equal rights with men . . . [and] the trade union movement's opposition to discrimination and progress made towards fuller participation by women members in the general work and direction of the movement.' Such expressions of faith were mingled, in the proposing speeches, with more sophisticated arguments: there were no 'women's problems' as such, said one delegate; education and child care were the concern of men as much as women. Against the motion, it was argued that women would continue to need a special platform until they really were equal, and the conference was saved by a decent majority. The delegates went on to vote for 'at least seven additional seats for women on the General Council' of the TUC. (There was no action on that until 1981 — and then only five seats were added.)

In the late 1970s, support gathered for positive action in the unions — as feminist influence grew and it became increasingly hard to deny that here, as in the field of employment opportunity, women could make no progress unless special efforts were made to shift entrenched patterns of discrimination.

The white-collar engineers' union, AUEW (now TASS), acted earlier and more thoroughly than most, appointing a national women's organizer in 1974. TASS had a network of women's sub-committees from 1922, when the all-female tracers' union merged with the engineers' and draughtsmen's union (then the AESD). Unlike the women who joined the National Union of General Workers in 1920, the tracers insisted on maintaining a degree of separate identity within the larger organization (perhaps because theirs was a distinct craft). In the early 1970s, TASS began to recruit clerical workers in engineering firms, which led to an increase in its female membership from 3.3 per cent in 1968 to 15 per cent in 1979. Its leaders realized that the membership drive would be assisted if the union made a positive effort to cater for the special needs of women workers. This coincided with a growing awareness of the women's liberation movement and sympathy with some of its more pragmatic demands. Thus, the women's sub-committees at national and divisional level, each with a special seat on its parent body, were given a new significance. The union began to run annual weekend women's schools, and to produce an impressive range of literature on women's issues. TASS has developed a large and vocal contingent of female activists.

The National Union of Public Employees commissioned a study of its structure from Warwick University. In their report, published in 1974, Bob Fryer, Andy Fairclough and Tom Manson of Warwick's sociology department argued:

> We do not believe that the [existing] under-representation has anything to do with 'women's nature' or lack of interest in the

affairs of NUPE . . . It has to do first with the position of women in the wider society and at work. All women come through a process which emphasizes domestic activity as a prime virtue, especially supportive of and secondary to the activities of men . . . The structure of the union can either be designed to alleviate the effects of such disadvantages or else it can operate on the basis of accepting subordination as a 'fact of life' which is only confirmed by the low degree of female participation in the union at all levels.[12]

On their advice, NUPE reserved five seats for women on its national executive council from 1975 onwards.

Nalgo set up a National Equal Opportunities Committee, urged its twelve districts to do likewise and began to publish a regular equal opportunities bulletin. Two other white-collar unions, APEX and ASTMS, established similar networks of national and regional committees in the mid 1970s; and by 1980 the two largest blue-collar unions, the Transport and General and the General and Municipal, had begun to set up equal rights committees in their regions. The TUC and a number of individual unions began to provide crèches at their larger meetings; some branches set about negotiating work-time meetings specifically for the benefit of female members; and at least one office committee bargained successfully for baby-sitting payments to cover union meetings outside working hours.

The TUC charter, *Equality for Women within Trade Unions*, adopted in 1979, urged unions to take positive steps such as these to increase women's participation. It recommended special seats on national and local bodies where women were under-represented, special advisory committees, paid time off for union meetings in working hours, child care arrangements for meetings, special encouragement for women to attend union training, and non-sexist union publications. It was mildly worded, leaving unions free to ignore it if they wished. Nevertheless, it provided a legitimate base from which campaigns for positive action could be launched.

Most promising of all was the spread of women-only meetings and courses (or, put another way, the introduction of consciousness-raising into the trade union movement). By the end of the decade, these were being provided regularly by several unions — notably the GMWU and TASS — as well as by the TUC. Jenny Owen, who was responsible for setting up TUC weekend courses for women in Manchester and Liverpool, described the response of her students in terms that no feminist who has spent time in a women's group could fail to recognize: 'It works every time. At the end of two days they're high on the experience of being together — and they all say what a difference it makes to have just women on their own.' A NUPE women's school that we visited in Kent was attended by twenty-five women — nurses, caterers, cleaners, a road sweeper, a gardener and others. They all said they found it invaluable, they'd learnt a great deal and they wanted to come back again. 'We couldn't have spoken freely if men had been here,' said one. Another explained that she'd discovered for the first time that other women shared her ideas and feelings: 'I used to think it was just *me*!'

In 1981 the Yorkshire region of the GMWU planned a series of factory-based discussion groups for women only — the first such project to be launched in Britain. The region had been active on the equal rights front for at least four years, holding regular meetings of its equal rights committee and special training courses for women. It had learnt not only that women found it immensely valuable to get together, but also that the great majority of female members could not take up the opportunity while meetings were held outside working hours and away from the workplace. The solution was to take the opportunity into the workplace, by training women in the GMWU to lead discussions among groups of their own workmates, in working time.

Resistance to change

As these and other new measures were introduced, they inevitably encountered some resistance. Poor communication was a serious obstacle — especially in the larger unions where members were scattered around small workplaces, with no centralized bargaining structures. The two groups of GMWU women whom we interviewed in the North-west had never heard of their union's national women's officer, Pat Turner, nor did they know that their own region employed an equal rights officer and had recently held a regional equal rights conference. Marjorie Harrison, who conducted a study of women in ASTMS, found that letters from the ASTMS National Woman's Advisory Committee were often blocked by unsympathetic branch secretaries:

> It was discovered that some Secretaries were not passing on the information at all and others, instead of reading from the letter (which was deliberately low-key), were mentioning almost in passing that 'two women's libbers want to come and talk to you about women's lib', which got the reaction it was geared to receive — rejection.[13]

Harrison also found that while the Women's Advisory Committee had scored some considerable successes on 'social issues' such as the defence of abortion rights and the campaign for child benefit, its impact was minimal when it came to industrial matters such as pay and maternity leave — because it had no direct links with the officials responsible for negotiations. In ASTMS as in many unions, there remained a strong distinction between 'women's issues' and industrial matters over which men retained firm control.

NUPE's allocation of special seats on its executive council was said to have encouraged the election of three additional women who stood in competition with the men — so in that respect the experiment was a success. However, links remained weak between NUPE's ordinary female members and the women on the executive, and the latter seemed to exert little influence when it came to policy-making on issues of special concern to women. This was partly because NUPE lacked a network of women's committees, which would have spurred on the executive members and made them more accountable. To rectify this the union began to set up women's committees at divisional level in 1981.

In the giant Transport and General Workers' Union, progress was especially slow. The union was proud of its internal democracy and when its 1979 biennial delegate conference voted to set up regional equal rights committees, it could not *instruct* the regions how or when to do so. The results were patchy. Officers in charge of each region were free to invite whom they pleased to attend the inaugural meetings. Some went into action right away, others dragged their feet for eighteen months or more. The huge membership of the T&G made it prohibitively expensive to mail directly to shop stewards from head office — let alone directly to members. Consequently, most of its female members were unaware of what was going on and had no say in the development of equal rights committees in their areas.

Women who had reached positions of prominence in their unions were not always the best supporters of new measures to encourage female activism. Some, who had fought for most of their lives to 'make it' on men's terms, grew comfortable as token women near the top and lost sight of their sisters' need for a helping hand. Others held on to their commitment, but were driven, in their relative isolation, to degrees of paranoia and over-caution. It was not the women themselves who were to blame, so much as the character and structure of their organizations, which tended to isolate and intimidate them. It seemed that the problem would only diminish if stronger women's networks were developed in the unions, if more women were appointed to senior positions, and if union hierarchies kept in much closer touch with the grass roots.

By the end of the 1970s, it was apparent that women were still a long way from equal participation and equal power, and it would be a long time before they ceased to make special demands on the trade union movement. ('Okay brothers, we think you've got the hang of it now. Let's scrap the men's conference and merge it with ours!') It was also apparent that the more positive action a union undertook, the faster its female members would progress towards fuller participation. As women became more aware of their powerlessness — and their potential — they would make more demands on their unions.

By this time, though, the unions had at least begun to acknowledge that the causes of women's inactivity were deeply rooted. Women had begun to talk openly about the links between their lack of power and their own domestic arrangements. At the TUC's conference on positive action in November 1980, one delegate demanded: 'When will our unions start telling our members to do their fair share of work at home, so that our members can get out to meetings?'

Developments in the 1980s

By the mid-1980s, significant changes had taken place in the trade union movement. Legislation introduced by the Thatcher government had weakened the unions' bargaining power, placing severe restrictions on the way they conducted industrial disputes, and making them liable to heavy fines and sequestration of their assets if they disobeyed the courts. The political and economic climate had forced the unions on to the defensive: as unemployment continued to rise, most negotiators gave priority to saving jobs rather than to improving wages and conditions or promoting equal opportunity; they also had to contend with falling membership — an inevitable consequence of a shrinking job market. None of this augured well for women; nor did the fact that more and more women were moving into part-time work and homework — fields in which most unions had poor achievement records.

Nevertheless, moves to promote women's participation in the unions continued. The unions were, by their nature, slow to respond to external social and economic change and during the 1970s women had often found this extremely frustrating; now, ironically, they saw it working to their advantage. Women had made huge efforts during the 1970s to spread some awareness of 'equality' issues and to develop policy initiatives. They built up a momentum that was not to be easily stopped, even as conditions deteriorated.

This is not to say that great achievements were made — simply that more unions were apparently making an effort. Measures pioneered by white-collar unions in the 1970s were adopted by many of the blue-collar unions. The shop workers' union USDAW, for example, appointed a national Women's Working Party in 1982, which in turn recommended a network of divisional women's committees as well as a full-time official with special responsibility for women; these changes were implemented in 1984/5.

Positive action at last became widely accepted as a strategy, and was promoted by the Women's Advisory Committee of the TUC. Policies became more sophisticated as different measures were tried and tested and women learned from experience. NUPE found that its reserved seats for women on the national executive council were not helping women at branch level. In 1982 it set up a National Women's Advisory Committee, appointed a National Women's Officer and instituted Women's Advisory Committees in each of its divisions. It also resolved to provide specialized women's courses in all divisions. In 1984 the national WAC made extensive recommendations for increasing women's participation throughout NUPE. Branches should negotiate time off with pay for meetings, or, failing that, provide child care and transport so that women could attend. Meetings in pubs and clubs were discouraged on the ground that they would effectively exclude Asian women. Other proposals included smaller and more informal meetings with a rotating chair, and a women's liaison officer for each branch to ensure communication between the Women's Advisory Committees and the members.

There isn't room here for a comprehensive account, but gradually during this period, more unions were setting up women's committees and working parties, appointing women's officers, providing child care facilities at conferences and meetings, introducing special training for women, publishing documents on issues relating to equality, analysing the extent of women's membership and participation, re-evaluating their structures and rule books, and so forth. It was hard to judge how far these moves increased women's power in the unions; harder still to assess their impact on women's pay and conditions. Much depended on whether unions were prepared to put funds behind these initiatives, on whether the new women's committees had a direct influence on union policy, and on whether women were able to gain a real voice in the bargaining process.

Much depended, too, on bringing the techniques and policies of women's liberation into the centre of the trade union movement. Women trade unionists had to develop the habit of gathering together, discussing their common experiences, setting them in a political framework and, on that basis, working out ways of achieving their objectives. By the mid-1980s, this was happening more often: both within and between unions, women were meeting *as women* and exploring common ground. The need for such meetings was more likely to be taken for granted; the question of whether they threatened trade union solidarity by excluding men was not debated with the passion that it had been in the 1970s.

It became more apparent, as time went by, that women would have to insist on making the inequality of domestic labour a primary concern of the trade unions. Only if men were obliged to stop claiming the right to be breadwinners-in-chief, and to see themselves as equal, active parents and home-makers, would they start to view their interests from a new perspective. Trade unionists, after all, were not just workers, but people with children and homes — members of communities who had lives to lead outside their factories and offices. Their needs as workers were inseparable from needs which arose from other parts of their lives.

The traditional priorities of union bargaining — focussing on the wage and the maintenance of differentials — had not helped to lift women out of low-paid areas or to alleviate their domestic responsibilities. On the contrary, they had primarily defended the interests of male workers.

For all workers, but especially for women, the benefits, services and facilities provided by the state (the 'social wage') were as vital as the earned wage — and these needed to be vastly improved. At the same time, women needed a strong voice in the way industries and services were designed and run, and in the way jobs were organized. In effect, this meant politicizing and feminizing the trade unions. Bargaining priorities had to be transformed, both at the level of negotiations with employers and at the national level, where unions had a key role to play in bargaining with government for the kind of social and economic planning that would redistribute wealth between women and men, and within the family, as well as across society.

Two terms of a Thatcher government certainly had a devastating effect on the unions and on the 'social wage'; they did, however, create conditions that could, in the longer term, force the kind of transformation that was needed. For one thing, Tory legislation forced unions to carry out secret ballots of their members. This concentrated union leaders' minds on the need to improve contact with individuals who were not activists and who had not previously been involved with decision-making: many were women. At the same time, Tory policies hastened changes in the character of the job market, which in turn weakened the traditional sources of trade union recruitment. This focussed unions' attention on the need to appeal to part-timers, homeworkers, and others in fields not traditionally organized: here, too, many were women. Also, the Tories' attempts to dismantle the welfare state encouraged certain public sector unions to rethink their priorities: they were no longer concerned mainly with wages; they had to develop new policies on how to defend the social wage and how to reconstruct public services in the event of a change of government.

This new approach could be found in the 1984 report of NUPE's Women's Working Party, which stressed the need to 'get the particular perspective of women into the forefront of our thinking and the mainstream of the Union's work'; it recognized that

> the development and quality of public services is not only a question of paid employment but also a major factor in the domestic lives of women which may enable us or not to seek paid employment in the first place and determine the type of job and hours we can do . . .

NUPE's deputy general secretary, Tom Sawyer, writing in *Tribune* (21 December 1984) expanded the theme. Women's demands, he said, 'put politics into collective bargaining':

> They don't just go for the biggest percentage rise that can be obtained for the biggest group of workers every time . . . Can the radicalism of women become a major rather than a minor force in the unions? If it can, our future is assured.

Another sign that attitudes were changing came from John Edmonds, who in 1986 took over as general secretary of the General, Municipal, Boilermakers' and Allied Trades' Union. GMBATU was Britain's second-largest union and by no means a radical trail-blazer. But writing in *New Socialist* in June 1986, Edmonds called on unions to reassess their approach. 'The old model of a Negotiating Man's Union — dispensing from above policies, bargaining solutions and the maintenance of a well-oiled procedural machine — has to go,' he said. Unions had to cater for what he called the new 'servant' economy, comprising millions of newly-exploited workers, 'overwhelmingly women working part-time in service industries or service occupations in other industries'.

> The priority will be bringing together isolated and fragmented groups, helping to enforce their rights and, most important, giving them for the first time the self-confidence to do it

themselves . . . Equal rights, health and safety, the working environment and very basic concerns of pay, conditions and the way in which workers are treated by employers . . . all these will rise to the surface . . . Unions must increasingly find a stronger place in the non-work areas of the lives of members and potential members . . . Unions can and should provide benefits for members not only as workers but also as consumers, as holiday-makers, as parents . . .

Edmonds was responding to a crisis brought about by seven years of Conservative rule. What is significant is that he (and other leaders such as NUPE's Rodney Bickerstaffe) were able to tap into the political and economic insights — as well as the vocabulary — that had already been developed by the women's movement. The debt was not, however, readily acknowledged.

The 1980s were characterized by a conspicuous militancy among some groups of women, around trade union issues. It is almost impossible to trace cause and effect, but it would be fair to suggest that a decade of women's liberation had created a climate in which women who did not see themselves as feminists nevertheless found a new strength and confidence. Women were in the forefront of key disputes which were not simply about defending jobs, but about the quality of state services — at Barking hospital, East London, for example, where a group of 42 women domestic staff stayed on strike for more than a year, after their hours of work had been cut to make their service more competitive. They protested not just about drastic reductions in their own pay, but also about deteriorating standards of cleanliness. But the most remarkable expression of this new militancy occurred during the miners' strike of 1984—5.

Women Against Pit Closures

The National Union of Miners began its strike against pit closures on 9 March 1984. The stage was set for a major confrontation with the government, which was bent on breaking the back of the militant and powerful NUM, and loosening Britain's economic dependence on domestic supplies of coal. Social security regulations had been changed to minimize the amount of benefit received by strikers' families — strikers themselves received nothing.

The strike got underway in the traditional manner: a men-only affair, with increasingly violent confrontations between pickets and police. It was almost certainly anticipated in government circles that the miners would be forced back to work by pressure from their wives, in the face of growing poverty and debt. There had been a few well-publicized cases in the past of women leading back-to-work campaigns. This time, however, the very reverse happened. Women in mining communities all over the country organized to support the strike. At first it was a relatively low-key business: the women wanted to show that they stood by their men. The men were not always keen that their wives should get involved; women had to win battles at home before they could play a part. They began to feed the strikers, opening kitchens and distributing food parcels. But before long the activities of the women transformed not only the strike, but the relationship between the mining communities and the left, and the lives and politics of the women themselves.

For the miners to hold out against the Coal Board over a long period, solidarity in the villages was every bit as important as numbers on the picket lines. The women banded together to organize feeding on a collective basis, not just for the men, but for families too. It soon became clear that this was more than a matter of 'stand by your man'. They took it upon themselves to fight for the survival of their communities. They were responsible for raising money, getting in supplies, cooking and distributing meals on a massive scale — demonstrating that this kind of work, which was normally 'invisible', had a central role in the economy of the strike. Thus, the women broadened out the meaning of the strike — it was clearly about more than the right to work; it was about the dignity and identity of the mining communities. They also established an autonomous and influential role for themselves as insubordinate women against the values of the Thatcher government.

Because they had the job of collecting money and food supplies, it fell largely to them to make links with supporters outside the mining villages. They travelled all around the country, speaking at meetings and rallies, making links with other political groups, many of whom had very different backgrounds and lifestyles — including Black activists, lesbians and gay men, and the Greenham women. They brought about an extraordinary cross-fertilization of left politics, introducing working-class families into middle-class homes and vice versa, and connecting the issues of the miners' strike with other issues of the left — notably anti-racism, gay and lesbian rights and the peace movement. Had the strike remained a men-only affair, not only would it have failed within a few months, but also these broader political links would never have been made.

This sudden uprising of working-class women did not happen in a vacuum; nor was it just a fluke that this strike, unlike previous ones, did not witness a 'petticoat rebellion' of wives urging their men back to work. It was an expression of changes that had taken place over a decade. Pauline, the wife of a striking miner from Blidworth in Nottinghamshire, explained it this way:

> I think women have been gradually asking more and more questions over the last ten years or so. In the last strike the women didn't ask any questions, it was all left to the men . . . But now women wanted to be more involved in the decision making, we wanted to know why the men were going on strike, so we could understand and support them . . . it was like wanting to know what's beyond that fence. When we first went on the picket line, it was because we wanted to know . . . what was over that fence . . . The more we found out the more we wanted to do as well.[14]

The women themselves changed dramatically during the year-long strike. They found their own strength, they found each other; many found confidence to speak in public and to travel for the first time beyond their own neighbourhoods. Many experienced a revolution in their domestic relations — as their husbands were left to do the housework and child care while they ran the kitchens and attended meetings and rallies. Pauline's experience was not untypical:

> We all knew that we had become fully active people, who had to be reckoned with not just ignored as we had been when we were housewives . . . Before the strike I thought I was quite content just to be in my own little kingdom, or my own little cell, whichever you want to call it, at home looking after the kids, doing washing, ironing and general chores . . . my involvement in the strike meant that Alan took on a lot of the looking after the kids and they were just as happy as when I did it. In fact I realised it was good for them, good for Alan and good for me . . .
>
> The issues of the strike really ate at me inside, really made me want to stand up and say, 'All right, enough is enough, I won't take this, I will do something to change it.' Once you've felt that once, you can feel it again over other things and we all knew that we'd never be the same again, that we'd always fight, when we saw something we thought was wrong. Already there were other issues which we knew we wanted to get involved in . . . the peace movement and campaigns against cuts to the health service . . . The situation of black people in Britain and the situation in Northern Ireland . . . we knew that the only way they could be

solved was by everybody standing up and fighting. Just as we knew we could only win our strike if everybody stood up and fought.[15]

In August 1985, five months after the strike ended, around 1,000 miners' wives and support groups attended the first annual conference of 'Women Against Pit Closures', a national co-ordinating body dedicated to keeping the women's fight going. Before the strike ended, one Kent miner had said during a meeting, 'Please, Mr Chair, when this strike is over, can I have my wife back? Not this one, the one I had before.' Half-joking, half-earnest, his wish expressed the feelings of many of the men. No doubt, many of the women did return to pre-strike patterns of domestic activity, but there was no returning to pre-strike consciousness. They had created their own political movement that could outlive the immediate struggle that brought it into being.

Table 10 Women in the unions

Union	Membership			Executive members		Full-time officials		TUC delegates	
	Total	Women	%	Total	Women	Total	Women	Total	Women
APEX	95,049	50,594	53.2	15	3 (8)	47	2 (25)	13	5 (7)
ASTMS	390,000	87,750	22.5	22	2 (5)	95	6 (21)	28	3 (6)
BIFU	154,579	78,765	50.9	32	4(16)	37	7 (19)	19	4(10)
CPSA	190,347	137,369	72.2	29	4(21)	14	3 (10)	30	9(22)
GMBATU	766,744	258,739	33.7	38	1(13)	287	12 (97)	86	4(29)
Nalgo	766,390	390,859	51.0	71	20(36)	191	20 (97)	72	23(37)
NUPE	680,000	455,600	67.0	26	10(17)	180	12(120)	34	10(23)
NUT	250,499	180,179	71.9	41	8(29)	27	2 (19)	37	10(27)
NUTGW	76,509	69,319	90.6	15	8(14)	38	4 (34)	13	10(12)
TGWU	1,490,555	228,750	15.3	42	1 (6)	500	9 (75)	92	9(16)
USDAW	392,307	239,170	61.0	18	1(11)	122	10 (74)	35	5(21)

Figures in brackets show how many women there would be if they were represented according to their share of the membership.
All figures are approximate and the most recent that were available in January 1985.
Source: EOC data

Table 11   Factors which 108 female respondents from the five union branches believed would encourage participation in union activities

Personal	No.	%	Union	No.	%
Fewer home responsibilities	51	55	Meetings held in more convenient places	34	37
Giving up other activities	15	16	Meetings held at a different time	11	12
Feeling more confident	41	44	Meetings held in work time	59	64
Going to meetings with someone I know	34	37	Make union matters easier to understand	57	62
My husband agreeing to me being active in the union	11	12	Provide child care facilities so I could come to meetings	5	5
Knowing that women can be as competent as men in union affairs	37	40	Make more information available about how unions work	52	56
Male union members giving me a chance to air my views	25	27	Organize more social events	14	15
Having a greater interest in union affairs	52	56	Running education courses	22	24
Nothing would make it easier	10	11	Creating opportunities so women could get together and discuss matters of interest to them	43	46
Other	4	4	Other	3	3

Source: Hear This, Brother: Women Workers and Union Power, ed. Coote, A. and Kellner, P. *New Statesman*, 1981.

Notes to chapter 5

1 Benton, S. *Patterns of Discrimination*, ACTT, 1975.
2 *Negotiating for Equality, Workplace Nurseries, Rights for Working Parents*, Nalgo.
3 *Charter for the Under-Fives*, TUC.
4 Kellner, P. 'The Working Woman: her job, her politics and her union' in *Hear This, Brother: Women Workers and Union Power*, Coote, A. and Kellner, P. (eds), *New Statesman*, 1981.
5 Quoted in Boston, S. *Women Workers and the Trade Union Movement*, Davis Poynter, 1980.
6 Ibid.
7 Land, H. *The Family Wage*, Eleanor Rathbone Memorial Lecture, University of Liverpool, 1979.
8 Kellner, P. 'The Working Woman'.
9 Campbell, B. and Charlton, V. 'Work to Rule — Wages and the Family', in *Red Rag*, 1978.
10 See also Coote, A. 'Powerlessness and how to fight it' in *Hear This, Brother*. New Statesman, 1981.
11 Stageman, J. *Women in Trade Unions*, Hull University, 1980.
12 Fryer, R., Fairclough, A. and Manson, T. *Organization and Change in the National Union of Public Employees*, NUPE, 1974.
13 Harrison, M. *Women in ASTMS*, Warwick University, 1980.
14 Beaton, L. *Shifting Horizons*, Canary Press, 1985, p. 213.
15 Ibid.

6   Learning

How much sex discrimination remained in British schools by the late 1970s and early 1980s? According to three separate surveys, a majority of teachers said that they were opposed to it, that they personally did not engage in such practices, and that they treated students fairly and provided girls and boys with equal educational opportunities.[1] In spite of being treated 'equally', girls and boys continued to perform unequally at school — especially in maths, science and technology. In 1983, for example, girls accounted for 27.9 per cent of O level passes in physics and only 19.6 per cent of A level passes in computer studies. (In 1977 the equivalent figures were 22.7 per cent and 20.9 per cent respectively.) For every girl who enrolled in non-advanced engineering and technology further education courses in 1983, there were 73 boys. In universities the same year, girls accounted for less than half of science undergraduates and just under 10 per cent of undergraduates in engineering and technology.

An attempt to explain this persistent 'under-achievement' was made by Mr R. R. Dale in *Educational Review*. 'A preponderance of androgen is responsible for the relative aggressiveness of the male,' he declared, 'and the reverse for the comparative submissiveness and obedience of the female.' He went on to argue that man's 'natural' aggressiveness gave him a stronger drive towards success.[2] Another prominent educationalist, Mr J. A. Gray, pointed out in a book on girls and science, *The Missing Half*, published in 1981, that experiments on rats had shown a link between 'the presence of testosterone [a male hormone] in the neo-natal period' and spatial ability.[3] This, said Mr Gray, suggested an inherent difference in spatial ability between human females and males. In a nutshell, spatial ability is what a rat has if it is good at dealing with two- and three-dimensional shapes; in humans it is put to use in certain applications of maths and sciences.

So much for the second demand of the women's liberation movement, which called for 'equal education opportunity'. The opportunity was there, apparently, but girls (or girl rats in any case) were naturally disinclined to take advantage of it . . .

As women fought for equality at work and for an equal voice in the unions, they found themselves contending with a social and economic system which had been constructed by men to express and sustain male power. Laws against discrimination could do no more than ruffle

the surface of this system, which designated women as unpaid domestic labourers, and effectively barred them from mainstream union activity and higher-paid, skilled jobs. But women were not simply excluded by force. They learned their place. The training was long and thorough. Lessons were accumulated hour after hour, year after year, and they were assimilated deep into the subconscious. Some of the learning was formal and institutionalized; much of it occurred informally, as ideas were passed on from one generation to the next, through the media, by word of mouth, by signs and gestures.

This was the construction of feminine psychology (to which we refer in chapter 1). It had been central to the process of female subordination. It prepared women for their appointed role and left them poorly qualified to perform any of the roles that men had reserved for themselves. It ensured that women acquired certain kinds of knowledge and skills, but not others, and it equipped them with a sense of what was appropriate and possible for women in general, and thus for themselves. The notion that British education treated girls and boys fairly and equally, and that girls were naturally worse at some things than others, was part of a constant battle, fought on many levels, to pre-empt and quell female resistance to the supremacy of men.

In this chapter we look at institutionalized learning, at the formal and informal ways in which girls and boys have been schooled in their respective roles. In the next, we examine some of the teaching that has gone on outside the education system, through different manifestations of our culture.

Women who were engaged in education — as teachers, students, publishers of school books and so forth — were active in the women's liberation movement from its inception. Women's groups devoted to equality in education, the elimination of sexism from school texts, and the promotion of women's studies, proliferated in the 1970s. A bi-monthly newsletter, *Women in Education*, was launched in Manchester in the autumn of 1973. The same year, the October issue of *Shrew*, the magazine of the London women's liberation workshop, produced the first thorough survey of sexist children's literature.[4] On 23 February 1974, in London, 85 women attended the first national feminist conference on education.

Activities such as these multiplied as the years passed. In themselves they amount to a remarkably intensive and productive educational exercise. As women learned in more detail how the education system operated, so their own policies towards it developed. The very experience of trying to introduce feminist ideas into an allegedly liberal education establishment, and meeting constant rebuffal, was instructive. Early in the 1970s, the emphasis of feminist campaigning was on equal access for girls to the education boys received and equal treatment within it, as well as on proving once and for all (or so it was thought) that girls were not inherently inferior. This was an important step; however, it gradually became evident to more feminists that what girls needed was not simply access to boys' education, but for education to be redefined and transformed, and then to be made available to both sexes on an equal basis, in such a way as to intervene against inequality.

Did we fall or were we pushed?

During the 1960s and 1970s, feminists on both sides of the Atlantic made considerable progress towards a new understanding of sex differences in learning. Thanks to Eleanor Maccoby, Carol Jacklin, Carol Dweck, Alison Kelly and others, evidence was accumulated to counter the arguments of Messrs Dale, Gray and others that males were *naturally* better suited than females to certain academic disciplines.[5] First, the effect of hormonal differences on the mental processes of females and males was shown to be slight — so slight that it could not possibly account for the gap between girls' and boys' performances in science subjects.

Secondly, researchers demonstrated that girls and boys were treated very differently from the moment of birth — in an infinite variety of ways, ranging from the tone of voice with which their first movements were greeted and the sex-typed colours of baby clothes and blankets, to role models presented by adults, older children and media characters, and rewards and punishments meted out for different forms of behaviour. Thus, whatever differences girls and boys may have been born with, these provided no more than a flimsy platform upon which society constructed the powerful ideologies of 'femininity' and 'masculinity'.

Thirdly, experiments in schools showed that with a little extra encouragement, girls could swiftly increase their spatial skills, bringing themselves into line with boys. And fourthly, attention was drawn to evidence that girls displayed superior verbal skills, a fact which suggested that certain testing techniques (such a multiple choice questions) had artificially enhanced the achievements of boys.

While the theorists were hacking their way through the undergrowth of prejudice, the great forest of educational practice remained almost entirely undisturbed. Young women and men continued to emerge from schools and colleges with different skills, qualifications, self-images and aspirations.

The arrival of the Sex Discrimination Act made virtually no impact, except in prompting a few schools to admit girls to 'craft' courses traditionally reserved for boys — and then usually only in exceptional cases, where girls applied for the privilege. In most schools, girls continued to be taught 'home economics', which equipped them for a lifetime of marriage, motherhood and household drudgery, while boys learned woodwork, metalwork and technical drawing, in preparation for skilled employment. For every boy who passed O level cookery in 1983, there were 39 girls; for every girl who passed O level technical drawing, there were 21 boys.

Teaching materials continued to reflect and reinforce traditional sex roles. In the early 1970s, Ladybird Books revamped their 'Peter and Jane' reading scheme, transforming Jane from a passive little cissy in a white dress to a 'modern Miss' in jeans and tee-shirt; however, the new Jane kept her feet firmly on the ground and looked on in admiration as her brother climbed trees and scored goals on the football pitch. Penguin's 'Breakthrough Reading Book', *Things I Can Do* (1970) showed a little girl sweeping with a broom ('I can be good'), while two little boys let rip with the androgen ('I can be very bad. I can fight.'). A book entitled *Tudor Britain*, in the Evans Brothers series of 'History topics and models' (reprinted 1974), contained no female characters at all, except for the 'queen' and the 'master craftsman's wife'; it gave directions for building Elizabethan houses and furniture, but suggested that 'the girls in the class should dress dolls in Tudor costumes.' These were typical examples of texts still used in schools in the 1980s.

Reporting her study of school text books in *Learning to Lose* (1980), Marion Scott noted that women's contribution to production and their role in society were rarely given proper acknowledgement: 'For example, in Third World countries women play a crucial role in farming but this was certainly not the impression which would be gained from the [geography] books'. In some books, said Scott, women were dealt with in a separate section or chapter, where coverage was usually superficial and often ill-informed:

A discussion of women's part in the labour market in the twentieth century . . . ends in an uninspired discussion of fashion (Robson, 1973). I also noticed a tendency to assume that by the twentieth century women had overcome most of the problems of inequality.[6]

Illustrations in science text books rarely featured females — and then only to demonstrate typically 'feminine' pursuits, such as blowing bubbles, mixing puddings and vacuuming. All this was rounded off with a blushing misconception of female sexuality. A typical sex education guide warned boys that they 'should not for a moment think that girls have no sexual physical sensations at all':

These sensations are different from yours in that they tend to be rather vaguely spread throughout the body and seem to most girls just general yearning feelings — rather like looking at a beautiful sunset and wanting to keep it but not knowing how.[7]

In most schools, careers guidance teachers continued to channel girls and boys into traditional sex-typed occupations.

Dale Spender, who was responsible for one of the surveys we reported at the beginning of this chapter, carried out, along with other feminists, extensive research into the way teachers behaved. It was discovered that teachers meted out preferential treatment to boys on an astonishing scale, without realizing that they were doing so. They spent more time talking to boys, and allowed boys to talk more. By taping lessons, Spender found that 'in general . . . teachers spend about two-thirds of their classroom interaction time with boys.' Girls had to wait longer to get the teacher's attention. Teachers were more likely to see boys as individuals and to differentiate between them: 'Whereas some teachers can readily provide the names — and frequently idiosyncratic and biographical details — of the boys they teach, they have difficulty providing the same information on girls.' It was a maxim in teaching to 'begin with the experience of the learner', yet it was usually male, not female, experience that teachers made the subject matter of their lessons. The majority of teachers of both sexes said they preferred to teach boys. They tended to enhance the achievements of boys, while underrating those of girls, and they *expected* boys to do better. Said Spender:

> I have found that there are occasions when the same feature is cause for commendation when thought to be the work of a boy, and cause for penalty when thought to be the work of a girl. Elaboration of presentation is one such feature, with teachers commenting on its excellence when they believe it to be the work of a boy, and dismissing it as superficial and time-wasting when they believe it to be the work of a girl.[8]

Why did teachers say they treated girls and boys equally when they evidently did not? It was not that they were deceived or being deceptive but because they operated in a social system which perceived 'preferential treatment for males as the norm, as the status quo, and therefore find such practices *fair*.' Spender reported that when teachers were asked to try to re-allocate their attention more equally, they found it very hard to give more than 40 per cent of their time to girls, and were then beset by feelings of guilt that they had been treating boys unfairly. 'A teacher who spends more than approximately one third of the time with girl students is perceived by herself and the students as spending too much time with the girls.' On the other hand, when students were told what was happening and encouraged to confront the problem of preferential treatment of males, it was found not only that girls were quite capable of asserting themselves and challenging the boys, but also that the boys themselves were less likely to complain.

A subsequent study suggested that this preferential treatment was not simply due to conscious or unconscious bias on the part of the teacher, but was 'in part attributable to sub-sets of boys engaging in strategies to secure that attention'. It was an interactional process, to which boys contributed (intentionally or otherwise) a sense of what they had already learned about their own power, and what was due to them as the dominant sex.[9]

Only rarely were trainee teachers made aware of these patterns, or encouraged to change their views or behaviour. The subject of sex-typing did not feature in the average teacher-training syllabus and it was not until the mid-1980s that some progress was made in this direction by the Inner London Education Authority (of which more later, p. 199). At a conference in 1980, Margaret Maden, then head of Islington Green comprehensive school, acknowledged that she had been surprised to find, after taping her lessons, that she had been paying considerably more attention to the boys than to the girls.[10] Most members of her profession would not have bothered to find out whether they did or not.

Of course, the intransigence of the education system acted as a brake on progress elsewhere. Educators were busy all the time, *actively* producing and reinforcing attitudes which perpetuated inequality and sexism. Even though there ceased to be any formal bars against women becoming astro-physicists or motor mechanics, schools still managed to ensure that girls were alienated from such 'masculine' occupations.

Liberalism and the patriarchal norm

During the 1970s, British educationalists moved slowly towards a new assessment of 'educational deprivation'. The introduction of comprehensive schooling was based on the premise that all children should have equal opportunity. Steps were taken to compensate for the environmental inequalities suffered by poor, working-class children — by setting up 'Educational Priority Areas' and allocating extra resources to them. It was gradually acknowledged that the 'under-achievement' of West Indian and Asian children was not due to innate inferiority, but to the failure of the education system to take account of their different backgrounds, or to accommodate their special needs. Thus 'multi-cultural' education was unleashed on some schools — a white concept and a mixed blessing, aimed primarily at bringing Black kids up to standards already set by whites.

Meanwhile, no special measures were introduced to help girls, in spite of clear evidence that they consistently 'under-achieved'. By the late 1970s, the idea that girls' talents were 'under-utilized' was gaining some credence, and this was being expressed in terms of 'society's loss' of potential scientists and technologists (in the 1980 Finniston Report on engineering, for example).[11] But there was a marked reluctance to do anything about it — especially anything that involved more than a superficial questioning of sex differences.

The British education system could not be seen as a blank sheet on which changes in society had been noted over the years. As Raymond Williams observed, we inherited an educational model which 'was essentially created in the nineteenth century, following some eighteenth-century models and retaining elements of the mediaeval'. Far from being neutral, it incorporated a set of beliefs which had grown out of those times. All that happened in the twentieth century was that amendments and additions were made where it was necessary to respond to social change and possible to do so without upsetting the basic structure of beliefs.

Large numbers of women had been involved in the development of the education system, but only as practitioners, not as policy-makers or administrators. Research by Eileen Byrne demonstrated that 97 per cent of the people involved in the 'government of education' were male.[12] Thus, the principles on which the system was based were devised by men. Its concerns and disciplines had been selected and designed from a male perspective, and underpinned by the values of a patriarchal culture. By the 1980s they were still widely accepted as objective, immutable and true.

Science, for example, had superseded religion as the fount of truth, and scientific methodology was generally assumed to be intrinsically objective, correct and unchallengeable, even though scientific 'truths' were disproved at regular intervals. Ruth Hubbard pointed out that scientists habitually selected evidence to back up their theories and discounted evidence that threatened them:

> Science . . . is made by a process in which nature is filtered through a coarse-meshed sieve; only items that scientists notice and structure into a cohesive system are retained. Since scientists are rather a small group of people — predominantly male — and mostly economically and socially privileged university-

educated males at that, there is every reason to assume that like all other human productions, science — and biology — reflect the outlook and interest of the producers.[13]

The interests of the white, male middle class were enshrined in the education system and remained undisturbed by gestures to mitigate the disadvantage of working-class and non-white students. The rules of nineteenth-century liberalism were deployed in defence of the status quo. What was normal was 'fair'. Attempts to change what was normal were condemned as 'social engineering' — the Big Bogey of the educational world.

Feminist researchers were finding that the alienation of female students from the study of science was intricately bound up with their sense of themselves as female and their idea of what constitutes 'femininity'.[14] If schools were to make it their business to challenge conventional ideas about female roles and 'femininity', and set about changing the 'masculine' image of science, then the girls' alienation might begin to decrease. However, it remained the dominant view in society that the female was the centre of the family, and that her function of wife and mother took precedence over any other. The men who governed the education system comfortably asserted that it was the duty of schools to *reflect* social values, not to change them. What they overlooked was that schools had been engaged in a massive exercise of social engineering for well over a century.

Eileen Byrne and others argued for a single 'core' curriculum, common to all schools, to be followed by pupils up to a certain age. Their purpose was to stop girls dropping out of subjects such as physics before they had a chance to find out about them.[15] Their opponents raised the spectre of 'Big Brother' imposing drear and dangerous uniformity, and carolled the virtues of 'individual choice'. Likewise, suggestions that sexist books should be banned, or at least energetically discouraged, were met with accusations of 'censorship'. (We return to the censorship debate in the next chapter.)

Liberal individualist arguments such as these were reinforced by another mainstay of the British education system: the man-made concept of professionalism. Teachers know best; their professional status embodied truth and authority; their freedom to conduct themselves as they wished in the classroom was sacrosanct and had to be defended — by employers as well as unions — at (almost) all costs. It certainly took precedence over the freedom of young people to question conventional wisdom and draw their own conclusions as they learned.

Such developments as there were in the seventies and eighties tended towards more rigid control and direction, although these remained under the cloak of liberalism. In her autobiography *The Tamarisk Tree 2*, published in 1980, Dora Russell suggested that there has been a 'glaring shift of values' in education since the 1960s. (To us it seemed more as if dominant values were briefly challenged — and then reasserted.) The ideas that Russell herself pioneered in the 1920s — that education should encourage self-discovery and self-expression in a non-competitive, egalitarian atmosphere — enjoyed a certain popularity in the 1960s, but soon fell back into disrepute with the onset of a new utilitarian stringency. She quoted Shirley Williams, speaking as Education Secretary in 1978 of the need for a 'coordinated approach by schools, teachers and industry'; and a 1976 directive from the EEC urging member states to provide 'appropriate preparation for working life at all stages of general education'. By the mid-1970s, as Russell said, teachers had become 'producers', ex-pupils the 'product': Children in school must therefore be regarded as the 'raw material' to be processed into manufactured articles.'[16] Had Russell's own values prevailed, schools might have responded more readily to new ideas from the women's movement. But a system which was supposed to groom young people to meet the requirements of industry would no doubt refrain from disturbing traditional sex roles. Modern industry was itself an expression of the patriarchal values that prevailed in schools, and it depended as much on the continuing unpaid domestic labour of women as on a steady supply of waged labour.

Cuts in education

The entrenched conservatism of the education system was hardened considerably by the economic recession and the policies of the Thatcher government. After 1974, government expenditure fell in real terms, with the worst cuts beginning in the late 1970s and continuing into the 1980s. When local authorities had their rate support grant from central government cut, education was a major victim, since it usually accounted for the largest slice of the grant. Between 1979 and 1983, the level of spending on education virtually stood still in real terms — but only because Labour-controlled local education authorities defied the government and exceeded their spending targets. The government responded by deciding to 'rate-cap' four Labour LEAs in 1985/6.

Schools found they could not replace essential textbooks which had worn out with use. One million fewer books were purchased by schools in the first three months of 1980 than in the same period in

1979. In spite of a sharp decline in pupil numbers, most education authorities found they could not improve their pupil/teacher ratios. Her Majesty's Inspectors of Schools reported in 1983:

> In some cases the circumstances in which education takes place and the availability of appropriate resources in the right quantity was found to be such as to make worth-while learning well-nigh 'impossible'.

In these straitened circumstances, plans to combat sexism in schools were unlikely to flourish.

Adult and further education were hard hit by spending cuts, too. These provided the main opportunities for women to make good their inadequate schooling, or prepare themselves to re-enter employment after raising their families. One of the first victims of local education cuts were discretionary grants, usually awarded to students in the arts, and in the para-medical and social services fields. (According to the Equal Opportunities Commission, the latter two fields were 'areas to which mature women are attracted and where they can use the expertise gained in the rearing of children and the care of families generally'.[17]) College crèche facilities were another early target, putting post-school education out of reach of many women with pre-school-age children.

As conditions worsened, schools felt they were hard pressed to maintain existing educational standards; the prospect of change became associated with deterioration rather than with progress, and this generally inhibited criticism of the status quo.

Beyond 'equal opportunity'

If schools were to stop reproducing sexist attitudes, and seriously set about promoting equal opportunity, they would need to do a lot more than to buy in new teaching materials and instruct their teachers in the evils of sex discrimination. Children arrived in school with attitudes and aspirations ready-formed; and throughout their formative years they continued to learn, from their families, from the media and from their day-to-day experience, that women and men had different functions and different aptitudes.

There were conflicting theories about how children adopted sex roles. 'Social learning' theories suggested that they were moulded by external forces: they acted in a manner which was socially acceptable in order to obtain rewards and avoid punishment. 'Cognitive' theories suggested they were more active participants in the process: once they had established a sense of themselves as female or male, they selected forms of behaviour which seemed appropriate to their gender. A more complex interpretation was presented by Rosie Walden and Valerie Walkerdine, whose research found that 'girls struggle to achieve a femininity which possesses the characteristics which are the targets of teachers' pejorative evaluations.'[18]

Ideas about how to intervene on girls' behalf varied accordingly. Alison Kelly pointed out in *The Missing Half* that if the 'cognitive theorists were correct, then it would not help simply to offer children alternative forms of behaviour ("Girls can be scientists; so can boys") as though sex distinctions were unimportant'.

> To attempt to eliminate sex distinctions may make children more conformist to those distinctions they can establish, and may even cause them anxiety over their gender roles.[19]

It followed that children should be brought to realize as soon as possible that it was not their behaviour which made them into boys and girls, but their physical (genital) formation.

> They should also be encouraged to see cross-sextyped behaviour as not only pleasing to adults around them, but as competent behaviour for their own sex. This suggests that, in the short term at least, we should be aiming not towards a neutral or sex-free conception of behaviour, but towards reversed or dual-sex typing.[20]

Kelly confirmed that the principle of affirmative — or 'positive' — action (which we have already explored in the context of employment) should be applied to education. Walden and Walkerdine, however, were critical of 'a model of rational change through the provision of information', which operated by changing stereotyped images, for example, and allowing greater curriculum choice. They argued that no amount of information would produce change by itself, and could even provoke resistance:

> Often, when approaches to change which use stereotyping fail, the automatic response is to argue that, after all, girls' femininity is 'natural' and therefore unchangeable . . . We would support interventions which attempt to work *with* the contradictory positions in which girls (and their female teachers) are placed. We would support approaches which examine girls' own fears and feelings as well as their performance.[21]

In addition, schools would have to change their own patterns of employment, which reproduced within almost every school in the country a standard pattern of inequality. Eighty-nine per cent of infant and primary school teachers were female. Male teachers predominated in secondary schools and in senior posts — more often than not teaching maths, science and other typically 'masculine' subjects. More than three-quarters of all female teachers were in the lowest-paid jobs (scales 1 and 2), compared with less than half of all male teachers.[22] Among non-teaching staff, the division of labour was even more pronounced, with male caretakers in positions of authority over teams of female cleaners and 'dinner ladies'.

Few children would identify this as sex discrimination. Nevertheless, they all learned from it. They gained the impression, for instance, that caring and servicing were functions of the female and that authority was ultimately vested in the male. For most of them, this reinforced what they had already learnt at home. In particular, the exclusively female regime in primary schools was likely to have a far-reaching effect on female and male patterns of learning. As Elinor Kelly explained in her contribution to *The Missing Half*, primary school teachers frequently demanded obedience, silence, passivity and conformity from their pupils — all features of traditional female behaviour:

> Many boys as a result of this process, which risks alienating them from school, are actually being trained to a degree of independence and initiative which encourages analytic thinking later in life. By contrast the girls, by conforming to femininity, are discouraged from originality and experimentation.[23]

Any serious attempt to help girls (and boys) realize their full potential would have to include a concerted attack on job segregation in schools; and this would need to be carried through to all levels of the education hierarchy. Ideally, a positive action programme in employment, combined with intervention strategies in teaching, was needed throughout the country. And neither would succeed unless the need for positive action — and all that that entailed — became a central part of the curriculum in teacher training.

A feminist model of education

Yet it was not enough simply to adjust the education system in order to enable girls and boys to compete on equal terms. While the aims and methods of teaching continued to reflect patriarchal values, the education system continued to stifle the development of children and sustain male control. The component parts of the system needed to be dismantled and rebuilt. Schools were intensely hierarchical institutions; learning took place in a stratified order, and in an atmosphere of competition, in which students strove towards standards of 'achievement' built on male-defined criteria. A girl who dropped out of physics was defined as an 'under-achiever'; yet she might have rejected it for valid reasons — for instance, because it seemed to her to bear no relation to everyday life. Her striving to relate science to humanity was an 'achievement' of another kind, just as a boy's view that cooking was 'cissy', or his lack of interest in language, was another form of 'under-achievement'. Educational values needed to be redefined.

Teaching had become a process by which 'experts' handed down information to the uninitiated. As Dale Spender suggested in *Learning to Lose*, a feminist approach would be quite different:

> If students deny their own experience and accept that of the experts then hierarchical structures are strengthened on many fronts: if, however, they do not accept the judgement of experts, then a novel form of interaction . . . can emerge. This has become the basis of understanding within consciousness-raising groups.[24]

A feminist model of education would be non-hierarchical and non-competitive, because it sought to change, rather than reproduce the present structure of society. 'In order to reproduce the social hierarchical order,' said Spender, 'a fundamental educational principle demands that most people fail — sooner or later.' Standards of excellence by which success and failure were judged were not objective, but had 'their origins in a culturally specific view of the world':

> Feminist educational ventures have 'proven' by the cooperation they have structured and fostered that the concepts winners and losers are meaningless and useless. If the traditional educational system is as inadequate as some critics claim and most evidence suggests, then there is an alternative model, which stresses cooperation, available. Such a model will not, however, reproduce the existing divisions and inequalities within society.[25]

It would be an uphill battle to redefine and reorganize education along such lines. A recognition that it was necessary to do so had developed in the course of the 1970s, as feminists experienced the resistance of the education system to their demands, and observed the limits of each small, piecemeal advance they were able to make. But their achievements should not be underestimated. Slowly, they were changing attitudes and broadening their influence. Many of their ideas became current in education circles even if they are not accepted. By the mid-1980s, most secondary school girls had access to information about women's changing role in society, even if they still saw marriage and motherhood as their main goals. These developments carried a momentum of their own, which led to a clearer perception of what needed to be done: that was to refurbish the image of 'free education' (tarnished by a reaction to the 'alternative' culture of the 1960s), reassert the values of Dora Russell, and go beyond that to create a model of learning which actively contributed to the liberation of women.

Experiments in positive action

The first major research project which set out to investigate attitudes and intervene to change them was 'Girls into Science and Technology', funded by the Equal Opportunities Commission and the Social Science Research Council. In a number of Manchester schools, the researchers scrutinized the developing attitudes of girls and boys to gender roles and to particular craft and science subjects, and employed positive tactics to improve girls' take-up of science and craft subjects. Their strategies included making science more relevant to the experience of girls; accentuating skills which girls had already developed; playing down aspects of science which they found especially difficult; presenting more female role models; discouraging opting out; and experimenting with single-sex sessions where it seemed that girls were inhibited by the presence of boys. It was hoped that after four years there would be tangible results — in the form of more girls opting for science and technology courses. It appeared that while the GIST interventions reduced pupils' general gender stereotyped attitudes, they had little effect on gender differences in attitudes to particular subjects; nor did they increase girls' take-up of science and craft subjects.[26] Almost certainly, though, the GIST project had an important (and unquantifiable) 'ripple' effect, raising awareness and interest far beyond the Manchester schools used for the research.[27] The lack of practical results could not prove that intervention didn't work, only that it didn't have the immediate impact the researchers had originally anticipated, and that different kinds of intervention might need to be adopted.

On quite a different scale, a major initiative was launched by the Inner London Education Authority in the early 1980s. A one-day conference on girls' education was held in March 1982, attended by representatives of women's organizations, teachers, ILEA members, inspectors and officers. Discussion focussed on the school curriculum, on career education, on 'external influences' and on the attitudes of men and boys. The conclusions drawn from these discussions were reflected in a report from a working party of the school inspectorate, *Equal Opportunities for Girls and Boys*. The report contained 98 detailed recommendations on every stage of education and teacher training. For example, it suggested ways of ensuring that schools implemented the Authority's policy by:

- encouraging equality of treatment and opportunity and avoiding sex-stereotyping in all teaching and play activities;
- using positive action where needed to ensure equal participation in all activities;
- reviewing all books and teaching materials and their curriculum content;
- avoiding timetabling arrangements which could affect choice along sexist lines and by regular monitoring of options available;
- making a senior member of staff responsible for monitoring equal opportunities; and by establishing guidelines for good practice;
- involving parents as well as all teaching and non-teaching staff in providing equal opportunities.[28]

It also recommended 'positive training' for all adults concerned with the community of the school; resource centres, in-service training and compulsory components on equal opportunities in initial teacher training courses.

ILEA set up an Equal Opportunities Unit, appointed an inspector with special responsibility for promoting equal opportunities for girls and boys, and established a 'Girls' Education Fund' to provide grants for school-based projects designed to promote sex equality. Then, in January 1985, ILEA published a formal 'Anti-Sexist Statement'. In her introduction, Frances Morrell, Leader of the Authority, paid tribute to those who had inspired ILEA's new commitment to equal opportunity:

> For many years, individual teachers, youth workers and others have been promoting and developing an approach to education, which promotes equal opportunities for girls and women by producing materials, arguing for changes and fighting for resources. These individuals have been in the main feminists, whose commitment to equal opportunities in education has often been pursued in the face of resentment and hostility . . . The Authority owes a great debt to their persistence, imagination

and commitment. Their collective pressure over the years has undoubtedly succeeded in shifting the official perception of sex equality from a fringe element within education to part of the definition of mainstream good educational practice . . .[29]

Thus ILEA became one of the first public bodies to launch a major policy initiative (in an area not specifically designated for women) that was consciously and overtly inspired by the women's liberation movement. The Anti-Sexist Statement, with its supporting arguments, was quite a sophisticated document. It stressed that 'passive support for equal opportunities' was not sufficient, and that it was necessary to fight actively against sexism. It linked the drive against sexism with ILEA's anti-racist policy, in such a way that the two ran in tandem without fudging the difference between them. It recognized that the problem was not simply one of the girls 'under-achieving', but was also one of girls' achievements being undervalued:

It is important to avoid the trap of . . . defining sexism as a girls' or women's problem, which can be overcome if only *they* adjust. Anti-sexism does not make girls and women just like boys and men. It does, however, ensure that women have access to the power, decision-making and earning capacities currently enjoyed by men. Equally important, it can also ensure that female experiences and perspectives are used to examine, and if necessary redefine, what constitutes power, skill and achievement.[30]

Perhaps most important, ILEA was prepared to back its policy with financial resources, to staff its Equal Opportunities Unit, to provide materials and training courses, and to fund a variety of school-based projects. Unlike the GIST project, which had a fixed time-limit (four years) and a specific target (getting girls into science and technology), ILEA apparently aimed at transforming the basis of education in the long term. By the mid-1980s, it was too early to assess the effectiveness of the policy but the Authority had, at least, done some useful groundwork. It had begun to create conditions for change — not only in London but also — as the idea spread — in other education authorities.

Notes to chapter 6

1   Clarricoates, K. 'Dinosaurs in the Classroom' in *Women's Studies International Quarterly*, 1(4), 1978; Spender, D. *Men's Education — Women's View*, Writers and Readers, 1981; Stanworth, M. *Schooling and Gender: A Study of Sexual Divisions in the Classroom*, Women's Research and Resources Centre, 1981.

2   Dale, R. R. 'Education and Sex Roles' in *Educational Review*, vol. 22(3).

3   Gray, J. A. 'A Biological Basis for Difference in Achievement' in Kelly, A. (ed.) *The Missing Half*, Manchester University Press, 1981.

4   Women's Liberation Workshop, *Shrew*, vol. 5(4), October 1973.

5   See Dweck, C. S. and Coetz, T. E. 'Attributions and Learned Helplessness' in Harvey, Ickes and Kidd (eds) *New Directions in Attribution Research*, vol. 2, Halsted, New York, 1978; Dweck, C. S. 'Learned Helplessness and Legative Evaluation', *Educator*, vol. 19(2), 1977; Fennema, E. 'Influences of Selected Cognitive, Affective and Educational Variables on Sex-Related Differences in Mathematics Learning and Studying', *Women and Mathematics: Research Perspectives for Change*, NIE Papers in Education and Work, no. 8, 1977; Fennema, E. and Sherman, J. A. 'Sex-Related Differences in Mathematics Achievement and Related Factors: A Further Study', *Journal for Research in Mathematics Education*, no. 9, 1978; Fox, L. H., Fennema, E. and Sherman, J. *Women and Mathematics: Research for Change*, NIE Papers in Education and Work, no. 8, Washington D.C. National Institute of Education, 1978; Maccoby, E. E. and Jacklin, C. N. *The Psychology of Sex Differences*, Stanford University Press, 1974.

6   Scott, M. 'Teach Her a Lesson: Sexist Curriculum in Patriarchal Education' in Spender, D. and Sarah, E. (eds) *Learning to Lose*, The Women's Press, 1980.

7   Jackson, S. 'Girls and Sexual Knowledge', in *Learning to Lose*.

8   Spender, S. Unpublished paper delivered to a seminar in Copenhagen in 1981.

9   French, Jane and Peter 'Gender Imbalances in the Primary Classroom: An Interactional Account'. Unpublished paper.

10   Speech at National Housewives' Register conference, St Albans, October 1980.

11   *Engineering Our Future*, report of the Committee of Inquiry into the engineering profession (Chairman Sir Montague Finniston), Cmnd. 7794, HMSO, January 1980.

12   Byrne, E. *Women and Education*, Tavistock, 1978.

13   Hubbard, R. 'The Emperor Does Not Wear Any Clothes: The Impact of Feminism on Biology' in Spender (ed.) *Men's Studies Modified: The Impact of Feminism on the Academic Disciplines*, Pergamon Press, 1981.

14   See Kelly, *The Missing Half*.

15   Byrne, E. *Working the System: A Strategy for Action*, paper presented to the Feminist Summer School, Bradford, obtainable from Women's Research and Resources Centre, 190 Upper Street, London N1.

16 Russell, D. *The Tamarisk Tree 2*, Virago, 1980.
17 EOC *The Effects of the Government's Financial Policy on Educational Provision*, 1979, from EOC, Overseas House, Quay Street, Manchester M3.
18 Walden, R. and Walkerdine, V. 'Girls and Mathematics', *Bedford Way Papers*, 24, 1985.
19 Kelly, A. 'Science Achievement as an Aspect of Sex Roles' in *The Missing Half*.
20 Ibid.
21 Walden, R. and Walkerdine, V. 'Girls and Mathematics'.
22 *Promotion and the Woman Teacher*, a National Union of Teachers Research Project, published jointly with the EOC, 1980.
23 Kelly, E. 'Socialisation in Patriarchal Society' in *The Missing Half*. See also Maccoby, E. 'Women's Intellect', in Hinton, K. (ed.) *Women and Science*, SISCON project.
24 Spender, D. 'Educational Institutions: Where Cooperation is called Cheating' in *Learning to Lose*.
25 Ibid.
26 Equal Opportunities Commission, *Ninth Annual Report*, HMSO, 1984.
27 Whyte, J. *Girls into Science and Technology*, Routledge & Kegan Paul, 1986.
28 Inner London Education Authority, *Education for Girls: What Do You Think?*, 1983.
29 Inner London Education Authority, *Race, Sex and Class. 6. A Policy for Equality: Sex*, 1985.
30 Ibid.

7 Culture

Looking beyond the institutions of formal learning at the tangled and uncomfortable relationship between the female sex and the media, it is possible to detect a pattern similar to that in education. Men controlled the means of expression — from the press and broadcasting, to advertising, film, publishing and even criticism — by occupying dominant positions within them, and by using the power this gave them to convey the ideas and values of a patriarchal order. Women were excluded from the formulation of policy and the execution of business. An intensive war was being waged against women, to degrade them as human beings, to deny their ideas and achievements, and to suppress their own perspectives on the world.

The women's liberation movement exerted some influence on the media from the early 1970s, and encountered some formidable resistance. It took more than a decade for feminists to measure the extent of male control, to assess the nature of it, and to work out strategies for overcoming it. The process was still under way at the time of writing.

To illustrate some of the general problems, we focus on an area we both know well: the news media. The treatment of women in this field was a target of feminist campaigning from the early 1970s. *Women's Report* kept up an exasperated commentary on Fleet Street's excesses in its column, 'Thanks and a free consciousness-raising session to . . .'. *Spare Rib* did the same in its regular feature 'Tooth 'n Nail'. In July 1973, *Women's Report* offered 'Thanks . . .'

> And seventeen blows with a wooden Japanese abacus to Robert Lacey, intrepid editor of the Sunday Times Look! Section. Only the redoubtable Mr Lacey could decide that the way to break down sexist barriers against female mathematicians was to (wait for it girls) HOLD A BEAUTY CONTEST TO FIND THE PRETTIEST MATHS STUDENT!!![1]

Even the redoubtable *Sunday Times* could not stoop to that by the end of the 1970s. Nor could the *Daily Mirror* report a debate between Margaret Thatcher and Barbara Castle as it did on 1 October 1974,

SOMEWHERE ON FLEET STREET.. THE THINKING MAN'S DAILY.

when political editor Terence Lancaster informed his readers: 'Redhead took on honey-blonde yesterday.'

In October 1975, the National Union of Journalists' Equality Working Party (which had close links with the women's movement) published its first edition of *Images of Women*,[2] subtitled 'guidelines for promoting equality through journalism.' The guidelines pointed to different ways in which women were ignored, trivialized and stereotyped in newspaper reporting, and suggested alternatives where possible. They dealt with grammatical conventions, such as the use of 'he' and 'his' to describe human beings of either sex:

> This . . . gives an impression that women are absent, silent, or simply less important than men . . . 'they', 'their', 'them' and 's/he' can often be used instead . . .

They urged journalists to avoid 'the gratuitous display of women's bodies' as well as 'clichéd references to "dumb blondes", "nagging-wives", "the fair sex", the "little woman"', and 'sex-typing of jobs, except where reference is specifically to men'. The tone of the first edition was cautious, even defensive. 'Some of you may laugh,' said the Working Party's introduction:

> Some may find our suggestions odd, unnecessary or extreme. But these guidelines are a serious attempt to show how everyday words and phrases . . . help to form and perpetuate a discriminatory, patronizing attitude to women.

By January 1977, the second edition displayed a more confident tone, reflecting a shift in public attitudes. This time, the introduction cited clause 10 of the NUJ's Code of Conduct:

> A journalist shall not originate material which encourages discrimination on grounds of race, colour, creed, gender or sexual orientation.

Later this was extended to read: 'A journalist shall only mention a person's race, colour, creed, illegitimacy, marital status (or lack of it), gender, sexual orientation or disability if this information is strictly relevant. A journalist shall neither originate nor process material which encourages discrimination on any of the above-mentioned grounds.' In theory NUJ members who broke the Code could, at the end of a long complaints procedure, be fined or suspended from membership — and suspension could mean the loss of their jobs.

The efforts of the Equality Working Party (which became the Equality Council in 1982) and the influence of the Code of Conduct, together with campaigns outside the NUJ by groups such as Women in Media, helped to raise the consciousness of many individual journalists — and, in some newspapers, even altered the style of reporting. However, the guidelines continued to be widely ignored. By the mid-1980s, only a handful of complaints under Clause 10 had been pursued, and most of these had failed to reach any conclusion. Yet there had been no shortage of material that encouraged discrimination on the grounds laid out in the Code of Conduct. The NUJ established an Ethics Council in 1986, to promote the Code and receive complaints from the public as well as from NUJ members; it was designed to deal with breaches of the Code through conciliation and education, rather than by disciplining individuals.

It was not easy to engage in ideological battle with Britain's newspaper barons. Their well-paid editors and columnists leapt into print with warnings of *Pravda*-style conformity or McCarthy-style witch hunts, at the first hint of any effort to interfere with their glorious 'free' press — just as in education, the vocabulary of liberalism was used to defend the status quo, and the dominant assumption was that what was normal was fair. When it came to the crunch, journalists — like teachers — usually defended the 'professional' autonomy of their colleagues. Well-meaning, socialist-inclined men who had jobs on the *Mirror* and the *Daily Star*, and local papers which modelled themselves on Fleet Street's popular tabloids, would shake their heads and shrug their shoulders earnestly: of course they loathed the tits and bums and the trivialization, but what could they *do*? They had to earn a living, after all. The less well-meaning ones accused their feminist colleagues of 'losing their sense of humour', or 'getting things out of perspective'. Many women in journalism were induced to share these attitudes.

By the end of the 1970s, the national press had its own equivalent to *Women's Report*'s 'Thanks . . .' column: 'Naked Ape', every Monday in the *Guardian*. That was progress of a kind. But 'Naked Ape' provided regular reminders that even the *Guardian* itself could print horrors like this, by a Peter Dobereiner, in November 1980, on the subject of a golfing holiday:

On no account consider taking along wives or mistresses. Women can be admirable creatures in their own way but the female who is content to pull your trolley for 36 holes a day without speaking, without deserting to the shops, without wanting to pinch the car for excursions to the beach, without complaining about the service and without generally fouling up a golf trip has not been born.[3]

And what the *Guardian* could still do, the *Daily Express* could do still better. When pilot Judith Chisholm completed a round-the-world-flight in November 1980, the *Express* revealed that underneath her canvas, fur-lined jump suit, 'the blonde' had been wearing 'a pair of frilly black pants and bra'.[4]

Mercifully, though, such crude and offensive reporting had by the 1980s become less common — doubtless due to the influence of the women's movement. In the 'quality' newspapers, it was less common to find women referred to purely in terms of their 'vital statistics' or the colour of their hair, or even (gratuitously) in terms of the number of children they had. Clichés like these would still appear in the tabloids, but less frequently. Newspapers learned to report feminist issues without any mention of 'bra-burning', although most found new ways of distorting or trivializing such matters. The women at Greenham Common came in for a particularly nasty brand of misogynist reporting, which characterized them as dirty, violent scroungers who were probably in the pay of Moscow. Worse still, the homophobic press invariably described them as lesbians in such a way as to denigrate all lesbians and, by association, all of the Greenham women.

Women's pages occasionally gave extended and sympathetic coverage to campaigns of the women's movement. However, these were often printed alongside soft-porn photographs of women in underwear, thinly disguised as 'fashion reports'. And the *Sun* and the *Star* showed no signs of reconsidering their policy of printing huge pictures of 'lovelies', 'dazzlers', 'sizzlers' and 'tantalizers' — allegedly servicing a daily need of their readers. Indeed, it was during the 1970s that the idea of a 'newspaper' became inseparable, in the minds of many millions of British readers, from the idea of naked female breasts. (See p. 221 for further discussion of this issue.)

The male perspective on news values

The traditional values of news reporting, and the balance of power between women and men in the newspaper and broadcasting industries, remained almost entirely unchanged. In a sense, this had implications as dangerous as the tabloid newspapers' unashamed policy of exploitation. For while the tabloids were hard at work building false images of women, they were joined by the rest of the news media in a combined attempt to keep real women out of sight altogether.

A spot check on two national 'quality' newspapers on 14 July 1986 revealed that the news pages of the *Guardian* included reports of 182 named individuals, of whom 21 were female. The *Daily Telegraph* on the same day featured 30 women among 193 named individuals. (Names occurring twice or more were counted only once for each story in which they appeared; business, sport and feature pages were not included.) Of the 144 news stories carried by the two newspapers,

15 made no mention of human characters at all; 19 were all or predominantly about women; 36 gave equal coverage to women and men; and 78 were all or predominantly about men. But there were signs of a slight increase in reports on women when these figures were compared with a similar survey carried out in 1981 for the first edition of *Sweet Freedom*: *Guardian*: 19 women out of 237 named individuals; *Sunday Times*: 14 out of 181. 109 news stories carried by both news-papers: 3 made no mention of human characters; 4 were all or predominantly about women; 12 gave equal coverage to women and men; 90 were all or predominantly about men.

The pattern remained typical of news coverage throughout the media — especially in the 'serious' newspapers, and on radio and television. A 1980 study of one local station, Radio Nottingham, found that men's voices occupied seven-eighths of the two-and-a-half hour morning news programme.[5] Women were featured more regularly in the 'popular' press, but these were almost invariably 'wives', 'mums', 'brides', 'mistresses', victims of crime or misfortune, TV stars, or 'sizzlers'. Reports were written from a male perspective, almost obliterating female experience. When a woman, a man and two children died together in a caravan fire in January 1981, the *Daily Mirror* told its readers: 'An RAF officer and his family were found dead . . .' The *Daily Telegraph* in July 1986 reported that Doncaster council had offered to purchase the house of a local family who complained about noise from the Civic Theatre: 'Mr Philip Young, 32, a personnel officer, his wife and 18-month-old daughter live next to the theatre . . .'

Women as autonomous human beings rarely featured in the news media. Their multi-faceted experience as women (individually and collectively) was seldom reported at all — and almost never from a female perspective.

A standard response to criticism of this kind was that women didn't get mentioned as often as men because they didn't do as many important things. That was true enough — if one accepted the pre-vailing definition of what was important. Where did that definition come from? Who decided what was 'news' and what was not; what was a 'hard' story and what was a 'soft' one; what was central and what was peripheral? Who set the standards by which certain everyday events, but not others, became 'human interest stories', worthy of public attention?

The prevailing values of the news media did not fall from heaven into the laps of editors: they were manufactured by successive generations of white, middle-class newspapermen, who handed them on, intact, to their counterparts in radio and television. So solidly were these values established that it became hard to imagine any other way of conveying information. Most journalists sincerely believed that there was such a thing as 'objective' or 'unbiased' reporting, when in fact the most they could do was to communicate events as fairly as possible, from their own point of view, according to the journalistic conventions they had learnt, and in a manner which was acceptable to their editors. For their readers, listeners and viewers, the product of journalism *became the real world* — even though it was nothing more than one cockeyed version of it.[6]

More women gradually became involved in journalism but they were never able to set the pace, or imprint their character on the news industry. They always lacked the power to challenge the dominant view of what mattered, or develop a tradition of reporting which consistently interpreted events through their eyes.

To make it in journalism, women had to strive to be as good as men, according to male standards. This was not easy, and so women remained in a minority in journalism, occupying the lowest-paid and least influential jobs. A 1977 survey by the National Union of Journalists found that among 314 journalists employed on seven newspapers in the North of England, 279 were men and 35 were women. All editors and deputies were male; all sports specialists were male; all photographers but one were male; there were 69 male and 11 female sub-editors; 42 male and eight female features/specialist writers; and 99 male and 23 female reporters. That pattern had changed very little by the 1980s. A more detailed national survey, published in 1982, looked at how women were employed on newspapers throughout the country. It revealed that women accounted for 97.2 per cent of women's page and fashion writers, 35.7 per cent of general news reporters, 29 per cent of feature writers and 25 per cent of design and art staff; yet only 8.8 per cent of senior editorial staff were women, only 5.2 per cent of industrial and financial specialists, 2.3 per cent of photographers and 1.6 per cent of sports writers. A far higher proportion of all female newspaper journalists was to be found in general news reporting (70.6 per cent, compared with 36.2 per cent of males) — and consequently far fewer women were dispersed through other occupational categories. The report concluded:

> This finding would seem to confirm the belief that many women have about their career prospects in the newspaper press — that they are predominantly taken on to fill low status 'dogsbody' roles, and have a much lower chance of career progress than males.[7]

Our spot check on the *Guardian* and the *Daily Telegraph* in 1986 found a total of 5 female and 77 male by-lines.

With the arrival of the women's movement came a growing awareness that certain items were being left off the news agenda. The media made minor adjustments but managed all the while to identify women as a sub-category of a male universe — both in the style of reporting and in the allocation of space. Thus, a news report would inform us that 'many people, including women' were injured in an accident. News editors felt free to insist that one story about women was quite enough for one day. Television executives might arrange for an occasional documentary on women, or even a series. But they retained a clear view that programmes about women had their special place and could be over-done. Endless programmes about men were, of course, quite acceptable.

In some newspapers, items about women were published mainly in the 'women's pages' — which robbed them of their status as news, implied that they were of no import to men, and identified them as stories of special rather than general interest. There were debates within the women's movement about whether or not women's pages should be abolished. Without them, most newspapers would not have raised feminist issues at all, and a wide range of important events would have gone unreported. It was broadly agreed that the best strategy was not to call for an abolition of women's pages, but to extend them, raise their status, and at the same time put pressure on editors to hire more women in the newsroom and to redefine editorial priorities. Here, as in education and other fields of employment, 'positive action' policies were badly needed.

In December 1980, Jeremy Isaacs, new chief of television's fourth channel, gave the first indication of some willingness among the media's power élite to alter the standard approach. He announced in an interview with the *Guardian*'s then women's editor Liz Forgan:

> We have got Panorama and World In Action on our screens already. I don't see why my weekly current affairs programme shouldn't be produced by women. I would like to get women to make such a programme which depends for its success on its ability to interest viewers, not to promote a cause, but which has the added bonus that it comes from people who are standing at a different angle to the universe from the male sex. It may therefore come up with a different set of attitudes, a different mix, a different set of priorities.[8]

Isaacs followed this up by hiring Liz Forgan as a commissioning editor for Channel Four. And, indeed, the channel did include in its first year's schedule a weekly current affairs programme made by women. The slot was divided between two companies, both run by women, who produced alternating series, *Broadside* and *20/20*. While *Broadside* concentrated mainly on what might be called 'women's issues', and often took an overtly feminist line, *20/20* produced a series which resembled such mainstream programmes as *World In Action*, but with female reporters and more frequent references to a 'women's angle'. Between them, they gave women an unprecedented voice in television's current affairs coverage; they produced some programmes that were excellent and innovative, as well, of course, as some that were not. They provided invaluable experience for a number of women who would not otherwise have got that kind of career break.

A year, however, was not long enough for these women to build the necessary confidence and skills, and to challenge and change the deeply entrenched traditions that men had built up in the area. After the first year, neither company had its commission renewed. *Broadside* fell apart after bitter internal rows. Gambles Milne, producers of *20/20*, went on to make further documentaries for Channel Four, but by this time had employed male producers and had ceased to be identified as a source of women's programming. Channel Four hired a special commissioning editor for Multicultural Programmes, but not one for women. The year 1986 saw the start of a new current affairs series made by an independent company run by Blacks and Asians — a welcome development. But it seemed that the channel's 'experiment' with women's current affairs was over. Its defenders would argue that women were integrated into the mainstream — that there were women working on other current affairs series, and that women's issues were covered by the channel's general output of documentary programmes. Both claims had some truth to them, but it was also true that Channel Four failed to give women sufficient power to redefine priorities, to find new meanings in events, to transform the conventions of programme-making — in effect, to reinvent current affairs.

Clear parallels could be drawn between the intransigence of the news media and that of the education system. In both cases, men held a monopoly of power. In both cases, men *claimed* the exclusive right to define what was objective and real, defending this with quasi-liberal appeals against 'censorship'. In both cases, too, feminist analysis developed along similar lines: beginning with calls for equal opportunity and a challenge to sexist content, it led to an acknowledge-ment that the whole system needed to be unravelled and re-knit into a new shape, which would allow no less than equal room for the experience and needs of women.

Channel Four almost certainly had a better record than the BBC or the big ITV companies, who did not make even token gestures towards women's programming. Inevitably, though, the new channel came in for greater scrutiny because early statements by its chief executive had encouraged greater expectations.

The Women's Film, Television and Video Network — a feminist organization — asked Channel Four's commissioning editors what proportion of their budgets were taken up by independent productions 'involving women'. (This was not a demanding criterion: a production with only one female presenter or producer would count.) In eight out of ten of the commissioning areas, the proportion had declined: News and Current Affairs, for example, had gone down from 20 to 11.02 per cent between 1984 and 1986; Independent Film and Video from 47.8 to 27.7 per cent; Education from 44 to 27 per cent; Light Entertainment from 17.1 to 12.9 per cent. In Arts there had been a slight increase. Only in Documentaries had the proportion increased substantially, from 22 to 50.13 per cent. The WFTVN also looked at Channel Four's internal employment policy and found that in 1985, while women made up 57 per cent of the channel's workforce, only 8 per cent of its 144 female employees held senior management posts and 28 per cent held middle-management posts. Of the 119 male employees, 28 per cent were in senior management and 49 per cent in middle management.[9]

From the early 1970s, feminist groups such as Women in Media and (later) the Women's Film and Broadcasting Lobby campaigned to get women better represented at all levels within the media industries. A certain amount of lobbying was also done by the media unions. ACTT and the NUJ each took on a full-time Equality Officer. By the mid-1980s the emphasis of lobbying had changed — away from fighting just for women, towards a broader approach. This was reflected in the NUJ's Campaign for Real People, launched in 1985, to combat all forms of stereotyping in the media — not just sexism, but racism and stereotyping of lesbians, gay men and people with disabilities. The WFTVN was set up in 1981 with a grant from Channel Four and later received funds from the GLC, as well as inspiration from the GLC's initiatives in developing equal opportunities policies. Its aims included not only building a national organized network of women, but also challenging 'hierarchies based on class, race or sex' and making positive efforts to counteract racism and discrimination against people with disabilities.

By the mid-1980s more women wielded influence in the media industries than in the early 1970s, although their numbers were still small. Some had absorbed male values on their way to the top, while others retained a female perspective but were isolated and could not make an impact. There was, by this time, a sprinkling of female technicians, whose numbers were beginning to grow, albeit at a slow pace. There remained a conspicuous absence of Black and Asian women. And there was still no sign of women being present in sufficient numbers to change the unwritten rules of cultural production.

Screen images

In television drama, attempts were made to co-opt the 'liberated' woman and enlist her in the male cause. Women were allowed to appear strong and independent without seeming freakish, but only on certain conditions. They had to be women who wanted to get on in a man's world. The strongest examples — *Policewoman, Juliet Bravo, Charlie's Angels* — were all busy enforcing rather than challenging the system which oppressed women in general. As Helen Baehr noted in her critique, 'The "Liberated Woman" in Television Drama', these are strong women 'reconstructed into redeemers of the patriarchy'.[10]

Some profound and sympathetic portrayals of women's *problems* occasionally surfaced in slots such as BBC's *Play for Today*, but as Baehr demonstrated, plays which addressed themselves directly to women's liberation usually descended into parody and ended by reaffirming the values and conventions with which feminism took issue.

Underlining all this was what the former newscaster Anna Ford referred to as 'body fascism'. For a woman to make it on TV, her body and her demeanour had to conform to a rigid set of standards. Men could be short, fat, ageing, bald, have misshapen noses and crooked teeth, warts, specs and straggly beards — and still spend hours in front of television cameras. A woman who was neither young, slim nor even-featured would be lucky to get a bit-part as a victim, a villain or a lunatic.

The double standard in women's magazines

Elsewhere in the media, the ideas of the women's movement met with an intriguing range of responses. Most magazines for teenage girls ignored it altogether. A typical episode in *Jackie*, taken from the issue of 31 January 1981, tells the story of schoolgirl Caroline, who misbehaved in a science lesson and got detention for it: leaving school

late, she met a good-looking boy at the bus stop . . . almost lost him to
Beastly Barbara . . . but triumphed in the end.

I wondered fleetingly whether there was a school rule about
being kissed in school uniform. If so, Daniel and I had just
broken it.

This was rich with lessons for the reader of *Jackie*. Science was alien,
and opposed to the ideal of femininity; rejection of it brought the
reward of a romantic encounter. A girl was not expected to be
interested in academic attainment: finding a boy/man to love was the
main thing, and in this quest, other females represented the enemy.

Meanwhile, some of the grown-up glossies were performing
precarious balancing acts. *Cosmopolitan*, launched in Britain in 1973,
initially based its character (as did the highly successful US original)
upon a corruption of the 'liberated' idea. It peddled the image of a
'free' and 'independent' woman, whose freedom and independence
were expressed almost exclusively through her (hetero)sexuality, and
who toiled endlessly towards that goal. *Cosmo* woman laboured day
and night to conjure from each separate part of her body, and from
every nook and cranny of her psyche, enough sexual allure and
energy to get her next man. For this she needed not only a steady flow
of advice on how to have 'relationships', but also a formidable array of
artificial aids — hair colourings and conditioners, anti-spot cleansers,
bust conditioning creams, de-flaking lotions, moisturizers, hypo-
allergenic skin tonics, deodorant tampons, electric muscle-toners,
depilatories, rouges, vitamins, mud-packs, breath fresheners, quick-
set nail repairers and cosmetic tooth-whiteners — all advertised in
Cosmo. Yet at the same time, *Cosmo* woman was intelligent, she went
out to work, and she was open to new ideas.[11] As the years passed and
the influence of the women's movement spread, the features on sex,
beauty, fashion, men and relationships were mixed more and more
with straightforward feminist writing. One issue in July 1986 included
articles on how to get a 'dental facelift', whether divorced men were
'worth the emotional investment', the secrets of 'good sex in bad
relationships', and how to get a date. ('If a girl walks round with her
head down, blinkered, as if she's dead from the ankles up, then she is
neither attractive nor approachable . . .') Yet it managed to combine
all this, and lots more of the same, with advertising *Cosmo* courses on
computer skills, public speaking and setting up a business, with an
item on men-only clubs which argued for extending the Sex
Discrimination Act, and with a distinctly feminist account of rape
trials ('. . . as long as our courts continue to put the rape victim on trial

. . . many women will still lack the courage to bring their rapists to justice.')

Having built a commercial success on a corruption of feminist ideology, *Cosmo* then tried to incorporate the real thing — and this was at least partly a result of feminists being involved editorially, in the planning and production of features for the magazine. However, the need for advertising revenue dictated that the magazine had to remain contradictory, pushing images of femininity that feminism was bound to reject. Other women's magazines were caught in a similar dilemma.

New and old games for advertisers

Advertisers went to town on the 'liberated' theme — using it to sell everything from kitchen units to jeans and perfume. In her book *Decoding Advertisements*, Judith Williamson explained how advertisements became 'hollowed-out systems of meaning' by referring to things — and people — in a way which robbed them of their own significance; this, in turn, affected the way we experienced our own lives and those of others. The people we saw in advertisements didn't 'do half the things *we* do: they don't sweat, neither do they go to work and produce.'

> Most of our lives are the 'unlived' lives of advertisements, the underside of their world picture. So this reality becomes almost literally unreal — sublimated, unconscious. As a teenager, for example, it is really possible to live almost totally in a sort of dream world of magazine stories and images, and this seems *more real than reality.*[12]

The dream world of advertisements had a stronger pull because the dream was a shared one. Even though people's real experiences were often very similar, these seemed isolated, while the impact of the media and social images was a truly universal experience.

Not only could advertisements take the meaning out of 'ideas, systems and phenomena in society', but they did so all the more successfully when they were dealing with something which was hostile to advertising itself. The women's movement, said Williamson,

> has provided advertisements, one of the most sexist fields of communication there is, with a vast amount of material which actually enhances their sexist stance. There is a television ad for an aftershave 'Censored' where a woman is beating a man at

chess. But then he puts on the aftershave and she is so wildly attracted to him that she leaps up, knocking over the chess board where she had him check-mated, and jumps on him like a wild animal. Now, far from the effect being to make us realize how inadequate the man is if he cannot stand being beaten at chess by a woman, her 'cool' and intelligence and obviously 'liberated' image are in fact made to devalue themselves: because the point is that *even* a cool, 'dominating' woman, an intellectual threat to a man, even she will become little more than an animal, and a captivated one, on smelling 'Censored' cologne for men. It is obviously more of an achievement to win over a 'liberated' woman than one who was submissive all along. Many ads are based on this sort of line: 'she's liberated *but . . .*'[13]

Meanwhile, the *un*liberated woman and uninverted messages of female passivity, dependence and sexual availability, still came in very handy for the advertisers. Naked women continued to be draped over hi-fi equipment; cars were portrayed as 'mistresses' and 'seductresses'. Advertisers had their own non-statutory code, administered by the Advertising Standards Authority: ads were meant to be 'legal, decent, honest and truthful' and they were not supposed to cause 'grave or widespread offence' in the light of 'prevailing standards of decency and propriety'. Many feminists took the view that a lot of ads fell short of the mark, and complained regularly to the ASA.

In 1980, the Authority looked into 37 complaints based on allegations that ads were offensive to women. Of these, 29 were dismissed. Typical of those not upheld was an advertisement for Kawasaki motorbikes, which pictured a woman's legs and feet (in stiletto-heeled shoes) with her knickers around her ankles. The caption read: 'We'll never let you down'. The Authority 'deplored the advertiser's low level of taste' but 'considered the advertisement was unlikely to cause grave or widespread offence'.[14] Also unsuccessful was a complaint from the Equal Opportunities Commission and the TUC against an insurance advertisement depicting a scantily clad woman. The headline warned: 'Guard Your Goods . . . A Lorry Load of Goods — Like a Beautiful Girl — Will Vanish If You Don't Look After It.' The ad was intended for lorry drivers and the ASA 'did not believe that it would be offensive to those who received it'.[15] Another 'scantily dressed female' was featured in an ad for cut-price carpets, under the caption: 'My business is on the floor'. The complaint was dismissed on the ground that the ad 'had been appearing from time to time and neither the publishers nor advertisers had received any previous complaints'.[16]

By the end of 1980, the Authority was prepared to admit that 'the portrayal of women in advertising was a matter of concern'. About a tenth of the 6,500 complaints it received (on average) each year related to advertisements thought to be distasteful, indecent or in some other way offensive — and more than 40 per cent of those were complaints about the way women were depicted. Rather than responding directly to the complaints it received, however, the ASA decided to carry out a survey to find out whether they reflected public opinion generally. In April 1982, it was able to report that the survey did not 'reveal widespread dissatisfaction about advertisements' among the women questioned; where offence was caused, it was not 'sufficiently widely shared . . . to be declared offensive in terms of the British Code of Advertising Practice'; and there was no need for new rules to be introduced.

While the ASA took no action, the Women's Committee of the Greater London Council succeeded in getting London Transport to adopt a code against sexism, covering ads on tubes and buses. It included the following conditions:

- [Ads would not be accepted if they were] likely to offend the general travelling public, or offend ethnic, religious or other major groups, on account of the nature of the product or service being advertised, the wording or design of the advertisement or inference contained, or the possibility of its defacement.

- Advertising content should not depict, refer to or imply violence specifically against women.

- Advertising which seeks to depict women as sex objects is unacceptable.

An exhibition on sexist advertising was subsequently mounted by the GLC Women's Committee, where it was reported that 'the number of sexist ads did drop significantly after the new conditions were introduced. Even though some have crept back, the very violent and brutal ones appear to be a thing of the past.' The anti-sexist specifications were retained by London Regional Transport, which took over London Transport after the abolition of the GLC. The Women's Media Action Group, a feminist collective which had been influential in raising the issue of sexist ads with the GLC Women's Committee, went on to launch, in 1986, a new campaign for a code against sexism, directed at the Advertising Standards Authority.

Pornography and censorship

On the question of pornography, the women's movement found itself trapped between the libertarian devil and the deep, Tory-blue sea. There was broad agreement among feminists that pornography was exploitative and undesirable; but what should be done about it? They didn't want to be pressed into service with the Mary Whitehouse brigade or the authoritarian right, who stood for a moral and political order which denied the very essence of feminism. Their more natural allies, perhaps, were the libertarians, with whom they shared anti-authoritarian instincts. But the libertarians were more interested in fighting censorship — at all costs — than in tackling the problems of women's oppression; and in any case they had difficulty understanding that 'women's liberation' was not the same as that fine old 1960s notion of 'sexual liberation'. The libertarians were in favour of photographs of women's genitals (or whatever) being published and displayed, as long as the women didn't mind being photographed and nobody was physically hurt in the process.

Standing aloof from the libertarians, but with one foot bravely in their camp, were the liberals. They weren't exactly in favour of pornography, but they weren't against it either, provided it was kept in its proper place. The liberals were the driving force behind the Williams Committee, which reported in 1980, with a recommendation to lift censorship on pornography, but to restrict sales to specially designated places and to ban any public display.[17] Unlike Whitehouse and the authoritarian right, they did not believe that pornography induced violence or other anti-social acts, and maintained that it was a relatively insignificant problem.

Many feminists saw a link between pornography and anti-social behaviour, but had quite a different idea from Mary Whitehouse of what kinds of behaviour were anti-social. And there were different opinions within the women's movement over what should be done about it. Some radical and revolutionary feminists took a pro-censorship position:

> When we became, or were brought up as 'liberals', 'no censorship' was one of the ideals we learnt . . . To launch an attack on porn we have to make a stand, to say that it is not the god-given right of any ruling group with money and power to plaster the environment with their sadistic, dehumanising and degrading view of a less powerful section of society. If this is to advocate censorship, then that is what we must do.[18]

These women cited the Race Relations Act, which made it a legal offence to incite racial hatred, as a useful precedent. It should also be an offence to incite sexual hatred, they argued. Other feminists disagreed. Legislation, in their view, would mean extending the power of the patriarchal state, and relying for enforcement on the police and the courts, whose past record in protecting women's interests had inspired little confidence. 'It is one thing to campaign against the ways in which the state is an instrument of male power, it is quite another to call upon it to ban, censor and proscribe in our name.'[19]

Then there was the question of how much would be achieved by simply sweeping pornography off the streets and into the sex shops; what mattered was changing attitudes and transforming the power structure of which pornography was an expression. And in this context, where did pornography begin and end? Wasn't a pin-up in a newspaper, or a salacious report of a sex crime, as degrading to women and as likely to condone and encourage oppressive male behaviour as the technicolour detail of a hard-porn magazine?

At the same time, there were disagreements within the women's movement about the nature and effect of images representing women. An artist who had her sculptures damaged by feminists in Leeds wrote to the magazine *Spare Rib*:

> We must have the courage to depict ourselves honestly in our art. If this is forbidden, we tread a dangerous and ever narrowing path. The field will be left to pornography. If some women are to have dictatorial jurisdiction over other women, I have misunderstood the whole aim of the movement.[20]

It was difficult to see a way out of the dilemma for feminists who opposed censorship *and* pornography. Susanne Kappeler wrote in 1986 of the need to reclaim the feminist critique of pornography from the argument about censorship. The important debate, she said, had been silenced, because anyone who spoke out against pornography was condemned for being in favour of censorship and against freedom of expression. Yet what was the point of free expression, if it did not safeguard a critique of pornography? What mattered was not passing laws, but exposing the political role of pornography:

> It has emerged and thrived in a patriarchal culture in which men have social, political and economic supremacy. The power arising from this social organisation has enabled them to suppress the ideas and opinions of other groups without the help of a political instrument, such as state censorship. The instrument of suppression lies in the control of the access to the market and to the 'ideological state apparatuses' where ideas and opinions are disseminated.

Women, typically, have not been involved in the production of ideas, just as black people or the poor have not. Pornography, as the expression of a particular set of ideas and opinions, centres on women, a class of people who have no access to the means of production of ideas. They are the *objects* about whom the ideas expressed are formed.[21]

As Kappeler pointed out, what women found objectionable in pornography, they had learnt to accept in 'high' art and literature: 'the systematic objectification of women in the interest of the exclusive subjectification of men'. The message was not about sex, but about subjugation.

The question remained — what was the most effective response? To raise awareness among women and men was vital, of course, but it did not tackle the immediate offence of publication and display. Was legal censorship appropriate in any circumstances? What other strategies could be employed?

As feminist analysis developed to the point where it no longer recognized a clear distinction between 'pornography' and other representations of women, the question of how to respond became all the more complex. It ceased to be a problem about specific products; it became a struggle against all forms of sexism.

Clare Short MP put forward a Private Member's Bill in 1986 to ban the 'Page Three' nudes from newspapers. Her Indecent Displays (Newspapers) Bill sought to make it an offence 'to publish in newspapers pictures of naked or partially naked women in sexually provocative poses'. It was partly intended to draw attention to the hypocrisy of men like Winston Churchill MP, who was trying at the time to extend censorship from print to broadcasting with an amendment to the Obscene Publications Act 1959.[22] Ms Short took the view that definitions of obscenity were too narrow if they failed to take account of the daily diet of female flesh served up by the tabloids. Her Bill received considerable support from women in general and from many feminists. It was opposed by the civil liberties lobby, which included some feminists, on the grounds that any extension of censorship was undesirable. They found themselves uncomfortably allied with male MPs from both sides of the House, who simply liked the tits and bums. The Bill never made it to the statute books, but provoked an intense debate. It showed just how widespread was the sense of outrage among women about the way they were represented in the press. It also demonstrated that, if definitions of pornography could not be confined, and if pornography were to be met with censorship, then the scope for censorship was without bounds.

Another possible strategy was to apply pressure through the political mechanisms of local authorities — just as the Women's Committee of the GLC had in the case of London Transport advertising. When the Labour Party won control of Brighton, following the local authority elections of May 1986, the new council banned a film called *9½ Weeks*, about a woman's fantasy of rape, following protests from women's groups. Banning a film turned out to be far more controversial than banning advertisements. It led to the local women's movement (and, by implication, all feminists) being charged with authoritarianism: 'Both [Ronald] Reagan and modern day feminists are attempting to deal by suppression with what they, rightly or wrongly, find abhorrent,' wrote one male opponent. 'The only way for the supposedly correct position to achieve supremacy is through co-ercion . . .'[23] Such arguments were inevitable, and were as likely to come from other feminists as from men. The advantage of this strategy of campaigning through local authorities was that it ensured that the debate remained in the political arena and allowed change to occur with the ebb and flow of local opinion. Legislation passed through Parliament took on a greater permanency and shifted responsibility away from the political process, into the courts.

The Campaign for Press and Broadcasting Freedom, which had a strong feminist element and set up a Women's Group in 1984, launched an investigation into media sexism and censorship, which included a questionnaire sent out to women's groups. It asked whether they would favour state legislation, other than existing laws such as the Obscene Publications Act. If so, 'What form should it take? Who should be responsible for drafting it? Who should enforce it? What should be the penalties attached? What effect would you hope it would have?' Results were expected in late 1986.

Meanwhile, a popular response among feminists continued to be direct action — fly-posting advertisements in the underground, spray-painting hoardings, showering blue-movie screens with paint-filled eggs and marching through Soho and other red-light districts to insist on the right to walk safely at night. Protests of this kind enabled them to express their anger and assert their power, without recourse to the male-dominated forces of social control.

Women Against Violence Against Women

In November 1980 Leeds University student Jacqueline Hill became the thirteenth victim of the man known as the 'Yorkshire Ripper'. Women in that part of the country had been living in fear of the 'Ripper' for at least three years — and the fear escalated with each new, brutal, ritualized attack. They had been advised not to go out alone at night by the gallant detectives of the 'Ripper Squad', who let it be known that 'no woman was safe' until the man was caught. Leeds had long been the centre of much feminist activity and now there was an explosion of rage. Women were furious that yet another murder had left the police wildly guessing. They were angry that their freedom had been further curtailed, while men were still at liberty to walk the streets. They were angry at the way in which the 'Ripper' story had been turned into gruesome entertainment by the media, while rapes, assaults and murders that were regularly committed by other men received so little attention. They were angry that newsagents and booksellers were all the while doing a roaring trade in sadistic pornography, and — perhaps most sickening of all — that the latest cult in films just happened to be one which gloried in violent attacks on helpless women. As Sally Vincent wrote at the time, there was a new trick to these films, designed to overcome audience immunity to all the 'mad axemen' movies that had gone before. They were shot entirely from the angle of the axeman himself, 'thus indicating, with no trouble at all, the universality of man as Ripper' and inviting the audience to 'identify and empathize with the killer':

> We see and hear the women in the film as though we were eavesdropping on them. We peep through the undergrowth to overhear their irreverent girlish chatter about men and male sexuality. We tippy-toe up behind them while they amuse themselves heartlessly upon the altar of masculine passion. And while we spy on them we learn they are naughty girls. They have no proper respect for men. They are *asking for it*! The audience is both voyeur and aggressor.[24]

On 27 November 1980, ten days after the death of Jacqueline Hill, 500 women attended a Sexual Violence Conference in Leeds. This brought together a number of feminist groups who had been organizing against male violence since the 'Reclaim the Night' marches of 1977 — including Women Against Rape and Feminists Against Sexual Terrorism — and they became linked in a new campaign, Women Against Violence Against Women. It marked an important stage in the development of feminist politics, in that different forms of male violence were identified as part of the same system of dominance and control. Some women in Leeds wrote this report of the conference in *Spare Rib*:

We agreed that as women gain greater independence, so men use more sexual violence to maintain their position of power over women. Sexual harassment at work undermines our confidence; rape and sexual assault keep us off the streets; sexual abuse in the family cripples our lives and teaches us our place in the world. Obscene phone calls, pornography, rape in marriage (unrecognized in law), gynaecological practice which violates women's bodies, prostitution which exploits women and shows how perverted men are — we discussed them all. [We] planned campaigns to combat male violence and asserted every woman's right to defend herself against it.[25]

There continued to be disagreements among feminists about the universality of male violence. Some asserted that all men were potential 'Rippers'; others saw violence more as a symptom of the political relationship between women and men than as something inherent in all men. All would agree that women were invariably the victims and men the aggressors.

At the Leeds conference, women planned action in cities throughout the country. In London, thirty feminists occupied the offices of the *Sun* newspaper to protest at its use of rape stories for titillation. In Leeds itself, a local 'Porn Group' leafleted outside a suburban 'family' newsagent stocking pornographic magazines and video cassettes, and collected more than 600 signatures from women passing by. Elsewhere, women demonstrated outside cinemas, glued up the locks of sex shop doors, smashed windows of strip clubs, daubed angry messages on walls ('MEN off the streets'), and marched to 'Reclaim the Night'. For once, the attention of the general public was focussed not on crimes against women as isolated, entertaining horrors, but on the anger of women at the systematic nature of those crimes. The political point surfaced briefly, then sank out of public view as the tide of complacency swept in again. Police told the press: 'These women are dangerous.' There were fifty arrests.

It seemed that only by continuing — and probably only by escalating — direct action of this kind could women sustain a distinctly *feminist* attack on sexual terror and pornography. Predictably, they were vilified and punished by the press and the police for 'anti-social' behaviour, while liberals clicked their tongues in disapproval and blamed them for whipping up a double-edged backlash, repressive on one side, misogynist on the other.

Art and literature

The clash between the women's movement and the liberal/libertarian left over 'cultural' matters was crucial. For if feminists were to cause any noticeable shift in public attitudes, they would need to win support at that point of the political spectrum. Liberal opposition was at its most robust in the area of art and literature — and its most glamorous moment was probably when Norman Mailer took Kate Millet to task for being irreverent about D. H. Lawrence.[26]

Feminists were not generally in favour of banning books, except possibly when it came to early reading schemes and some non-literary texts which formed a compulsory part of the school syllabus. However, they developed their own modes of literary and art criticism, which they regularly employed. And they made it clear that they wanted to encourage the writing and publishing of new non-sexist books, especially for children. The liberals were not simply offended by the idea that certain kinds of books might be encouraged or discouraged (although that was bad enough in their view); what they could not swallow was the suggestion that any work of art — any act of creative imagination — could *be sexist*. They often respond immoderately, throwing words like 'censorship' around in an indiscriminate fashion.

A staunch exponent of the liberal line was the writer and literary editor David Caute, who in November 1980 launched an attack on publishers' guidelines for children's books. A working party had been set up under the auspices of the Equal Opportunities Commission to devise non-sexist guidelines for the UK, following the example of American publishing houses, notably McGraw-Hill. The guidelines would be advisory and voluntary. They would not dictate what could or could not be published, but merely suggested an additional criterion by which works could be judged. They were intended (rather like the NUJ guidelines for journalism) to break some of the old habits of a man-made tradition, and to encourage a new approach. For example, the US McGraw-Hill guidelines counselled:

NO: Pioneers moved West, taking their wives and children with them.
YES: Pioneer men and women moved West, taking their children with them.

Caute (writing in the *New Statesman*) saw the whole thing as a sinister threat. He was especially worried that the working party was 'not confining its reforming zeal to picture books for toddlers':

> it will also pass broad judgement on how to evaluate works of history, fiction and poetry (including the 'classics' of literature) offered to teenagers in secondary schools.[27]

Literature was sacred, apparently; it was above this kind of analysis. Any attempt to evaluate it from a feminist perspective smacked (in Caute's view) of totalitarianism: 'What we don't need is a new generation of Young Pioneers spoon-fed in one-dimensional virtue.' What made David Caute (and other liberals) act like jealous lovers when feminists took an interest in their favourite Muse? Were they not suffering from the same syndrome as the journalists who believed in the objectivity of their own news values, or the teachers who thought they had a hot-line to the truth?

In the past, men alone had the power to define what was 'literature' and what was 'art'. Knowing no other order, they assumed that *their* view was *the* view; and that only from their position — at the centre of the cultural universe — could truth and beauty properly be judged. Feminists were trying to assert a woman-centred view alongside theirs, perhaps with the hope of eventually producing a synthesis of the two. But since men believed so deeply and unconsciously in their right to occupy the central space, these efforts of women could only be perceived as an invasion, an attack on their 'freedom' to impose their meanings on the rest of the world.

From their privileged perspective — and only from there — it looked as though there was quite enough scope for everyone. Feeling themselves unjustly nudged out of place, men found it appropriate (in an 'artistic' context as well as in education and journalism) to invoke the defensive vocabulary of liberalism: 'Social engineering' . . . 'threats to press freedom' . . . 'censorship' . . . 'Young Pioneers'. They would tar the women's movement with the brush of totalitarianism to quell an uprising against their own cultural empire.

Dislodging the emperor was a necessary goal for women, of course, but it was not the final one. Ultimately, they had to imagine and create in their own, free space and on their own terms. It was one thing to rediscover and reassess the forgotten or undervalued traditions of 'women's art' — a job done well by the feminist publishers Virago, for example. It was another thing to encourage new female authorship and to fight for greater female control of the media. And it was yet another to explore the possibilities of creative expression from a position of real strength.

Aesthetic values needed to be redefined. What were the differences between 'women's art' and 'feminist art'? Could, or should, a line be drawn between 'art' and 'politics'? How important was it for women to foster collective, rather than individualistic, techniques and modes of expression? Debates on these and other questions gathered momentum within the women's movement in the late 1970s and early 1980s.[28]

The process of redefinition was inextricably linked with the process of changing the political and social role of women. In the visual arts, for instance, women had to find new ways of seeing and representing themselves: in the past these had always been dictated by the status of women as objects of the male gaze — and this set up within the female a contradiction between her sense of herself as subject, and her sense of herself as object. As John Berger observed:

> A woman must continually watch herself . . . From earliest childhood she has been taught and persuaded to survey herself continually. And so she comes to consider the surveyed and surveyor within her as two constituent yet always distinct elements of her identity as a woman.[29]

Women and men saw themselves and each other in such profoundly different ways that women could not reclaim themselves in art simply by appropriating and adapting artistic modes developed by men. For example, there was no women's equivalent to the female nude — whether in High Art or in 'dirty' magazines. How could female sexuality be expressed in female terms? There was no female equivalent to the male tradition of erotic art. How, for that matter, could *femaleness* be expressed in female terms?

In 1980 Judy Chicago's massive exhibition, *The Dinner Party*, opened in San Francisco. It consisted of a triangular dinner table, with thirty-nine place settings. The table was vast, almost fifty feet along each side. Each place setting was about three and a half feet wide and consisted of an embroidered runner, cutlery, a goblet and a plate, whose different designs evoked the characteristics of a famous woman. They ranged from pre-Christian goddesses to Sappho, Boadicea, Susan B. Anthony and Virginia Woolf. The main feature of each setting was the 'plate', which was, in fact, a painted ceramic sculpture, based on the shape of a vagina. The names of 999 other women, also well-known, were inscribed on the 'heritage floor' in the centre of the triangle. The exhibition was completed with banners designed for the entrance, documentation of the five years' work by Chicago and her team of helpers, and a display of congratulatory telegrams from feminist artists all over the world. Its goal, said Chicago, was 'to ensure that women's achievements become a permanent part of our culture'. It was magnificent, flamboyant, confident. It was widely acclaimed. Many women reported that they found it profoundly moving and inspiring — breathtaking in its scale. When was there ever such a work by women, for women, celebrating femaleness? Others criticized it. For instance, the feminist sociologist Michèle Barrett questioned the 'dictatorial zeal' with which Chicago commanded the whole operation; her satisfaction in winning respect from, rather than challenging, the established institutions of the 'art world'; her ranking of women in hierarchical order and her use of vaginal imagery.[30] Disagreements over *The Dinner Party* did not reach a swift resolution. The exhibition and the critiques that followed were part of a process of change which was vital to the development of feminism as a political force.

By the mid-1980s, women were involved — on an unprecedented scale — in writing and publishing, in music, theatre, cabaret, film- and video-making. Some of it was mainstream, some of it marginal: the margins were bulging with activity. Much of it was feminist; some, arguably, was not — and the argument itself belonged to the process. A new feminist criticism was being developed, that not only explored what women were doing, but also set about considering popular culture, so that soap opera and other aspects of TV and radio, as well as music, art and design, were examined from a female perspective. Thus, cultural production became an increasingly important vehicle for the ideas of the women's liberation movement, as the movement itself — in an organizational sense — fragmented and dispersed.

Notes to chapter 7

1   *Women's Report*, vol. 1(5), July/August 1973.
2   *Images of Women: Guidelines for Promoting Equality in Journalism*, from NUJ, Acorn House, 314 Grays Inn Road, London WC1.
3   *Guardian*, 24 November 1980.
4   *Guardian*, 15 December 1980.
5   Lee, N. *One Eighth of a Say, The Place of Women on BBC Radio Nottingham's Morning News Programme*, from 118 Workshop, 118 Mansfield Road, Nottingham.
6   See also Coote, A. 'The Meaning of Man-talk', *New Statesman*, 2 January 1981, followed by Page, B. 'Sense and Sensibility', *New Statesman*, 9 January 1981, and Letters, *New Statesman*, 16 January 1981. See also Spender, D. *Man-Made Language*, Routledge & Kegan Paul, 1980.
7   Smith, R. *Women in the Press*, NUJ, March 1982.
8   *Guardian*, 1 December 1980.
9   *Channel Four Television and Equal Opportunities*, 1985, from Women's Film, Television and Video Network, 79 Wardour Street, London W1V 3PH.
10 Baehr, H. 'The "Liberated Woman" in Television Drama', *Women's Studies International Quarterly* vol. 3(1), 1980.
11 See also Coward, R. '"Sexual Liberation" and the Family' *m/f* 1, 1978.
12 Williamson, J. *Decoding Advertisements*, Marion Boyars, 1978.
13 Ibid.
14 ASA Case Report 68.
15 ASA Case Report 67.
16 Ibid., p. 5.
17 Report of the Committee on Obscenity and Film Censorship, HMSO, November 1979, Cmnd. 7772.
18 Rhodes, D. and McNeill, S. *Women Against Violence Against Women*, Onlywomen Press, 1985.
19 Loach, L. 'Censorship on a Short Fuse', *New Socialist*, June 1986.
20 Ibid.
21 Kappeler, S. 'Censored: The Porn Debate', *New Socialist*, March 1986.
22 *Indecent Displays (Newspapers)*, HMSO, March 1986; *Obscene Publications (Protection of Children, etc.) (Amendment)*, HMSO, March 1986.
23 Miles, P. 'Shock! Labour Bans Film', *New Statesman*, 11 July 1986.
24 Vincent, S. 'Women who ask for it', *New Statesman*, 19/26 December 1980.
25 *Spare Rib* 103, February 1981.
26 Mailer, N. *Prisoner of Sex*, Little and Brown, 1971.
27 Caute, D. 'No more firemen', *New Statesman*, 14 November 1980.
28 For example, see Coward, R. 'Are women's novels feminists' novels?', *Feminist Review* 5, 1980; and Barrett, M. 'Feminism and Cultural Politics' ed. Brunt, R. and Rowan, C. Lawrence & Wishart, 1982.
29 Berger, J. *Ways of Seeing*, Penguin 1972. See also Tickner, L. 'The Body Politic: Female Sexuality and Women Artists since 1970', *Art History*, vol. 1(2), June 1978.
30 Barrett, M. 'Feminism and the Definition of Cultural Politics' in *Feminism, Culture and Politics*.

8 Sex

In *The Dinner Party*, the idea of female power was conveyed through the imagery of female sexuality. As the artist Judy Chicago was suggesting, the relationship between power and sex lay at the heart of the struggle for women's liberation.* What distinguished this from other political movements was that women were beginning to confront the physical and psychological aspects of human life and to challenge conventional notions about sexuality. One such notion was that sexuality belonged to the private sphere which floated free of economic and political affairs. Another was that it was simply an expression of economic relations, which would be altered as a result of economic transition.

The issue of sexuality loomed large in the women's liberation movement. It was at the centre of some of the fiercest disagreements, while at the same time lending an important new dimension to feminist politics. In this chapter we look at some of the ways in which feminists challenged the meanings imposed upon sexuality by a patriarchal society; at how they developed political perspectives on sex, power, pleasure, and the construction of human identities.

Recipe for a heterosexual woman

Feminists had to contend with some powerful myths. One was that sex was a purely natural phenomenon and therefore apolitical (like the multiplication of cells, perhaps, or the fall of snow in winter). Another was that the natural expression of sexuality was a narrowly defined convention of heterosexual practice. A third was that a woman's sense of her own sexuality was natural, rather than something constructed by social and economic factors.

In fact, there was very little that was 'natural' about a woman's sense of her own sexuality. Consider the teenage girl who was taught the 'facts of life' in a school biology lesson, tracing cross-sectional diagrams of ovaries and testicles, with the penis fitting neatly into the vagina

---

* For those readers who have turned straight to the chapter on sex, you'll find our description of *The Dinner Party* at the end of the previous chapter.

and the spermatozoa zooming up to fertilize the egg. She might add this wisdom to her personal experience of the monthly 'curse' or 'period': a time of physical discomfort and fear of being betrayed by shameful smells and stains. Her favourite magazines would urge her to paint her face and shave her legs and trap her breasts in polyester lace — for these, not the natural features of her body, were the signs of 'femininity'. She would learn to smile and speak softly, listen and flatter, dress with care and move with grace — because this, rather than her own spontaneity, would make her desirable. She would be drilled in the protocols of physical interaction: all that kissing and cuddling and feeling and fondling led inexorably to the Sexual Act, when the biology lesson sprang triumphantly into 3-D. She learnt that 'losing her virginity' was one of the most significant moments of her life. *This* was sex!

How often she performed the Sexual Act, by what means and with whom, thereafter determined whether she was 'bad' or 'good', a 'tart' or a 'tease', 'easy' or 'frigid'. She was not expected to initiate the action, except with such subtlety that the other imagined it was *his* idea. He would 'give it to her' while she 'gave herself'. There was even a danger that he might force it upon her whether she liked it or not, and there were ways in which she could be deemed to be 'asking for it' that were beyond her immediate control. To guide her through the snakepit, she had the catechism of Romantic Love, which taught that one day, if she followed the correct path, she would find the right man, to whom she could belong and so live happily ever after. The sources of her own erotic pleasure remained an awkward half-secret.

Of course, if she were not careful, she could find herself pregnant and pressed into motherhood and marriage before she was entirely sure that she had found true happiness with Mr Right. She might find, whether by dint of her economic dependence, or for fear of physical force, that she was obliged to remain with a man she did not especially like. If, as she performed the Sexual Act in the marital bed at more or less regular intervals, she managed to express herself freely without shame or fear and enjoy herself to the full, when she herself wanted to, it would be *in spite* of what she had learned, not because of it. She wasn't born to practise sexuality this way, nor did she achieve it; she had it thrust upon her.

If the lessons of her formative years failed to bring her physical or psychic fulfilment, they achieved a lot else instead. They endowed her with a sense of herself which had a profound effect on the way she led her daily life — how she perceived and behaved towards men, women and children; her domestic arrangements; how she sought and gained affirmation; what she dared — and dared not — do. And (as we have seen in earlier chapters) the patterns of everyday life greatly influenced the kind of work women did, their economic strength and weakness and their capacity to shape their own future.

The modern myth of homosexuality

Modern mythology presented not only a distorted account of 'natural' sexuality, but also a rigid picture of different types of people: there were heterosexual people and there were homosexual/lesbian people.

There were arguments about how these apparently opposite conditions were arrived at, but everyone was supposedly identified as one or the other. 'She *is* a lesbian . . . she or he *is* a heterosexual . . .' (Even people who fell between the categories were defined in those terms: 'She *is* bisexual.' Such a person could be neither heterosexual or lesbian *because* she was a bit of both.)

The idea was, in fact, relatively recent. Lilian Faderman showed in her book *Surpassing the Love of Men*, that passionate friendship between women — whether or not it involved physical love — had in the past been accepted as something (many) women did, and had not always been seen as a threat to the social fabric. This was partly because the idea of women having an autonomous sex drive was, until recently, beyond the grasp of those who had power to make and enforce society's rules. But it was also because that kind of behaviour, if it did occur, was not seen as defining the subject as a certain type of person, nor as undermining her femininity:

> There were in several eras and places many instances of women who were known to engage in lesbian sex, and they did so with impunity. As long as they appeared feminine their sexual behaviour would be viewed as an activity which women indulged in when men were unavailable or as an apprenticeship or appetite whetter to heterosexual sex. But if one or both of the pair demanded masculine privileges, the illusion of lesbianism as *faute de mieux* behaviour was destroyed. At the base it was not the sexual aspect of lesbianism as much as the attempted usurpation of male prerogative by women who behaved like men that many societies appeared to find most disturbing.[1]

The idea of what homosexuality stood for had changed dramatically over the last century. Laws against male homosexual acts, passed in the last quarter of the nineteenth century, were intended to prohibit non-reproductive sex. The concern was with sinful behaviour, which belonged to the panoply of sin to which we were all heir. It was quite distinct from the twentieth-century concern, which was about a certain type of person, and which was based on the more recent idea that homosexuality was an 'unfortunate condition'.

As Jeffrey Weeks argued in *The Making of the Modern Homosexual*, the 1957 Wolfenden Report represented the final acceptance of this definition, which signalled a homosexual *type* — that is, one who suffered from the condition.[2] The definition was extended to lesbians as it gradually came to be recognized that women were capable of erotic pleasure, and of actively seeking that pleasure. It served to regulate the distribution of sexual practice, for if homosexuality was something that only 'homosexuals' or 'lesbians' did, it followed that others did not. Thus the construction of a homosexual identity entailed the construction of a heterosexual identity, and served to police the behaviour of all people.

Lie back and think of England

Unfortunately for many women, conventional heterosexual practice wasn't always a great deal of fun. As an erotic sensation, penetration of the vagina by the penis could leave a lot to be desired. The incidence and intensity of the female orgasm preoccupied sex reformers and psychoanalysts throughout the twentieth century. Its low incidence or non-occurrence ('frigidity') was identified as a major cause of sexual maladjustment and marital breakdown. Some investigators reckoned that it signalled lack of consent, others imagined it was part of the feminine condition. Generally, it was assumed that female orgasm was something that did not occur spontaneously: it had to be *mobilized*.

All the major studies of female orgasm recorded mammoth failure rates. In the 1930s, Dickinson and Beam reported in the first substantial analysis of marriage, *A Thousand Marriages*, that in nearly two-thirds of their cases, sex was not satisfactory.[3] Hannah and Abraham Stone, popular sex counsellors of the post-war era, said in their widely read book *A Marriage Manual* that failure to reach orgasm was 'the most frequent sexual complaint among women who are otherwise entirely normal'.[4] The British sex reformer Eustace Chesser, who wrote many popular manuals on sex and carried out his own survey of sex and marriage in the 1950s, known as the Chesser Report, concluded from surveys of Britain and American literature that 70 per cent of women never reached satisfaction.[5] Seymour Fisher's study, *The Female Orgasm*, estimated in 1972 that only 39 per cent of women had orgasms during intercourse.[6] A feminist heir to this tradition of sexual investigation, Shere Hite, showed in *The Hite Report* (1978) that only 30 per cent of women had orgasms 'during intercourse without direct manual stimulation'. From this she drew the conclusion that:

> not to have orgasm from intercourse is the experience of the majority of women . . . often the ways in which women do orgasm in intercourse have nothing to do with intercourse itself.[7]

She went on to throw down the gauntlet to the investigators:

Even the question being asked is wrong. The question should not be: why aren't women having orgasms from intercourse? But rather: . . . why have women found it necessary to try everything in the book, from exercises to extensive analysis to sex therapy, to make it happen?[8]

Alongside this steady accumulation of evidence, new concepts of female sexuality gradually developed. Even before the mass surveys got under way, British feminists such as Dora Russell, Marie Stopes and Stella Browne were asserting women's rights to sexual pleasure, free from fear of unwanted pregnancy. 'There has grown up a masculine mythology suppressing and distorting all the facts of women's sexual and maternal emotions,' wrote Stella Browne in 1917.[9] In *Married Love*, which took the world by storm in 1918, Marie Stopes went so far as to assert that a man might stimulate his wife to orgasm during pregnancy without penetrating her:

the time will come when it will be sufficient for him to be near her and caress her for relief to take place without any physical connection.[10]

Yet while feminists in the early part of this century campaigned for female pleasure, they saw sex essentially as part of a maternal cycle. Their ideal was the sexually satisfied earth mother; their ideas were anchored more in eugenics and evolution than in eroticism. They played an important part in constructing the modern ideology of heterosexuality, popularizing in a plethora of marriage handbooks the notion that women's pleasure must be mobilized to match the man's, for successful execution of the Sexual Act.

The ideal scenario was described by Dr Helena Wright in *The Sex Factor in Marriage* (1920): the sole purpose of the clitoris was pleasure, she observed; man had the joy of arousing woman and 'creating in her an ardour equal to his own' . . . at the moment of sufficient excitement the woman was ready to receive the male and the mutual climax consummating the act was completed. 'Thought is abandoned, a curious freeing of the spirit, very difficult to describe . . . a pleasure of the soul.'[11] Having dished out advice on how to achieve the ideal mutual orgasm, Dr Wright was eventually prompted to revise her prescription. She worked in one of London's first family planning clinics and heard the experiences of many men and hundreds of women who visited it: they had tried the recipe and it didn't work. In 1947, in *More About the Sex Factor in Marriage*, she condemned the notion that 'women will have an answering orgasm felt in the vagina induced by the movement of the penis'. This misconception was so widespread, she said, that it amounted to a 'penis-vagina fixation', and she expressed doubt about 'the efficacy of the penis-vagina combination for producing orgasm for a woman.'[12]

Her observations were vindicated six years later when, in 1953, Alfred Kinsey published his massive study, *Sexual Behaviour in the Human Female*.[13] As a result of his findings Kinsey shocked the West and especially Freudian orthodoxy by suggesting that there was no difference between the 'infant' and the 'adult' orgasm: this was heretical because it dissolved the ideological barrier between the allegedly 'immature' clitoral orgasm and its 'mature' vaginal version. It implied that penetration of the vagina did not, after all, add a superior quality to the female climax. Freud had maintained that maturity in a woman was symbolized by the transfer of her erotic interests from the clitoris to the vagina.

Again in 1966 William H. Masters and Virginia Johnson pointed out in their substantial work, *Human Sexual Response*,[14] that 'the primary focus for sexual response in the human female's pelvis is the clitoral body'. Even though the clitoris had been recognized as a site of pleasure, they observed, it tended to be consigned to a supporting role in 'foreplay'. As soon as the woman was aroused, it was bypassed on the way to penetration, instead of being given the attention it deserved, as a source of pleasure in its own right, more exciting and excitable than the vagina.

Most commonly, the conclusion was drawn that if women were discontented with their sex lives, the problem lay chiefly with them; it was interpreted as a failure of female physiology or psychology, not of the Sexual Act itself. Masters and Johnson claimed the problem could be solved by synchronizing vaginal penetration with stimulation of the clitoris by means of genital 'traction' during intercourse. Thus, female orgasm was still to be orchestrated to coincide with the male orgasm.

Under the collective microscope

This was the state of play when the women's liberation movement began to take shape in the late 1960s. As we have seen, a key feature of the movement was its insistence that 'the personal is political'. In the safe space of small groups, women started to share their secrets — and what emerged, among much else, was an epidemic of sexual failure. Women were bored with their husbands in bed; or their husbands were bored with them; or they only had orgasms when they masturbated; or they felt awkward and humiliated; or they hated their own bodies; or they feared they were frigid. There they were, at the height of the Permissive Era, when everybody was supposed to be having such a terrific time, and yet . . . fucking was a let-down. It wasn't true for all the women. Some were evidently satisfied, but so far, this knowledge had only enhanced the others' sense of failure and fear of being 'abnormal'. In spite of *all* the evidence to the contrary, the dominant view remained that the Sexual Act should consist of penetration of the vagina by the penis, ideally culminating in mutual orgasm; any other activity, regardless of how it benefited the female, was peripheral or compensatory.

The effect of discussing the problem in consciousness-raising groups was to start to politicize it. As sex, love and monogamy were scrutinized under the collective microscope, they were seen not simply as autonomous functions of 'human nature', but as aspects of a power struggle. Women began to interpret conventional heterosexual practice as the glue which held together the patriarchal order — by symbolizing and reinforcing male power and female dependence, by regimenting social relations and by helping to set the patterns of everyday life.

It was this perspective that Anne Koedt expressed in her paper 'The Myth of the Vaginal Orgasm', in which she drew political conclusions from existing evidence about the role of the clitoris in female sexuality, and from the suppression of that evidence.

> One of the elements of male chauvinism is the refusal or inability to see women as total, separate human beings. Rather . . . men have chosen to define women only in terms of how they benefit men's lives. Sexually, a woman is not seen as an individual wanting to share equally in the sexual act, any more than she was seen as a person with independent desires when she did anything else in society. Thus, it is easy for men to make up what facts are convenient about women, as society is controlled so that women have not been organized to form even a vocal opposition to the male 'experts'.[15]

Koedt suggested that 'the establishment of clitoral orgasm as fact would threaten the heterosexual *institution*,' and that men were too fearful of losing their hold over women to imagine 'a future free relationship between individuals'. Male power relied heavily on the continued sexual dependency of women and this became more crucial as women sought greater social and economic independence. 'What we must do', Koedt insisted, was to 'redefine our sexuality'.

We must discard the 'normal' concepts of sex and create new guidelines which take into account mutual sexual enjoyment. While the idea of mutual enjoyment is acknowledged in marriage manuals, it is not followed to its logical conclusion. We must begin to demand that if a certain sexual position now defined as 'standard' is not mutually conducive to orgasm then it should no longer be so defined.[16]

By pursuing the 'logical conclusion' of the evidence, the women's liberation movement began to question the priorities and protocols of heterosexuality and challenge the supremacy of the Sexual Act. Perhaps penetration wasn't *the* magic moment after all. Perhaps the vagina's acceptance of the penis was only one of many sexual acts — which could not be ranked in order of importance, nor mapped out in stages like an assault course up a mountainside. If this was so, traditional notions about sexual desire and fulfilment lost credibility. Women's pleasure need not be seen as dependent on men's. And if penetration did not 'complete' the sexual act, then physical relations which omitted it could not be dismissed as incomplete or immature. Female sensuality and female eroticism could assert their own meanings and horizons. They might meet and mingle pleasurably with men's, but they were neither defined nor patrolled by them.

Breaking out of the old routine

The possibilities for change and development seemed infinite in the early years of the movement. At the second national women's liberation conference in Britain, in 1971, there were workshop discussions on sexuality which ranged over far more complex territory, and were far more creative and radical than anything that had gone before. Everything was open to question: marriage, monogamy, heterosexuality, lesbianism, bodies, babies . . . nothing was sacred or fixed. Marion Thomas recalls the effect of reading 'The Myth of the Vaginal Orgasm':

It was my first discovery of my own sexuality. I was sleeping with men and not coming. I was allowing them to be the ones who knew about lovemaking and running the show. And I just kind of joined in. That pamphlet pointed out that you could have pleasure on your own, with another woman or with a man, and that you didn't *need* to have a man there. Soon afterwards I had my first good sexual relationship with a man, at 23. I discovered I was a very sexual person who had a great deal of pleasure.

The movement enabled many women to question old routines and alter their perspective on sex — not uncommonly through encounters with other women. For some, these new love affairs were felt as an extension of sisterhood; they were simply about loving women. For others, they seemed a delightful alternative to their exhausted efforts with men. Geraldine Park was one who found that her identity as a fragile 'English rose' was transformed when she went to the States to stay with her new female lover:

> I wore jeans for the first time! I had a whole new conception of myself, my body, the way I could flirt with people — anybody. I felt I could be really raunchy, experience myself as both the seducer and the seduced. It was a way out of any set text. It was crucial, that experience, learning what a woman's body is like. All I'd had before was this mystified sense of myself, vicariously presented through my knowledge of how a man responded to a woman (who might be me or a fantasy figure for all I knew). That sense of the concreteness of my physical form has remained with me . . .

Both Geraldine Park and Marion Thomas alternated for a time between relationships with women and with men. 'Being with women', said Marion, 'I rediscovered the sensuality I knew I had. The lack of role-playing was very important — and the way sex and emotion were very bound up. I learned a lot about what it is to give as well as receive . . .'

This kind of exploration among feminists was not confined to bourgeois metropolitan circles. Pauline Barry remembers that in her women's group in Bradford in the early 1970s 'there were 45-year-old working-class women having lesbian experiences for the first time in their lives. Or people going out with a bloke one night and a woman the next.' It broke up some marriages, metamorphosed others, left some people frightened and hurt. But for most it was a positive development, which expanded awareness and pulled the rug out from under the old Me-Tarzan-You-Jane act, which once passed for 'making love'.

Some feminists continued to have sexual relations with women and not with men — because they desired women, because they managed to find a supportive milieu, or because they didn't desire men (even disliked or hated them), or because they felt that only thus could they express their sexuality and their politics — and for combinations of all these reasons. Angela Lloyd recalls that when she came out as a lesbian in 1971 the fact that her life was anchored in a supportive group of like-minded friends was vital to her:

> I loved the women-centredness of their companionship. They were all women who had left their homes and had this great struggle for freedom. They offered a personal and social life I'd never dreamed possible. I didn't make a political choice about lesbianism, but the political context of these women's lives had a great effect on me. It was very courageous to give up marriages, homes, take off with the kids, squat in women's houses, play in bands. Motherhood was such a meeting ground of feminism, yet that isn't in the histories . . .

Meanwhile, the majority of feminists, whose practice remained exclusively heterosexual, were learning and changing too — as a result of talking to other women, reading, experimenting alone or with lovers and (very often) fighting it out on a daily basis with their menfolk. It seemed possible in the early 1970s that the women's liberation movement could transform human sexual relations.

Opposing tendencies

Early initiatives which might have led to the development of a new feminist sexual politics were crushed, in the middle and late 1970s, between two opposing tendencies: the first was a defensive strategy which might be described as 'heterosexual chauvinism'; the second was separatism — in our view, defeatist. These probably didn't reflect the aspirations or experience of the majority of feminists, but they nevertheless had force because they suggested ways of dealing with sexuality which were relatively straightforward, since they did not break with traditional categories. Both were shaped and defined by the values of patriarchal sex: 'Do you fuck with men or don't you? Should you or shouldn't you?' For a time, these questions threatened to tear the movement apart.

At its most glamorous and flamboyant, heterosexual chauvinism appeared like a revamped *femme fatale*. It was the kind of feminism men liked best. It slapped their knees for being sexual slobs and chastised women for being sexual slovens. Above all, it promised the superfuck. Germaine Greer set the tone in her book *The Female Eunuch*.[17] Greer shared with the libertarians of the 1960s a faith in the naturally disruptive effects of a sexualized culture, and a concern with sexual repression in society. She shared with women's liberation a concern with power in sexual relations: 'Men have commandeered all the energy and streamlined it into an aggressive conquistadorial power.' But the burden of her argument, like that of Masters and Johnson, was to protect the conventions of heterosexuality, not to change them:

> If the right chain reaction could happen, women might find that the clitoris was more directly involved in intercourse and would be brought to climax by a less pompous and deliberate way than digital massage . . .

(The Sexual Act, apparently, had not a shred of pomposity about it, and was never done deliberately.) The clitoris would be merely an object of scorn — all digits and spasms in Greer's world — if it weren't perceived as such a terrible menace:

> The banishment of the fantasy of the vaginal orgasm is ultimately a service, but the substitution of the clitorial spasm for genuine gratification may turn out to be a disaster for sexuality . . . Masters and Johnson's conclusions have produced some unlooked for side-effects, like veritable clitoromania . . .

This notion of 'genuine gratification', which Greer insisted must involve the vagina, ran very close to the Freudian *faux pas* about mature and immature sexuality. She did not identify any difference between the vagina as *a* place of pleasure and *the* place; the hierarchy of sexual values remained intact.

Greer held out hope of some sort, however. Women could save themselves from the worst effects of male sexual power-play if they would only 'accept some part of the responsibility for their own and their partner's enjoyment':

> This involves a measure of control and conscious cooperation. Part of the battle will be if they can change their attitude toward sex and embrace and stimulate the penis instead of taking it . . .

According to the code of heterosexual chauvinism, fucking was what all the best women did. If one was clever, one's feminism could even enhance one's sexual prowess! But it was a delicate business. One was in the parlour of the male ego and must take care not to rumple the antimacassars or knock ash on to the rug. Germaine Greer made it plain that however many faults men had, they were indispensable when it came to sex, because penetration turned it into the Real Thing. The message had to be reinforced assiduously, or one risked being banished to the kitchen for failing to show proper respect. Any woman who had dared embrace another in her past would have to keep mighty quiet about it.

Shortly after Greer published *The Female Eunuch*, radical feminists in Britain began to prepare for their own intervention in feminist body politics, which took quite a different tack. *Thoughts on Feminism*, their paper published in 1971 for the November national women's liberation conference in London, argued:

> as long as the Sex Act remains the norm for sexual relations, we remain the habitual givers, pawns in the male power game. And we will continue to be dominated by men . . . as long as we have our closest emotional/sexual relationships with men, Women's Liberation can be no more than a hobby.

Heterosexual contact, the paper suggested, penetrated even the psyche: 'Our personality alters as we become less penetrable (vaginal) and increasingly self-contained (clitoral).' The answer was to give it up.

The mainstream of the movement baulked at the challenge. Its concern was with strategies which enabled women to survive *in* the world. This radical feminist paper amounted to revolutionary defeatism: run for cover and snipe at those who malingered on the front line.

Worse was to come. As we observed in chapter 1, there was a struggle in the early 1970s between socialist and radical feminists, over the structure of the London women's liberation workshop — and in particular over whether men should be allowed across the threshold. The radical feminists held out for exclusion and won a tactical victory. Thereafter, the workshop became an increasingly separatist enclave, with other feminists going their own ways. It was not the radical feminists' wish to retain space free from men that was damaging, but their assertion that separatism was the correct path for *all* feminists. In the summer of 1974, the workshop newsletter published a relentless attack on heterosexual women, reprinted from a document written by New York radical lesbians. Called 'The Clit Statement', it was run as a serial over many weeks: 'Straight women think, talk, cross their legs, dress and come on like male transvestite femme drag queens,' it accused and, in a later episode, described straight women as 'agents'.

Ironically, Germaine Greer said something similar herself — 'I'm sick of being a transvestite, I refuse to be my own female impersonator'

— but in that context, the sharing of discontent about inauthentic ways of being women was directed towards a restructuring of femininity. 'The Clit Statement' was an attack not only on forms of femininity, but on women themselves. As such, it contravened the founding principle of radical feminism. The New York Redstockings, who had formulated the 'pro-woman' line in 1969, issued a powerful riposte. But British radical feminists remained silent. Even in the mainstream of the movement, there was little open retaliation. Perhaps it seemed too difficult to sustain a political and personal critique of heterosexuality alongside a political and personal commitment to it.

The effect was to drive heterosexual women (a large majority among feminists, as among all women) on to the defensive. They felt roughed up by the very movement in which they had sought safety. Not only did they feel that they themselves were under attack, and their idea of what women's liberation stood for was on trial, but they were also required to defend heterosexuality — in a way that left them no room for their own manoeuvres against patriarchal sexual practices. The Greer style of defence held little meaning for most of them; it lay, unwelcome, in their line of retreat.

Groups began to disaffiliate from the London workshop; women stopped taking its newsletter. Many now found that their feminism was confined to campaigning corners or to the informal networks of their female friends. For a time, they felt they couldn't participate in the politics of the women's liberation movement, where the dominant question was whether one was for or against heterosexuality, rather than how to formulate strategies *within* it, or how to reform feminine psychology. Social feminists had not yet developed a positive perspective of their own. There were ritual rows at one national conference after another, until the last one in Birmingham in 1978 — when the split was so bitter and painful that no one was prepared to organize another such gathering.

In the late 1970s a new grouping, 'revolutionary feminism', emerged from the radical feminist current, generating yet more explosive texts. Leeds Revolutionary Feminists confounded an already depressed movement with a paper published in 1979, 'Political Lesbianism: The Case Against Heterosexuality'.[18] This asserted that penetration was 'an act of great symbolic significance, by which the oppressor enters the body of the oppressed'. It denied that heterosexual women were the enemy (hardly reassuring at this stage), but insisted that they were 'collaborators with the enemy':

Every woman who lives or fucks a man helps to maintain the oppression of her sisters and hinders our struggle.

All feminists, the Leeds paper claimed, could and should be political lesbians: 'Our definition of a political lesbian is a woman-identified woman who does not fuck men. It does not mean compulsory sexual activity with women.' When this was published in the movement's national newsletter, *Wires*, the challenge was taken up with more bravado than before. Lesbian and heterosexual women wrote letters, subsequently published in *Wires*, which attacked the Leeds Revolutionary Feminists for denying 'the principle that every woman's experience is real and valid', and for failing to understand the nature of the feminist fight against patriarchy — for mistaking (as it were) the edifice for the glue which held it together:

> Somehow they reduce the whole structure of male supremacy to fucking. Withdrawing sexual services from men becomes the total strategy — how exactly this will bring them to their knees is not explained. Of course, it is a lot easier to make heterosexual feminists feel guilty than it is . . . to confront the structures of the patriarchy which go beyond immediate personal relationships.[19]

The critics rejected the doctrinaire approach of the Leeds group as being inimical to women's politics. 'The only point in women changing their lives is if *they* want to . . . We have to discover, as we go along, what it is that women want, not to try to dictate it now.' It was pointed out that the paper denied the unconscious dimension of sexuality and, not least, that it implied that lesbianism had nothing to do with eroticism:

> In particular, it ignores the importance of women's sexual relations with other women whilst making the question of whether women have sexual relations with men central to the whole definition of political lesbianism.

One letter suggested that the paper was not about sexuality at all, but a political exercise in making the movement a 'closed group of cadre units'.

As before, however, the arguments about heterosexuality were defensive. They proposed no way out, no revision of the movement's aims, no redefinition of the terms of the debate. The old categories of 'gay' and 'straight' remained undisturbed and the questionable propriety of the Sexual Act continued to divide feminists.

Divide and rule

What was needed was an exploration of the experience that lesbians and heterosexuals *shared* and to build on this common ground a political understanding of sexuality. No doubt some women's groups looked into the matter, but this approach was not brought out into the open, to the forefront of feminist politics, where it needed to be. Instead, there were pressures on women to accentuate their sexual identity in traditional, polarized terms.

On one side, the political priorities of Gay Liberation impinged strongly on the feminist approach to lesbianism. This movement, which combined male and female homosexuals (the former predominating), emerged during the same years as women's liberation. It was based on a celebration of what was still felt to be a minority and deviant identity. The lesbians who were part of it in the early 1970s tended to be women whose homosexuality pre-dated their involvement with the women's liberation movement: they came to it by a different route from those who discovered a sexual desire for women in a feminist milieu. There was considerable tension between the 'old' and 'nouvelle' lesbians. 'Old' lesbians had a sense of allegiance to the homosexual community, to which they had paid their dues: in that setting, any intimation of androgyny or bisexuality threatened betrayal, because it was so often associated with not coming out — with plunging into the world of gay pleasure and never paying the price, never letting on to family, friends or employers. Their response to the 'nouvelle' lesbianism was to be highly suspicious of it; to any sign of bisexuality, directly unsympathetic.

As for the idea that feminism was the theory and lesbianism the practice, which began to be articulated by radical feminists in the early 1970s, some of the 'old' lesbians were unsympathetic to that too — because they were socialists, not separatists. Moreover, it was too threatening to the organizing principle of gay politics, which was about naming your gay *identity*.

Gay liberation did not leave room for the possibility of lesbianism being an alternative choice to heterosexuality (albeit an unequal one, bearing heavy risks), nor for the possibility of both being part of a spectrum in which the similarities were more significant than the differences. In that sense, it initially mirrored the way in which society marginalized homosexual desire as being something experienced only by homosexuals.

Lesbianism in the women's liberation movement was as much about women as about homosexuality, as it was conventionally defined. It was more about desire than about identity as one specific *type* or another. As such, it represented a challenge to the very *category* of 'homosexuality' — and a correlating challenge to the 'heterosexual' category. At the same time, however, the movement as a whole had to cope with the queer-bashing abuse that rained on it. 'They're just a bunch of dykes' was a typical slur. The manifest affection between feminists — all that 'huggin' and a kissin'' — got them labelled if nothing else did.

Trapped by the old patriarchal definitions, those who did not identify as lesbians and who did not want their feminist politics dismissed as symptoms of deviance, found themselves protesting that, even if some of their best friends were lesbians, they most certainly were *not*. But if a woman wanted to challenge the established protocols of heterosexuality, or admit the erotic imperfections of the patriarchal fuck, how was she to respond to her partner's benign murmur that maybe she didn't like it because . . . she was *really* gay? There was no confident feminist affirmation of heterosexuality to which she could refer, only the clitorophobic defence of the Greer school.

Feminists fighting for their children in custody cases were sometimes accused of being 'unfit mothers' — a charge levelled automatically against lesbians — and had to struggle to be recognized as 'real women', meaning unsullied by any traces of lesbianism.

Both Geraldine Park and Marion Thomas, whom we quoted earlier, resumed a fixed heterosexual identity. It wasn't because they stopped desiring women — but because they hadn't stopped desiring men, and found the combination of this urge and the urge towards social conformity irresistible. 'I had this very strong sense of how awful it would be', Geraldine explained, 'to be looked at by somebody who had none of the libertarian notions about lesbianism being a good and healthy thing, and to be found disgusting. I felt profoundly uncomfortable being subject to other people's destructive judgements. I don't believe there is an essential womanhood — we are constructed, held in place.'

'I want to be *in* the culture, not exiled from it,' said Marion. 'I did find lesbianism terribly painful. Terribly exiled. The intolerant, harsh world is beastly to homosexuals. The fact that I could handle relationships with men again, and that with men I do feel I have social acceptance — these things have been influential. But I really affirm and insist on my right to love women.'

Alongside these women were thousands of feminists who had never desired other women and who were committed to sexual relationships with men: when their feminism was challenged, the incentive to assert a heterosexual identity and to deny any personal association with lesbianism was probably even stronger.

These were the effects of what Adrienne Rich described as 'the lie of compulsory female heterosexuality', which afflicted 'not just feminist scholarship, but every profession, every reference work, every curriculum, every organising attempt, every relationship and conversation . . .' It caused, she said, 'an incalculable loss to the power of all women to change the social relations of the sexes, to liberate ourselves and each other'.[20]

That lie was chiefly to blame for the sense of betrayal which made the gay liberation movement so suspicious of bisexuality. It meant that, even in the women's liberation movement, lesbians were obliged to reaffirm and defend their homosexuality. As a result, the new feminist lesbianism developed its identity within the sphere of gay politics — which wasn't its home ground, whose priorities it didn't share and which didn't reflect the conditions in which it flourished. Women who desired women but couldn't identify with the 'lesbian' label were left in political limbo. As for bisexuality, it was dishonourably discharged. Even when radical feminists promoted the political choice of lesbianism, it was more as a correct way of life than as an expression of erotic desire.

No counter-strategy

Women warned each other, at the first national conference held by lesbians in Canterbury in 1974, that lesbianism was being used as a derogatory term to divide their movement. But no counter-strategy emerged to prevent this, except a determination to defend lesbianism, which was vital, but not enough. On that same occasion it was decided that lesbianism should be a major topic at the forthcoming national women's liberation conference in Edinburgh, on the ground that it was the most misunderstood issue of the movement and that existing aims expressed heterosexual priorities.

Out of the Edinburgh conference, after much heated argument, came the movement's Sixth Demand: 'An end to discrimination against lesbians, and for women's right to determine their own sexuality.' But unfortunately, since the movement didn't yet know what it wanted to say about sexuality, the demand tended to confuse the issue. It affirmed a commitment to lesbians' civil rights but ignored their erotic interests. By combining two separate aims, it seemed to associate self-determination with a specific lesbian identity, as though other less clearly defined expressions of sexuality were not relevant.

Neither the Sixth Demand nor the politics of gay liberation — any more than the perspectives of separatism or heterosexual chauvinism — expressed what was (potentially) revolutionary about the sexual atmosphere within the women's liberation movement. For here were the beginnings of a positive commitment to female eroticism, as something powerful and autonomous, which was shared by heterosexuals, lesbians and bisexuals — and which transcended all such definitions, robbing them of meaning except as barricades thrown up in defence of patriarchy. If the political significance of this could be seized, then femininity could be taken out of its strait-jacket and celebrated rather than shunned. It could be positive and strong as well as sensual, desiring as well as desirable. It would not deny men, and it would not rely on them. It would be what women wanted it to be, not what men decreed.

Questioning assumptions

By the mid-1980s, most of the heat had gone out of the row about the political rights and wrongs of lesbianism and heterosexuality. It faded in significance as the character of the women's movement changed, becoming less vulnerable to factional claims that there was one correct path for all. The argument was not resolved, but feminists were turning their attention to other aspects of sexuality, and questioning some of the assumptions which lay behind the debates of the 1970s.

As non-separatists no longer felt the need to defend heterosexuality *per se*, they began to explore it with more confidence — especially in seeking the political meanings of its psychological and social dimensions. This involved re-examining the motivations and desires of men — looking beyond the issues of aggression and violence, to male vulnerabilities and fears.[21] It also meant investigating the concepts of 'love' and 'falling in love'.[22]

Questions were raised about the way in which sexologists such as Masters and Johnson, as well as feminists who had drawn on their work, first reduced sexuality to the physical business of getting orgasms, and then elevated it to become the measure of female power and liberation. Knowing how to reach orgasm was nice, but was it liberating? What about the complexities of desire and love? It was important to explore the experiences that lesbians and heterosexuals shared, in order to reach a political understanding of sexuality, but there was a range of 'censored emotions', which belonged to that shared experience and which were more difficult to own up to — namely, 'masochism, self-objectification, domination, guilt, hostility and envy . . .' These required scrutiny too.[23] Increasingly, feminists drew on psychoanalysis to help explore the sources and meanings of female sexuality and eroticism; this was a dynamic process, as they were using psychoanalytic techniques to pose political questions about the patriarchal premises of Freudian theory.

We have pointed to some of the debates that were taking place, but these can only indicate the direction of new ideas and arguments. As the political atmosphere grew more repressive, with emphasis on 'family' virtues and 'Victorian values'; as the spread of publicity about sexually related diseases made sexual freedom seem more hazardous than liberating; as the tragedy of the killer virus AIDS fuelled homophobia . . . the challenge for feminists was to keep on asserting women's right to define their own sexuality (in line with the Sixth Demand), and to use the process of definition to extend understanding rather than to construct categories or boundaries.

The interventions of the women's liberation movement were hotly contested within the movement itself. The effect, over nearly two decades, was to defend lesbianism and make it visible; to support women's desire in the context of heterosexuality in a woman-centred way, which implied a radical reformation of heterosexuality; and to bring the creation of masculinity and femininity, as well as the question of pleasure, into the political arena. All in all, this was no mean achievement.

Notes to chapter 8

1 Faderman, L. *Surpassing the Love of Men*, Junction Books, 1981.
2 Weeks, J. 'Deviance, Desire and Sexual Deviance' in *The Making of the Modern Homosexual*, Hutchinson, 1981.
3 Dickinson, R. and Beam, L. *A Thousand Marriages*, Baillière Tindall & Cox, 1932.
4 Stone, H. and A. *A Marriage Manual*, Gollancz, 1952.
5 Chesser, E. *Marriage and Freedom*, Rich & Cowan, 1952.
6 Fisher, S. *Understanding The Female Orgasm*, Pelican, 1972.
7 Hite, S. *The Hite Report*, Hamlyn, 1978.
8 Ibid.
9 Browne, S. 'Women and Birth Control' in Paul, E. and C. (eds) *Population and Birth Control: A Symposium*, 1917.
10 Stopes, M. *Married Love: A New Contribution to the Solution of Sex Difficulties*, Fifield, 1918.
11 Wright, H. *The Sex Factor in Marriage*, Noel Douglas, 1930.
12 Wright, H. *More About the Sex Factor in Marriage*, Williams and Northgate, 1947.
13 Kinsey, A. *Sexual Behaviour in the Human Female*, Indiana University Institute for Sex Research, 1953.
14 Masters, W. and Johnson, V. *Human Sexual Response*, Churchill, 1966.
15 Koedt, A. 'The Myth of the Vaginal Orgasm' in *Notes from the Second Year*, 1970.
16 Ibid.
17 Greer, G. *The Female Eunuch*, Paladin, 1971.
18 Leeds Revolutionary Feminist Group 'Political Lesbianism: The Case Against Heterosexuality', first printed in *Wires* no. 81, reprinted in *Love Your Enemy?*, Onlywomen Press, 1981.
19 Reprinted in *Love Your Enemy?*, ibid.
20 Rich, A. *Compulsory Heterosexuality and Lesbian Existence*, Onlywomen Press, 1981.
21 Hollway, W. 'Heterosexual Sex: Power and Desire for the Other' in Cartledge, S. and Ryan, J. (eds), *Sex and Love*, The Women's Press, 1983.
22 Goodison, L. 'Really Being in Love Means Wanting to Live in a Different World', ibid.
23 Segal, L. 'Sensual Uncertainty, or Why the Clitoris is not Enough', ibid.

9　The future

We have tried to give an account of the development of feminist politics over nearly two decades, to show how much progress was made towards realizing the aims of women's liberation, and how far they met with resistance. We don't claim to have produced a definitive history; this is one version of events, which reflects the authors' own politics and experience.

Like other phases of the continuing women's movement, women's liberation had to assert its own meanings and resist those imposed on it by men. Although we were never informed of the fact by television news readers, or by the leader-writers of the national press, it was one of the most important political developments of this century. We have described many of its aspects and achievements in earlier chapters, and we cannot hope to give an adequate summary here. A few pointers will have to suffice.

The idea that women and men should be treated equally — an extreme aspiration in the late 1960s — was scarcely contentious (in theory, if not in fact) by the late 1970s. By the mid-1980s, the more sophisticated concepts of 'positive action' and 'contract compliance' were also quite widely acknowledged. A whole new library of books, papers and pamphlets had been produced by women, containing a new body of theory, a new perspective on contemporary society, a new sense of history. The mechanisms of male power and female subordination were opened up for scrutiny.

A revolution in consciousness affected women who had never been near a women's liberation meeting. Women felt proud of being women and of being among women in a way most had not felt before. The word 'sexism', barely invented in the 1970s, became a familiar part of our vocabulary. The concept of patriarchy gained recognition (on the left, at least) as a power system which pre-dated and shaped capitalism.

It was surely unimaginable in 1969 that women would stage a nationwide mass protest against male violence . . . that within a few short years there would be national networks of refuges for battered women and rape crisis centres . . . that 80,000 women and men would march to defend abortion . . . that trade unions would organize against sexual harassment . . . that feminist ideas would be given regular, serious coverage in women's magazines . . . that women would

transform a major strike of mine-workers against pit closures . . . or that a committee set up to further women's causes in Greater London would command a budget of £90 million . . . yet all these things happened, and a great deal more besides. It is important to safeguard this knowledge, especially as we know that women's rebellions have been buried and forgotten in the past.

Everywhere but nowhere

By the mid-1980s, 'women's liberation' was seen as something which belonged primarily to the 1970s. It represented a peak of intensity and activity in a continuing women's movement, rather as the suffragettes had done, more than half a century before.

There was no longer a single, tangible — if structureless — body, to which women felt they belonged. Gone, too, was a certain spontaneity and elation, which had been associated with the moment of discovery, when a new generation found its own strength and reinvented revolution. Perhaps there was also less optimism about the pace and character of change that could be achieved. This was not simply a consequence of two Conservative governments and economic recession (although they played their part); as the years passed, women had learned more about the nature of female subordination, the limits of reform and the incorrigibility of male resistance.

A generation of girls had grown up for whom the discovery of women's liberation was something that belonged to their mothers' time. They had not had to reinvent rebellion. As they reached adulthood, they found it in full swing. They also found Margaret Thatcher at Downing Street. Theirs was a profoundly different mix of experience from that of the generation which had grown up in the 1960s and early 1970s. If they subscribed to the aims of women's liberation — which many did — they did not join the struggle in the same way. They had to do it in their own style, which was not the style of the 1970s. And if some of their mothers had once felt that the women's movement was theirs to shape and steer, now they found that it had passed out of their hands; not simply to their daughters, but to others who hadn't been involved earlier, and who would take it in new directions.

A sense of identity with women's liberation had initially drawn together a remarkable diversity of groups and individuals. In the early years, because this phase of the movement was small and embattled, women closed ranks, fighting to establish the movement's ideas and make its presence felt. Over the next decade and a half, the movement flourished; its ideas developed and spread. As it grew in strength and confidence, energies which had been focussed inwards, on building a new politics, could shift outwards and diversify again, to carry those politics into other arenas. And as women's liberation made connections with ideas and struggles beyond its own frontiers, so there emerged new kinds of feminist politics, which would carry the women's movement, profoundly changed since the 1970s, into the 1990s and beyond. The Black women's movement, the peace movement, Women Against Pit Closures and the new municipal women's committees were all part of that development. So, too, was the renaissance of women's culture, which found expression in music, theatre and cabaret, books, film and video, criticism and a wide range of academic studies.

The strength of women's liberation lay in its diversity, its capacity to celebrate difference and its spontaneity. But here also lay its vulnerability as a distinct political force. Ideas and energies exploded and dispersed. By the mid-1980s, women's liberation was everywhere, yet it was nowhere. An era had passed. There would not be another major outburst of rebellion — on the scale of the 1970s — until another generation discovered its own need to re-ignite the fire. But feminist politics was still very much alive. It owed much of its character and most of its considerable influence to women's liberation.

After women's liberation

What survived the passing of the era of women's liberation was a continuing struggle, conducted by women individually and in groups, inspired by feminist ideas which had become current during the 1970s. It was in the nature of feminist politics that women were engaged at many different levels at once — trying to change themselves, to change society and to change their relation to society. Their struggle went on within the family, with parents, children, siblings, husbands — to transform oppressive relationships, to change patterns of behaviour, and to redistribute labour and wealth. It was also a struggle for cultural change: it challenged cherished traditions and powerful taboos; it asserted the value of the roles women already performed, while trying to create new ones, and to break into those traditionally preserved for men.

Meanwhile, women were fighting to improve the material conditions of their lives and, to this end, fighting for power within trade unions and political organizations, and against the vested interests of employers and international capital. As women entered into spheres of activity that were dominated by men, they had to transform these too, in order to survive without becoming surrogate men. They struggled to change the values and priorities of men, as well as the way they conducted themselves . . . in short, to change the world. And all this time, women were fighting to assert their own interpretations of what they were doing and their own definitions of who they were, against man-made accounts which tended to ridicule, belittle or ignore their efforts and achievements.

It was intrinsic to the experience of feminism that women went on learning and changing all the time, and that nobody had all the right answers. One of the chief characteristics of women's liberation was the process whereby personal experience — explored among women in a supportive context — could become the base on which theory and strategy were built. Women might cease to use the term 'consciousness-raising', and to organize 'consciousness-raising groups', but the process remained a vital political activity. It was a means of challenging and transforming women's constructed sense of femininity. It named and endorsed individual feelings and experiences and discovered how far they were common to women in general. It affirmed differences as well as similarities. It enabled women to go on working out their politics for themselves.

There had never been a single-slogan road to women's liberation (although some factions disagreed); nor was there One True Feminism. The women's movement continued to embrace a variety of theoretical and practical approaches to understanding female subordination and asserting the power of women — with individuals and groups forming different kinds of alliances around different issues.

Fighting with and against men

Some maintained a commitment to being separate from men — at home, at work and in their politics — and saw their struggle as being primarily against men. The majority, though, would go on fighting with men and against them, often at the same moment. They took the view that men as individuals could be economically oppressed, socially impoverished and psychologically cramped by a system which sustained the power of men in general. They felt that some men were genuinely committed to change and to ending female subordination. Women could accept their goodwill and excellent intentions, and work with them on common ground — but they would still have to deal with the (often subconscious) ways in which men resisted change, and their propensity to run for cover when things got tough.

The struggle against men involved much more than a pursuit of positive changes (new laws, benefits, services, and so on). Women had to engage with a constant offensive, waged by men through the education system, the media and other aspects of our culture. These were not just sources of resistance to change, but sites of active propaganda for male values and male views. It happened across a vast range of activity — from history lessons where children learned to disregard female achievements, to Page Three of the *Sun*, where readers learned about the nature and worth of 'femininity'. It penetrated deep into the psyche, through the system of grammar, for example, in which 'he' stood for *he* or *she*, and through the codes of advertising, which inverted the meanings of women's liberation.

So women had to be on the defensive all the time. They also had to cope with strategies employed by men to resist their efforts to move forwards. These strategies moved with the times. Once, men had argued that women were not their equals because God had ordained it. Later, they argued that women were 'naturally' inferior and that science had proved it. Later still, they were heard to say that women *were* equal, but would have to wait (until after the revolution or after the recession, or after the next election) to enjoy equal treatment. When the last of these arguments seemed to lose force during the time of women's liberation, men developed a new strategy of *passive resistance*.

This entailed agreeing that women were equal and agreeing that women should have equal treatment *now* . . . and then doing nothing about it. Many of the changes women wanted required action on the part of the institutions and organizations men controlled: men's inaction guaranteed the status quo. The strategy was also employed at a personal level — for instance by men who agreed that child care should be shared equally, yet absented themselves from their own responsibilities at home. It was particularly effective on the left, among men who professed to support women's liberation. Often, it was not a conscious tactic; it was a result of men not facing up to the fact that they would have to give up power and privilege, and even be inconvenienced, if women were to move towards liberation.

There were conflicts of interest between women and men which had to be openly confronted and explored. Women had to challenge men as men, and the politics they produced as men. Otherwise, it would be women, and not men, who were always seen as the problem. Men would have to put their own relationships to masculinity and patriarchal power into crisis if they were genuinely to support feminism. By denying that their relation to women was contradictory, they promoted themselves and their interests as universal. Those committed to class politics would have to recognize that their interests as men did not coincide in every respect with those of their class.

Into the mainstream

In its first decade, women's liberation remained on the edge of institutional politics, reflecting women's sense of being marginalized by the male-dominated mainstream. At the same time, it created a new politics with women at the centre, enabling women to develop a political culture of their own. Arising out of this came a strong move in the 1980s to get into the mainstream — not to abandon feminist politics, but to carry the form and content of feminism into political institutions, to transform their methods and objectives.

This was another key dimension of the continuing women's movement. It was a logical extension of the feminist-based campaigns for positive action. It began to happen in the Labour Party, in trade unions and local authorities, as we have described in earlier chapters. Grass-roots activity and self-help politics would always be a mainstay of the movement, but women had recognized the limitations of being in a pressure group. They knew they couldn't rely on those in power giving way to pressure: they had to engage with power directly. Since it was still hard for women to 'make it' on men's terms, they would have to change the terms. And women who went for power would need to be encouraged and supported, so that they remained accountable to feminism and sustained by it.

In the course of the 1970s, feminists developed a presence on the left, where they emerged as critics of policy and practice. Towards the end of the decade, they had begun to intervene in a more organized way in the Labour Party and in the formulation of policy for future Labour governments — in the hope that the Labour Party would eventually return to power. What would a feminist political strategy look like? In the following pages we set out our own approach. It is intended not to intervene in the politics of Thatcherism, but to help prepare a radical alternative by intervening in the politics of Labour. We don't claim that it is representative of feminist views in general, but it is an attempt to encompass some of the main insights and arguments developed by socialist feminists within the women's liberation movement.

A feminist political strategy

One thing that has been missing from planning on the left is a clear vision of what kind of society we want to live in. There is some talk of 'socialism', but little talk of what that might mean. What would be the

guiding principles? What would everyday life be like for ordinary
people? This sort of question must be asked in order to provide a
framework for policy-making.

We want a society in which men are not privileged and women are
not subordinate; in which women are free and powerful. This isn't all,
but we concentrate here on relations between women and men. These
cross barriers of race and class, and fundamentally affect other issues,
such as common ownership, democracy and freedom.

At the same time, we take the view that politics is not simply about a
set of ideals that will burst into reality at some future revolutionary
moment. That approach defers change; we are interested in building a
political practice which effects a continuing process of change, starting
now and moving towards goals, which are not cast in concrete for
eternity, but which may themselves be changed in the process. How,
then, to approach this process of change, and get it moving in the
direction we desire?

Feminist demands cannot simply be added, like a shopping list, to
any existing manifesto. We argue for a new starting point, a new set of
criteria, a new order of priorities. Patriarchal politics, especially on
the left, has a distorted perspective. Its analysis of what is wrong and
how things work in society, as well as its objectives, tend to focus upon
one relatively limited area of life: production. In developing an
'Alternative Economic Strategy' to counter the policies of the Labour
right and the Conservative government, the male left has begun with
the objective of regenerating industry and creating 'full employment'.
It has taken men's and women's relation to each other as given and has
proposed no change. This approach de-sexualizes politics, and in
doing so denies any political room for feminism. It is blind to the
existence of children and domestic work and thus has nothing to
suggest about transforming men's relation to children and child care.
And it characterizes the left's objectives in purely economic terms, so
that the politics of sexuality and culture are beyond its pale.

As women, we assert a different approach to politics, which has a
double axis: production and reproduction. This embraces domestic
work as well as paid work, and relations within the family and
community as well as relations between labour and capital. It also
recognizes the importance of sexual and cultural politics.

Set in the light of female experience, the aim of 'full employment'
takes on a different meaning. Most women are already over-employed,
working a 12- to 16-hour day. The real problem is what work they do
and how much they get paid for it — if they get paid at all.

Our strategy begins by asking a different question: not 'How do we
create full employment?' but 'How shall we care for and support our

children?' (We mean this not in the sense of private domestic choices, but in the sense of our collective responsibility towards the next generation.) Much turns on the question, not least the redistribution of labour and wealth within the family. It does not eclipse the aim of redistributing wealth between labour and capital; but in our view it is the appropriate context in which that aim should be set.

Beginning with the question of child care, we are convinced that it is to the benefit of children, no less than of parents, that children be looked after by men and women equally. Young children grow up with a limited picture of the respective characters and capacities of males and females; this is one of the ways in which sex stereotypes become rooted in people's minds. While men continue to segregate themselves from children, they are cut off from a range of experience which would broaden their understanding and change their political priorities (and which they might even enjoy). We would argue, too, that children benefit from the company of other children and adults, outside their immediate family, and that collective child care is a positive advantage, not just a means of compensating for the absence of wage-earning mothers. If there is anything wrong with nurseries and other child care facilities it is that they are under-resourced and poorly organized. (We have described in an earlier chapter, p. 33, the efforts of feminists to establish nurseries along democratic, non-sexist lines.)

Our feminist strategy would combine generous resourcing for child care facilities outside the home, both for under-fives and for school-age children outside school hours, with a commitment to reorganize paid employment so that parents of both sexes could spend equal time with their children. We are not suggesting that children should spend 35 to 40 hours a week in nurseries or day-care centres, but that there should be a combination of community-based collective care and home-based parental care.

The arrangement of time spent in paid employment is a crucial factor in changing the current pattern of male absenteeism from child care and other domestic responsibilities. It would be necessary, in our view, to reduce working hours substantially, aiming for a *maximum* thirty-hour week. There would need to be firm restrictions on overtime and an end to the present distinction between 'part-time' and 'full-time' workers, which has acted so much to women's disadvantage. All those working sixteen hours or more should have the same statutory rights. A shorter working week could help to create new jobs (although we do not imagine there would be a *pro-rata* increase). More important, it could *begin* to create the conditions in which men and women could participate equally in domestic work as well as in paid employment.

As we have seen, male absenteeism from domestic work has been one of the main causes of women's continuing low pay and powerlessness in the labour market.

If a new government were to embark on a public spending programme aimed at reducing unemployment, one possibility would be to limit all new jobs in the public sector to thirty hours per week. This would mean that more people could have jobs. It could be combined with a system of incentives and/or sanctions to reduce hours in the private sector — and this should be seen not as an emergency stop-gap, but as a positive alternative to future redundancy and a means of encouraging a permanent change in the pattern of working time. (The labour movement has made very slow progress towards even a thirty-five hour week: it has certainly never promoted it as a means of democratizing domestic life.)

These proposals obviously raise vital questions about pay. How can living standards be maintained and improved if working hours are reduced? We reject the traditional response of the male left that any proposal for change which threatens the wage is unacceptable. This springs from a fixed idea about the nature of family support — which is that each family has one main source of income, provided by a male breadwinner. As we have already shown, the 'family wage' approach perpetuates female dependency and male control. It discriminates against large families, since the individual wage does not vary according to the number of children the wage-earner has to support. And it is no help to the families of the unemployed. Moreover, it is based on a concept of the family as a harmonious economic unit, which takes no account of conflicting interests within the family.

The point is not to protect the male wage but to restructure family income. This can be done by strengthening women's earning power, by increasing state benefits for dependants and carers, and by improving the 'social wage'.

The earning power of women could be strengthened in several ways. The law could be used, backed up by collective bargaining, to ensure women get equal pay for work of equal value with men. Positive action programmes, and 'contract compliance' (see p. 142) would improve women's opportunities to break into higher-paid fields of work usually done by men. This need not entail discrimination against men at the point of selection for jobs, but if it is to be successful it *must* break down the infrastructure of male privilege, so that women have real equality of access to education and training, to the means of organization and to all levels of employment. The reorganization of working time and the provision of child care facilities are an essential part of positive action. It would also be useful to amend the Sex

Discrimination Act — for instance, to facilitate complaints against indirect discrimination and to provide statutory backing for positive action programmes.

These measures could be combined with a general strategy against low pay — since the problem of low pay is largely a problem of women's pay. The strategy would need to include an overhaul of the Wages Council system and the introduction of a statutory minimum wage, which the TUC finally came out in favour of in 1986.

The second element in restructuring family income involves state benefits. We would argue that it is not in the best interests of children to depend on their parents' wages as their primary means of support. It works to the disadvantage of children whose parents are out of work, and of those who have only one parent, or more than one or two siblings. Child benefit should be increased substantially — until it is commensurate with the real cost of supporting a child. This principle is already accepted in relation to one group of people who do not earn wages — pensioners. If it were extended to children, it would ensure greater equality between families as well as independent security for children, and it would help to break the economic control which men exercise within the family.

In addition to a realistic level of child benefit, there should be proper support for adults who have care of dependants. This would include an extended period of paid parental leave, available to the mother or the father, as well as a carer's allowance, available regardless of the carer's sex or marital status.

We have dealt so far with the purely financial aspects of family support. Clearly, the services and facilities provided by the state are of considerable importance too. Our feminist strategy would place a strong priority on extending the 'social wage' — by providing better housing, transport, health care, welfare and child care, as well as introducing new services to ease the burden of domestic work, such as community restaurants and laundries.

Just as incomes need to be restructured in order to minimize the economic dependence of individuals within the family, so state provisions must be reorganized in order that they are not conditional upon membership of a traditional family unit. People who live alone, or with a partner of the same sex, or with groups of friends, must be free to do so without suffering social or financial disadvantage. As we have seen, the welfare state is based on an assumption of female dependence, and its rules and regulations reinforce patriarchal control. Our strategy would seek to transform the principles on which the welfare state is founded.

A strategy which is informed by female experience and based on

feminist priorities looks to the state as much as to the employer to
maintain and improve living standards. (For many people, of course,
the employer *is* the state.) But we cannot rely on the state as benefactor,
any more than we can rely on employers. Trade unions would need to
extend the scope of collective bargaining to local and national
government, in order to win improvements in the social wage — and
to invest no less energy in this than in bargaining with employers
about pay and conditions. More important still, women themselves
need to gain power in the state, locally and nationally.

As we have already suggested, male privilege and female subordination are not simply by-products of economic relations. They
are intrinsic to our culture. They are actively promoted through
values inherent in the education system and the mass media, in social
traditions and taboos. Our strategy would make it a priority to
challenge and transform these values.

This would entail an anti-sexist policy for schools and colleges. It
would promote voluntary codes of practice against sexism in
advertising and the media, as well as against pornographic display. It
would seek to improve health care for women and to maximize
women's own control over their health and fertility. It would overhaul
family law and introduce family courts. It would promote women's
cultural activities. It would defend women's right to define their own
sexuality. It would take a woman-centred approach to male violence,
recognizing that men, not women, are the problem . . . These are just
some of the measures that would be included.

Our strategy would require substantial resources and we can expect
to meet objections on this ground. But resources could be found if the
political will were there. There could be some redistribution among
working people — for instance, by abolishing the married man's tax
allowance and increasing child benefit. There could be a major
redistribution of resources among different areas of public spending
— for instance, away from spending on nuclear arms and nuclear
power, from the Common Agricultural Policy, or from motorway
building programmes, towards child care, welfare services, public
transport and housing. And of course there could also be a
redistribution from employers to workers — by taxing profits, for
example, and by restricting the export of capital; by taking into social
ownership banks and other key concerns; by introducing a statutory
minimum wage; and by winning through collective bargaining (backed
up by legislation if necessary) a substantial reduction in working
hours without a commensurate loss in the value of earnings.

Finally, our strategy would need to ensure the full participation of
women as well as men in the implementation of policy. Locally and

nationally, women must participate at all levels of the decision-making process. The channels of democracy in our society — unions, political parties, local authorities, Parliament — have been constructed by men, for men. They are not designed to facilitate female participation, and they by-pass important areas of women's lives. They must be changed and here, too, men will have to relinquish privilege — the privilege of power. We are supposed to be living in a democracy. But we women are still fighting for the franchise. We may have the vote but we don't have the power to exercise our political will. Women's liberation has taught us that. We can no longer be the silent majority.

Index